The Gift

The Gift explores how objects of prestige contributed to cross-cultural exchanges between Africans and Europeans during the Atlantic slave trade. An eighteenth-century silver ceremonial sword, commissioned in the port of La Rochelle by French traders, was offered as a gift to an African commercial agent in the port of Cabinda (Kingdom of Ngoyo), in twenty-first century Angola. Slave traders carried this object from Cabinda to Abomey, the capital of the Kingdom of Dahomey in twenty-first century's Republic of Benin, from where French officers looted the item in the late nineteenth century. Drawing on a rich set of sources in French, English, and Portuguese, as well as artifacts housed in museums across Europe and the Americas, Ana Lucia Araujo illuminates how luxury objects impacted European–African relations, and how these economic, cultural, and social interactions paved the way for the European conquest and colonization of West Africa and West Central Africa.

Ana Lucia Araujo is a professor of History at Howard University, Washington, DC. A specialist on the history and memory of slavery and the Atlantic slave trade, she has authored and edited thirteen books.

Cambridge Studies on the African Diaspora

General Editor: Michael A. Gomez, New York University

Using the African Diaspora as its core defining and launching point for examining the historians and experiences of African-descended communities around the globe, this series unites books around the concept of migration of peoples and their cultures, politics, ideas, and other systems from or within Africa to other nations or regions, focusing particularly on transnational, transregional, and transcultural exchanges.

The Gift

How Objects of Prestige Shaped the Atlantic Slave Trade and Colonialism

ANA LUCIA ARAUJO

Howard University, Washington, DC

CAMBRIDGE
UNIVERSITY PRESS

CAMBRIDGE
UNIVERSITY PRESS

Shaftesbury Road, Cambridge CB2 8EA, United Kingdom

One Liberty Plaza, 20th Floor, New York, NY 10006, USA

477 Williamstown Road, Port Melbourne, VIC 3207, Australia

314–321, 3rd Floor, Plot 3, Splendor Forum, Jasola District Centre,
New Delhi – 110025, India

103 Penang Road, #05–06/07, Visioncrest Commercial, Singapore 238467

Cambridge University Press is part of Cambridge University Press & Assessment,
a department of the University of Cambridge.

We share the University's mission to contribute to society through the pursuit of
education, learning and research at the highest international levels of excellence.

www.cambridge.org
Information on this title: www.cambridge.org/9781108839297

DOI: 10.1017/9781108989756

First published 2024

Printed in the United Kingdom by TJ Books Limited, Padstow Cornwall

A catalogue record for this publication is available from the British Library

Library of Congress Cataloging-in-Publication Data
NAMES: Araujo, Ana Lucia, author.
TITLE: The gift : how objects of prestige shaped the Atlantic slave trade and
colonialism / Ana Lucia Araujo, Howard University, Washington, DC.
DESCRIPTION: Cambridge, United Kingdom ; New York, NY : Cambridge
University Press, 2024. | Series: Cambridge studies on the African diaspora | Includes
bibliographical references and index.
IDENTIFIERS: LCCN 2023024150 | ISBN 9781108839297 (hardback) |
ISBN 9781108989756 (ebook)
SUBJECTS: LCSH: Slave trade – Atlantic Ocean Region – History. | Presentation
swords – France – History. | Presentation pieces (Gifts) – History.
CLASSIFICATION: LCC HT1322 .A73 2024 | DDC 382/.44099–dc23/eng/20230830
LC record available at https://lccn.loc.gov/2023024150

ISBN 978-1-108-83929-7 Hardback

Contents

v

Maps and Figures

Maps

Figures

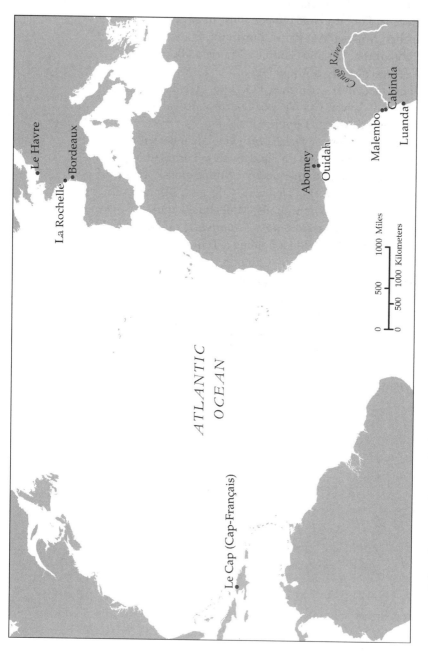

MAP 1 Selected ports and towns in the French Atlantic world in the second half of the eighteenth century: Abomey, Ouidah, Malembo, Cabinda, Luanda, Le Cap (Cap-Français), Bordeaux, Le Havre, and La Rochelle. Map by Tsering Wangyal Shawa, Geographic Information Systems and Map Librarian, Princeton University.

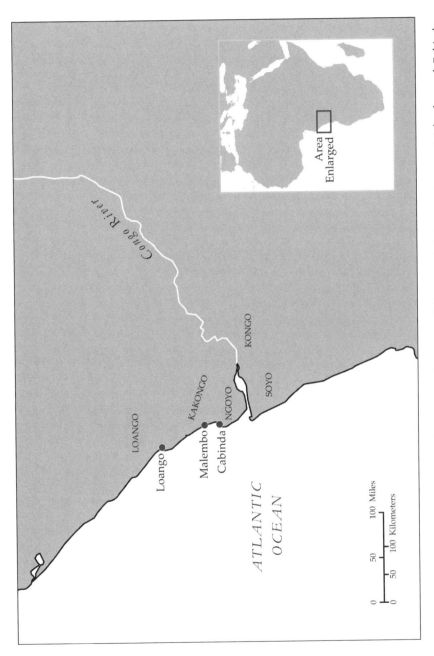

MAP 2 The Loango coast kingdoms of Loango, Kakongo, and Ngoyo and their ports Loango, Malembo, and Cabinda. Map by Tsering Wangyal Shawa, Geographic Information Systems and Map Librarian, Princeton University.

Acknowledgments

This book was made possible thanks to financial support from various institutions. First and foremost, Howard University has supported my work in multiple ways over the past fifteen years. I am indebted to the School of Historical Studies at the Institute of Advanced Study (IAS) (funding provided by the Gladys Krieble Delmas Foundation), Princeton, for awarding me a fellowship in the spring of 2022. Since I arrived in the United States in 2008, this was my first external fellowship, and I am deeply grateful for having spent time at IAS free from teaching and service obligations, while exchanging ideas with scholars from around the world. My time at IAS allowed me to write a significant part of this book. The College of Arts and Sciences of Howard University provided me with additional funding for research leave in the spring of 2022 and sabbatical leave in the spring of 2023. I am grateful to Nikki M. Taylor, the then Chair of the Department of History at Howard University, for her enthusiastic support of this project. I am also indebted to Rubin Patterson, Dean of the College of Arts and Sciences, to Associate Provost Kimberly Jones, and to Associate Deans Kim Lewis and Thomas A. Foster, who supported every stage of the process to get research leave and a sabbatical semester.

The American Philosophical Society awarded me the Franklin Research Grant to conduct research in France. My deep thanks to Kristin Mann and Randy Sparks, who supported my application for this grant. The Getty Research Institute, Los Angeles, CA, awarded me a six-month Getty Residential Senior Scholar Grant in the spring of 2023. I am particularly grateful to Mary Miller, Alexa Sekyra, Nancy Um, and Sabine Schlosser for their support and warm welcome at the Getty, where I worked to complete parts of the manuscript and the final revisions, and where I received great feedback from Getty scholars. In 2019, I was a Visiting Professor at the University of Paris VIII. During this short but very intense and productive period, I conducted research in Paris, Bordeaux, Nantes, Lisbon, Coimbra, and Tervuren, where I visited several museums and archives. I am grateful to historian Armelle Enders, who made possible this period in Europe that was crucial to my research.

When I started working on this project, I planned to study the demands for restitution of African art and heritage, a topic I started exploring on the eve of the grand opening of the Musée du Quai Branly in 2007, during a postdoctoral fellowship. However, I was never able to continue the project as it was originally conceived. In 2019, Gaëlle Beaujean, curator of the African collections at Quai Branly, called my attention to an object that she included in her PhD dissertation and later in her published book that deserved closer analysis. Thanks to her, I abandoned the broader project and decided to focus on the main object I follow in this book; as a result, Gaëlle became this project's godmother, by always offering her generous support.

Many colleagues and friends answered questions, suggested readings, and provided me with sources. Historian Roquinaldo Ferreira read the very first written paper drawn from this research. He answered my questions and pointed out primary and secondary sources. Without his support and advice, I could not have finished this project. Mariana P. Candido was an enthusiastic supporter of the book from its difficult beginnings. I asked her countless questions and she has read and heard my complaints over the past four years. She read the book proposal and the full manuscript and offered me precious criticism. While doing research, I often asked advice of Suzanne Preston Blier. Her work is obviously an inspiration for this kind of inquiry. Through our exchanges, I was encouraged to go down all possible rabbit holes. Suzanne also generously read the full manuscript, and I am grateful to her. Cameron Monroe also offered me feedback and advice on numerous occasions.

Robin Law and John K. Thornton also answered questions and suggested readings, read the manuscript, and provided criticism. Kate de Luna read the entire manuscript and offered precious suggestions and corrections. I am particularly grateful to Daniel Domingues da Silva, Alex Borucki, Nicholas Radburn, and David Eltis. They received emails and messages at unusual times of the day and night and patiently answered my questions regarding French slave voyages, ship captains, and slave ships. I am also indebted to Carlos Serrano, who provided me with numerous images of Cabinda's *bimpaba*. I am grateful to Jan-Lodewijk Grootaers, former curator at the Minneapolis Institute of Art, who kindly sent me several images of *bimpaba* housed at the institute and gave me permission to use one of the pictures presented in this book.

Susan Cooksey, curator of African art at the Samuel P. Harn Museum at the University of Florida, also offered guidance in the early stages of this project, when I gave a lecture at her university. Bayo Holsey, Kristin Mann, Anna More, Tatiana Seijas, and Rebecca Shumway also offered valuable comments on a precirculated paper about this project presented at the conference "Archival Lives: The Violence of History and the Transatlantic Slave Trade," at Emory University, in December 2019. I would like to thank Adriana Chira for organizing this event and inviting me to present my work. I am also grateful to Jorge Canizares-Esguerra. Although we have never met in person, he has supported this project.

Francesca Trivellato and the participants in the Seminar in Early Modern European History at the Institute for Advanced Study, especially Diana Kim, Karen Graubart, Emily Kadens, Peter Lake, and Byron Hamman, also offered me fruitful criticism on a long paper about this project. I am also indebted to the scholars at the Getty Research Institute who offered feedback, among them Mecka Baumeister, Cecilia Dal Zovo, Peyvand Firouzeh, and Rebecca Giordano. Their comments and questions helped me with revisions for the final version of this manuscript. Fellow scholars Patricia Martins Marcos and Allen F. Roberts, who attended a public lecture at the Getty, also offered useful suggestions. I also thank Alexandre Dubé, Christina Mobley, Sue Peabody, Sheryl Reiss, and Carlos da Silva Junior, who helped me by answering my questions at various stages.

Many scholars, colleagues, friends, archivists, and curators helped me to complete this book project. I am indebted to the two anonymous readers who read the book proposal during the difficult period of the global COVID-19 pandemic, and who later also read the full manuscript. These reviewers gave me numerous suggestions and generous comments. In Portugal, I am grateful to Inês Beleza Barreiros, who invited me to Portugal twice. During these two visits I was able to visit archives and museums in Lisbon and Coimbra. Inês became a friend and interlocutor, and I hope we will continue to collaborate in the future. I am also grateful to José Pedro Monteiro, who welcomed me in Coimbra, and arranged a visit to the Museu da Ciência da Universidade de Coimbra. I also thank Paulo Ferreira da Costa, Ana Botas, and Íria Simões at the Museu de Etnologia de Lisboa. In Belgium, Tom Morren, archivist at the Royal Museum for Central Africa, helped me to locate several records. Hein Van Hee, curator at the Royal Museum for Central Africa, guided me during a research trip to the museum's renovated exhibitions, gave me access to the collections in storage, and responded to numerous questions by email as well. Part of this research was conducted during the COVID-19 pandemic. Without the help and tireless support of archivists in various countries, the research for this book would have been impossible. In Lisbon, Portugal, I am indebted to archivists Paulo Pacheco, Maria da Graça Caldeira Alves da Palma, and Cláudia Marina Barata Moreschini at the Arquivo Histórico Ultramarino; Constança Rosa at the Fundação Calouste Gulbenkian; Helena Grego and Manuela Cantinho at the Sociedade de Geografia de Lisboa; and Paulo Manuel Lamuria Cascalheira Tremoceiro, Pedro Miguel Matos Judicibus, and Ana Maria Fernandes at the Arquivo Nacional da Torre do Tombo.

In France, where I conducted most of the research for this book, numerous archivists, curators, and fellow scholars helped me to find documents and objects. Krystel Gualdé, Directrice scientifique the Musée d'histoire de Nantes, responded to my questions about specific images and helped to obtain digitized documents. I am also grateful to Karine Garcia-Lebailly. At the Archives départementales de la Charente-Maritime, in La Rochelle, I am indebted to Etienne Petitclerc, who answered questions, found physical documents, and provided me with digitized copies of documents. At the Médiathèque Michel-Crépeau, also in La Rochelle, archivists Olivier Desgranges, Jefferson Tonneau, and Muriel Hoareau offered me unvaluable support. I cannot adequately express my gratitude to Florence Chabrier and Marie Chouleur at the Service historique de la défense aux Archives de la Marine, in Rochefort. They both offered me great support in person and remotely to locate records, by answering my numerous emails and offering digitized documents. I am also grateful to the archivists at the Archives nationales in Paris and Pierrefite-sur-Seine. At the Archives nationales d'outre-mer in Aix-en-Provence, I am indebted to Amélie Hurel. In Marseille, I thank Véronique Bernardet-Gaudy and Marie-Claire Pontier at the Archives départementales Bouches-du-Rhône, and Sylvie Drago at the Archives de la Chambre de Commerce et d'Industrie. At the Musée d'Aquitaine in Bordeaux, Laurent Vedrine, Paul Matharan, and Katia Kukawka welcomed me to the museum, where I was able to visit the storage rooms. Katia continued to answer my questions over almost three years and helped me to obtain permission to use an image of one of the museum's objects. At the Musée du Nouveau Monde in La Rochelle, Mélanie Moreau, director of the Musées d'art et d'histoire de La Rochelle, provided me with crucial information about the silver *kimpaba* examined in this book, and gave me permission to use an image of the object. I am also grateful to Jean-Pierre Lacoste, consultant on the arts of Africa, Americas, and Oceania at Maison Rossini in Paris, for the technical information regarding this silver sword. I am thankful to Marie-Cécile Zinsou, with whom I corresponded about the crowns of kings Béhanzin and Toffa.

Archivists and curators in the United States also supported my work. At the Baltimore Museum of Art, in Baltimore, Maryland, I am grateful to Brittany Luberba, Assistant Curator of Decorative Arts, and Kevin Tervala, curator of African Art, who met me in person, responded to my questions, and made the process of obtaining permissions to publish the photograph of an object from the museum's collections an easy one. At the Virginia Museum of Fine Arts, in Richmond, Virginia, I am indebted to chief curator Michael R. Taylor, who facilitated obtaining permission to publish a photograph of a museum's *kimpaba*. I am also grateful to Ashley Ledford and Kelly Powell, who welcomed me to the museum during a research visit. While at the Institute for Advanced Study, I also benefited from tremendous support from librarians. I am particularly thankful to Tsering Wangyal Shawa, Princeton University's Geographic Information Systems and Map Librarian, who designed the maps for this book. Marcia Tucker and Karen Downing assisted me in getting books as well as locating and digitizing images.

This book could not have been published without generous support by historian Michael Gomez, who accepted it for inclusion in his Cambridge Studies on the African Diaspora series. I have no words to express my gratitude to my wonderful editor Cecelia Cancellaro. An enthusiastic and responsive editor makes all the difference during the long, and sometimes painful, process of finishing a book manuscript. Cecelia supported and cared about this project from the day I submitted it to Cambridge University Press. I also thank Victoria Phillips for her assistance along the way. I am also grateful to Ruth Boyes, Ranjith Kumar Saravanan, and Alice Greaves who made the production process extremely smooth and efficient. I was able to start and finish researching and writing this book thanks to my husband, Alain Bélanger. Alain gave me love and unconditional support during this long journey. He went to the archives with me, held documents while I was photographing them, and listened with great enthusiasm to my questions and ramblings about new findings. He also supported me during my very long absences at home and abroad. This book is dedicated to him.

Introduction

On Gifts and the Atlantic Slave Trade

In 2015, the Rossini auction house put on sale a large and unusual eighteenth-century silver sword manufactured in France (Figure 4.1). On the false blade of this impressive object is an engraved dedication written in French that reads: "Andris Macaye Mafouque le juste de Cabinde." The inscription allows us to identify the sword as a present to a righteous (*juste*) dignitary based in Cabinda, a West Central African port in the era of the Atlantic slave trade. At first sight, the object could be seen as any other eighteenth-century silver artifact produced in Europe to be given as a gift to a prominent person. But accompanying the ceremonial sword was a sign covered with red velvet on which there was an ivory plaque stating "1892 souvenir de la campagne du Dahomey" (1892, souvenir from the Dahomey campaign). Whereas the engraved inscription suggests the sword was offered to an African dignitary, the plaque indicates that French officers who fought during the wars that led to the conquest and colonization of the West African Kingdom of Dahomey brought the object to France. The Musée du Nouveau Monde of La Rochelle in France made the highest bid and purchased the object.[1]

Since its acquisition, the silver ceremonial sword has been prominently displayed in one of the museum's main rooms. The stunning object is also featured in the modest guidebook that describes its permanent exhibitions.[2] How was an eighteenth-century object, given as a gift to a West Central African middleman, looted from Dahomey's capital at the end of the nineteenth century? This book attempts to answer that question. I use this gift, carried to different places by various peoples at several times, to tell the history of the French trade in enslaved Africans in the kingdoms of the Loango coast in West Central Africa and in the Kingdom of

Dahomey in West Africa. I also seek to understand how the societies of the Loango coast were impacted by a trade in which people were considered as commodities, in other words "objects of economic value ... and social potential."[3]

The Gift: How Objects of Prestige Shaped the Atlantic Slave Trade and Colonialism follows the tortuous trajectory of this silver ceremonial sword and examines its changing significances. Through its displacement, this object became a multilayered repository of words, images, shapes, materials, and meanings embodying the complex dialogues among different peoples and regions in the Atlantic world during the eighteenth and the nineteenth centuries. Yet, these exchanges could not exist without the long-distance maritime trade with Asia and the Mediterranean. French slave merchants were part of cosmopolitan networks. Traders from La Rochelle who sailed to the Loango coast, the Bight of Benin, and the French West Indies purchased people with a variety of currencies and goods, including European and Asian textiles, coral from the Mediterranean, and manufactured items made of silver mined in South America and Mexico. Therefore, despite of the small scale of this study, I frame this book as what Francesca Trivellato defines as a "global history in small scale."[4] In other words, instead of approaching the French silver *kimpaba* only through the lens of micro-history, my analysis is also guided by macrohistory.

Over the following pages, I examine how exchanges of prestige gifts had an impact on societies on the Loango coast and the Bight of Benin during the second half of the eighteenth century and the late nineteenth century. But before going further, it is important to make some distinctions. In the context of the Atlantic slave trade and the commercial exchanges within the African continent, depending on the period and the region, a variety of items such as certain European, African, and Asian textiles and even some kinds of alcohol could be referred to as "gifts" or "presents."[5] Gifts also included objects of prestige, manufactured items, very often especially created for their recipients. Thus, by using the French silver sword as a framework, I argue that objects of prestige embodied the new power acquired by African agents, because of the intensification of the Atlantic slave trade in the eighteenth-century. Following this artifact's trajectory allows us to explore how African and European authorities took decisions and how they positioned themselves when negotiating the terms of the Atlantic slave trade. It also permits us to interrogate how societies of the Loango coast and the Kingdom of Dahomey conceived ideas of sovereignty. Ultimately, I contend, the analysis of objects of prestige offers an opportunity to better understand how material culture shaped the Atlantic slave trade and colonialism, and how cultural artifacts were also modeled by the trade in enslaved peoples and the rise of European colonial rule in Africa.[6]

THE ATLANTIC SLAVE TRADE ON
THE LOANGO COAST

Travelogues, visual images, ship manifests, ship logs, ship captain journals, correspondence, and artifacts show that in their attempts to control the ports on the Loango coast, such as Cabinda, Malembo, and Loango, European slave traders engaged in close interactions with African rulers and brokers. These European agents acquired enslaved Africans in exchange for a variety of goods such as European and Asian textiles, handguns, iron bars, and cowry shells that served as currencies.[7] In these interactions, African agents developed tastes for specific European, American, and Asian goods, foods, and drinks, as well as for finery and luxurious objects made of precious metals, coral, ivory, glass, and porcelain. European traders sought to please African rulers and their intermediaries in order to obtain the best conditions to conduct the trade in enslaved Africans.

There is a growing scholarship examining the tastes and consuming patterns of West Central Africans and West Africans during the era of the Atlantic slave trade. Still, very few studies examine gifts of prestige among these items.[8] Whereas some goods provided to African traders were labeled as gifts, the nature of these presents is complex as, to both European and African agents, they were conceived as a form of tribute or tax that should be paid to each agent at specific stages of the commercial transactions that took place on the coasts of Atlantic Africa. But in order to obtain the support of local rulers and agents, European traders also offered valuable items, gifts of prestige that were manufactured in Europe, Asia, and sometimes also in the Americas. Shipowners who outfitted slave ships as well as the ship captains they assigned to sail to the ports on the Atlantic coasts of Africa understood the importance of offering presents that embodied symbolic elements that were meaningful to local agents.

Over the past years, several historians have examined the slave trade in the West African ports of Senegambia, the Gold Coast, the Bight of Benin, the Bight of Biafra, and the region south of the Congo River in West Central Africa.[9] But the Loango coast, the region north of the Congo River, remains understudied. Since the publication of Phyllis M. Martin's first research monograph investigating the external trade on the Loango coast five decades ago, very few scholars have studied this region.[10] Exploring the singularities of the ports of Loango, Malembo, and Cabinda allows us to understand how these ports, unlike other ports such as Luanda and Benguela south of the Congo River in twenty-first century's Angola, remained under the control of their respective local rulers, therefore often challenging European attempts to dominate the trade in the region.

The ports controlled by the Portuguese, such as Luanda and Benguela, exported an estimated number of 2,826,000 and 764,000 enslaved Africans, respectively, during the era of the Atlantic slave trade. Approximately 1,843,000 enslaved Africans were boarded on slave ships that left from the three African-controlled ports north of the Loango coast (Map 1). Cabinda, part of the Kingdom of Ngoyo, exported nearly 753,000 persons, and current estimates establish that 672,000 enslaved persons were deported from Malembo (the main harbor of the Kingdom of Kakongo) to the Americas and 418,000 from Loango, in the Kingdom of Loango.[11] The majority of these enslaved men, women, and children were initially sent to the Dutch, French, and British West Indies.

Moving west to the Bight of Benin (Map 2), until the eighteenth century, the French, English, Portuguese, and Dutch kept a sustained presence in the port of Ouidah that was part of the Kingdom of Hueda but was conquered by the Kingdom of Dahomey in 1727. In the eighteenth century, most slave ships trading enslaved Africans on the Loango coast were French. Captains from various French ports sailed to the region to purchase and transport African captives to Saint-Domingue, then France's richest colony in the Americas. But with the rise of the Saint-Domingue Revolution in 1791, the French presence dramatically declined both on the Loango coast and Ouidah, as well as in the other ports of the Bight of Benin such as Porto-Novo and Badagry, today respectively located in the Republic of Benin and Nigeria. At the turn of the nineteenth century, most slave traders acquiring enslaved Africans in these two regions transported these captives to Brazil and Cuba.

The Gift illuminates the complex mechanisms of the Atlantic slave trade in the eighteenth and nineteenth centuries and the rise of colonialism by following the trajectory of an eighteenth-century silver artifact fabricated in the port of La Rochelle, transported to the port of Cabinda (then part of the Kingdom of Ngoyo in twenty-first century Angola), brought to Abomey (the capital of the Kingdom of Dahomey in twenty-first century's Republic of Benin), and then carried back to France. The various chapters show how material culture and luxurious artifacts produced in Europe facilitated and sometimes also complicated the relations between African and European social actors during the era of the Atlantic slave trade. Through this analysis, the book aims to help readers to grasp how the rise and fall of the Atlantic slave trade in West Africa and West Central Africa paved the way for European conquest and colonization of the continent. Likewise, the book interrogates how the French slave traders from La Rochelle, the African traders from Cabinda, and the rulers of Dahomey invested this object with economic and symbolic value. By fabricating, manipulating, transforming, and displacing the silver sword, these various agents also gave to this object new meanings. The sword embodies Appadurai's approach, and that of many historians, that "we have to follow the things themselves, for their meanings are inscribed in their forms, their uses, their trajectories."[12] By centering material culture and objects of prestige, a dimension neglected by historians far too often, this book seeks to make two main interventions in the historiography of the Atlantic slave trade. First, it aims to show that gifts of prestige were central components in the economic, cultural, and human exchanges among Europeans and Africans during the period of the trade in enslaved Africans. I argue that gifts of prestige were neither ordinary goods nor currencies. Created and shaped to please the receiver, gifts of prestige changed over time to fulfill new goals and respond to new tastes. Therefore, they became tangible repositories of the tragic cross-cultural exchanges intended to provide an enslaved workforce to the colonies of the Americas. Second, through the study of the displacement of one single object, the silver *kimpaba* given as a gift to the *Mfuka* Andris Pukuta, the book shows that despite having been historically studied as two independent regions, the Loango coast and the Bight of Benin were linked by close and complex ties during the era of the Atlantic slave trade.

GIFTS IN CROSS-CULTURAL EXCHANGES

Gifts have been described as an institution by scholars in Classical studies. Starting in antiquity, the term "gift" could be associated with taxes, dowries, and offerings to the gods. Gift exchanges among rulers and visitors from distant lands have also been documented since antiquity, including in Homer's poem *Odyssey* written in the eighth century BCE. In these ancient accounts, hosts provided gifts to their guests upon their departure. The gift was then a memento of sorts, a keepsake that visitors from distant lands would carry back home. Menelaus, the King of

Sparta, welcomed Telemachus, Odysseus's son, in his palace and also offered him gifts: "Come now, stay with me here in my palace, until eleven days or twelve have passed. Then I will send you off with precious gifts."[13] As Telemachus just wanted treasure as a present, Menelaus enumerated the valued items he would give to his guest:

> I will give you different gifts, just as you ask.
> I will give you the finest piece of treasure
> Of all the hoard I have piled up at home;
> A finely crafted bowl, of purest silver,
> With gold around him.[14]

Alcinous, the king of the Phaeacians, pleased by Odysseus's wisdom, offered him gifts, "as hosts should do to guests in friendship."[15] Gifts sealed agreements and relationships. In Homer's *Odyssey*, gift givers were hosts and gift receivers were guests. In his classic work *Essai sur le don* (translated as *The Gift*), French sociologist Marcel Mauss reproduces a verse of *Hávamál*, a thirteenth-century Scandinavian poem that meditates on the problem of gift-exchanging:

> With weapons and clothes
> Friends must give pleasure to one another
> Everyone knows that for himself
> Those who exchange presents with one another
> Remain friends the longest
> If things turn out successfully.[16]

The poem emphasizes that presents at least indicate the intention of maintaining long-lasting friendships. Yet it also cautions about the risk that there could be obstacles along the path. In this context, exchanging gifts is a form of contract. Gift exchanges were also part of diplomatic exchanges in later periods, during the Middle Ages and the early modern era in Europe and Africa, as well as in the Mediterranean world more broadly.[17]

Exchanges of luxury objects as gifts also played a central role during the first commercial and diplomatic transactions between Asian and European traders in the Arabian Peninsula in the early modern era.[18] Portuguese explorers and the rulers of Atlantic African societies engaged in similar gift-exchanges as early as the fifteenth century.[19] The rise of the Atlantic slave trade emerged alongside these first contacts, sometimes marked by great violence. Of course, gifts could soothe these conflicts. As in previous periods and other cross-cultural contexts, gifts were treasured for their monetary value. African rulers often appreciated objects

FIGURE I.I Crown for the King of Ardra, copper (metal), glass, velvet, h.
II × d. 7 inches, England, *c.* 1664. Courtesy: Rijksmuseum, Amsterdam,
Netherlands.

made of precious metals as well as rare items from distant regions. In
the exchanges that developed throughout the modern era to this day,
unlike in antiquity, foreign guests are usually those who offer gifts
to their hosts. Atlantic interactions gave rise to new kinds of objects
such as crowns, swords, and scepters, adapted to the new context and
using forms and materials that engaged the new African recipients. For
example, when the English Royal Company of Adventurers sent an
embassy to the Kingdom of Allada (also known as Ardra) in the Bight
of Benin in 1664, they sent the king of Allada a magnificent copper
crown. Lined with red velvet, the crown is decorated with fleurs-de-lis
and four crosses-pattée, with a globe on the top (Figure I.I). The crown
was modeled after the St Edwards Crown made for the coronation of
King Charles II in 1661. But instead of a solid gold frame decorated
with rubies, amethysts, sapphires, garnet, topazes, and tourmalines, the
West African piece was in copper and ornated with colorful glass stones.
Although acknowledging the royal status of Allada's ruler, the crown

was not made of gold and diamonds, but rather in materials such as copper and glass, suggesting the West African ruler occupied a different rank than that of the king of England.[20] Unfortunately, the English crown never reached the Bight of Benin, as the vessel that carried the gift was intercepted by the Dutch in the context of the Second Anglo-Dutch War (1665–1667). Although the king of Allada never received the precious present, today the English-manufactured crown is prominently featured at the Rijksmuseum in Amsterdam, the Netherlands.

African rulers also offered presents to European rulers and agents. Enslaved African men, women, boys, and girls were considered as objects in the exchanges developed during the Atlantic slave trade, which is why African kings also gave slaves as gifts to European traders. In 1750, for example, King Tegbesu of Dahomey sent an embassy to Brazil to negotiate the terms of the Atlantic slave trade. At that time, before heading to Lisbon, the ambassadors stopped in Bahia, where the colonial government headquarters was located and from where the Portuguese fort of Ouidah in Dahomey was administered. The ambassadors brought with them several gifts to the king of Portugal, including two large boxes covered in iron with ornate locks and four enslaved children. Except for one girl who became blind, the other three children were sent as gifts to Lisbon.[21] Gezo, the king of Dahomey, offered a Yoruba enslaved girl named Aina as a gift to British Navy officer Frederick Edwyn Forbes in 1850 when he was visiting Abomey, the capital of the Kingdom of Dahomey (see Map 1). Forbes renamed her Sarah Forbes Bonetta after himself and the name of his navy vessel. Back in London, Forbes gave the enslaved girl to Queen Victoria, who paid for her expenses as she continued to live with the Forbes family.[22]

During the era of the Atlantic slave trade, gifts were valued for their symbolic meaning as much as for their pecuniary value. Hence, in the context of the trade of enslaved Africans that encompassed three continents, various peoples, and several societies over more than three hundred years, the role of gifts and commodities was not opposed, but rather closely related and often intertwined.[23] Therefore, the function of one object or a category of objects or things could also change depending on the agents, the region, and the period. As put by Mauss, although gift exchanges are voluntary, "in reality they are given and reciprocated obligatorily."[24] Of course, reciprocity is never guaranteed; therefore, a gift is always a bid, as the giver hopes to gain trust from the recipient.[25]

Drawing on Mauss and other theorists who have debated the position of gifts in global exchanges, I seek to understand how the French gift and by extension European gifts became prestige objects and royal insignias in African societies such as the Kingdom of Ngoyo and the Kingdom of Dahomey during the era of the Atlantic slave trade.[26] I also explore how stolen gifts became objects of power for African rulers and for European officers who invaded and colonized the African continent at the end of the nineteenth century.

Starting with Mauss, anthropologists have debated for decades the gestures of giving, receiving, and reciprocating as the three obligations associated with the exchanges of gifts.[27] Although these three dimensions are present in the context of the presents exchanged between European and African agents on the coasts of Africa, there is also a form of circularity that characterized these exchanges. In other words, once a present was reciprocated, another one would follow. Mauss also differentiates gifts given to humans and gifts that humans give to gods.[28] Still, in the two African societies studied in this book, kings, and to some extent their representatives, embodied divine qualities. Mauss also insists that the gift carries human attributes, part taken from the giver, giving the giver power or superiority over the recipient, creating a debt, of sorts. But in the context of the specific gift discussed in this book, at least to some degree, the French silver sword invested the West Central African recipient with power. Drawing on Nicholas Thomas, in the conflictual context of the Atlantic slave trade, the sword became a "crucial index of the extent to which those relations are sustained or disfigured."[29]

OVERVIEW OF CHAPTERS

The Gift is divided into six chapters. Chapter 1, "The Loango Coast and the Rise of the Atlantic Slave Trade," revisits the history of the three kingdoms of the Loango coast: Ngoyo, Kakongo, and Loango. I discuss the main institutions and social structures of these societies in order to explain how the three states, and especially Ngoyo and its port, Cabinda, developed commercial exchanges with the Portuguese, Dutch, French, and English agents. I explore how the three states of the Loango coast joined the trade in enslaved Africans through these interactions. I pay particular attention to the role of the *Mfuka*, the king's agent who oversaw the coastal commercial transactions, by seeking to bring to light his role as a middleman and slave trader. In Chapter 2, "La Rochelle and Atlantic Africa," I explore the history of the French port city of La Rochelle and its involvement in the Atlantic slave trade. By looking at the city's position vis-à-vis other French slave-trading ports, I examine the city's connections to Atlantic Africa and the commerce of enslaved people. I pay particular attention to the commercial activities of the shipowner Daniel Garesché and the ship captain Jean-Amable Lessenne, two important historical actors in the story told in this book. Next, in Chapter 3, "Slave Traders Turned Pirates," I explore the commercial activity associated with the trade of enslaved Africans in Cabinda in the Kingdom of Ngoyo on the Loango coast during the eighteenth century. I look at how European powers such as the English and the French competed to obtain the best conditions for their trade in enslaved people in the region and how wars fought in Europe affected their trade on the Loango coast. In addition, and more importantly, this chapter focuses on the competition among French slave traders in the ports of Cabinda and Malembo. The chapter tells the story of how ship captains from Bordeaux and Le Havre attacked two slave ships from La Rochelle. I explore how this conflict illustrated the enduring clashes among European powers in Cabinda. Here I emphasize that despite their continuous efforts, European states never succeeded in constructing permanent trading structures on the Loango coast, as they did on the Gold Coast and the Bight of Benin. Next, Chapter 4, "Deciphering the Gift," follows the conflict among ship captains discussed in Chapter 3 to explain how French traders returned to the Loango coast to offer a special gift, a silver sword, to Cabinda's *Mfuka*. I explore the various dimensions of this sword, its creation, production, migration, reception, and meanings for both the givers and the recipient. In Chapter 5, "A Displaced Gift," I discuss the various possible explanations as to how and when the gift given to Cabinda's *Mfuka* ended up in Abomey, the inland capital of the Kingdom of Dahomey, nearly 2,000 miles away from Cabinda. Chapter 6, "Ngoyo Meets Dahomey," studies how the silver sword was received and incorporated in its new home in the royal palaces of Abomey. The Conclusion, "Objects that Shaped the Slave Trade and Colonialism," discusses how the silver sword embodies the history and the legacies of the Atlantic slave trade and European colonialism in Africa. Thus, spanning West Africa, West Central Africa, France, and to some extent Saint-Domingue, this book aims to show how the study of material culture can complicate and nuance the study of the Atlantic slave trade and the ascent of European colonialism in Africa.

The Loango Coast and the Rise of the Atlantic Slave Trade

The French were not the first European traders to reach the coasts of Africa and more specifically the Loango coast. This region stretched from Cape Lopez (twenty-first century Gabon, in the north) to the Congo River (where twenty-first century Democratic Republic of the Congo and Angola intersect, in the south). Before them, in the early fifteenth century, Portuguese navigators had started to explore the coasts of North Africa and West Africa. First, they reached Ceuta, the North African port across the Strait of Gibraltar. Then they surveyed Madeira Islands, the Azores, and the Canaries. In the subsequent years, they reached the island of Arguim in twenty-first century's Mauritania, rounded Cape Bojador, arrived at the region of Senegal, and eventually passed Cape Verde. Moving east, after sailing along the Bight of Benin, Portuguese navigator Diogo Cão and his fleet reached the Loango Bay in West Central Africa in 1483.[1]

Sailing south, Cão's expedition met the mouth of the Congo River. On its southern bank near the harbor of Soyo, they found Mpinda, the coastal province of the Kingdom of Kongo, which is in twenty-first century Angola. To mark their arrival in this area, Cão chose a sandy beach surrounded by palm trees, where he placed a *padrão*, a monument of sorts consisting of a white stone cross carved with the Kingdom of Portugal's coat of arms. But the Portuguese navigator's expedition had only just started. One of the most important kingdoms in the region was located in the region:

Seeing the greatness and abundance of water that the river showed in its mouth, it seemed to him that such a great river had to be inhabited by many peoples;

and when he entered up the river ... he saw appearing on its banks many people, of those he was used to seeing back on the coast, all very black with their unruly hair.[2]

This first encounter propelled long-lasting exchanges between the Kingdom of Kongo's rulers, nobles, commoners, and slaves and Portuguese agents, who over the next decades expanded their presence along the coast of West Central Africa.

By the middle of the sixteenth century, there were three kingdoms along the Loango Bay. Each kingdom had its own port: Loango, in the Kingdom of Loango; Malembo, in the Kingdom of Kakongo; and Cabinda, in the Kingdom of Ngoyo (see Map 1). The Kingdom of Loango was the main state on Loango Bay. In 1575, the Portuguese founded Luanda, south of the Congo River. The capital of the Portuguese colony of Angola, Luanda gradually became the largest slave-trading port in West Central Africa.[3] In 1617, the Portuguese established Benguela. During the era of the Atlantic slave trade, Luanda and Benguela respectively became the first and the third largest exporters of enslaved Africans to the Americas.[4] But in 1641, the Dutch took control of Luanda for nearly seven years. As the Portuguese and the Dutch competed on the coasts of West Central Africa, the governor of Angola, Pedro César de Meneses, complained to King João IV that the ruler of "Cabinda" refused to pay allegiance to the king of Portugal, and instead had decided to be a vassal of the Kingdom of Kongo.[5]

The kingdoms of Loango, Kakongo, and Ngoyo were highly centralized states, a feature that may have favored their persisting autonomy from the sixteenth to the nineteenth centuries. Owing to a variety of internal and external factors, not only the Portuguese, but also no other European power managed ever to control the three main ports on the Loango coast during the era of the Atlantic slave trade, unlike the two Portuguese colonies of Luanda and Benguela. As Loango, Kakongo, and Ngoyo developed, the initial European demand for commodities such as ivory and copper was gradually replaced with the trade in human beings during the second half of the seventeenth century. This chapter revisits this early history, by examining how these states were structured, and identifying the main local agents involved in the commerce with Europeans I especially examine the role of the *Mfuka* (spelled in various ways, including *Mafuku*, *Mafuka*, *M-Fouka*, *Mafouque* in French, and *Mafoeke* in Dutch) in the Kingdom of Ngoyo, to understand the complex interactions among African rulers, their local agents, and Portuguese, Dutch, British, and French slave merchants, who were often in competition.[6]

1.1 AFRICAN AGENTS OF THE LOANGO COAST

West Central African agents were pivotal in these commercial and cultural exchanges. Although responding to the external demand for enslaved Africans, unlike other regions of West Central Africa that supplied African captives to the Atlantic slave trade, the three centralized states of the Loango coast controlled their trade in human beings and maintained their independence vis-à-vis European merchants. Another crucial factor to consider is that the inhabitants of the Loango coast never fully and officially embraced Christianity as did their neighbor, the Kingdom of Kongo. As European powers such as the Dutch Republic, Britain, France, and Portugal started to trade in enslaved Africans in the region during the eighteenth century, middlemen such as the *Mfuka* increasingly acquired wealth and political power vis-à-vis noblemen, therefore transforming the balance of power in these societies. In this process, European luxury gifts contributed to shaping the dynamics of the Atlantic slave trade, whereas the commerce in human beings also transformed African and European material culture.

In the early sixteenth century, the Kingdom of Loango was the dominant state on the Loango coast. The region's environment included fertile soil, forests, and savannas with rich wildlife, as well as a long shoreline and several rivers, all of which favored the rise of a robust and unified polity. By the time of the arrival of the Portuguese, the region was occupied by the Vili, a term that originally designated caravaneers.[7] The Vili people belong to "a branch of the large Kongo family of the West Central African Bantu," whose language Vili belongs to the Kongo clade, and is part of the Bantu group.[8] When discussing the origins of the Loango coast's peoples, Phyllis Martin relied on the premise advanced by the late historian Jan Vansina (1929–2017), who in turn drew directly on the work of Dutch physician and armchair geographer Olfert Dapper (1636–1689).[9] According to this hypothesis, the peoples of the kingdoms of Loango, Kakongo, and Ngoyo had a common origin in the region of Mpumbu (also referred to by Europeans as Pombo). This area is located north of the Pool Malebo (Lake Nkunda) at the border of the twenty-first century Republic of the Congo and the Democratic Republic of the Congo. Hence, the Vili, along with the Kongo peoples, may have migrated to the region in the early fourteenth century or even earlier. Martin states that the *Maloango* (ruler of Loango) claimed connections to the royal family of the Kingdom of Kongo, from which his polity became independent between the late fourteenth century and the early fifteenth century.[10] But Vansina questioned the claim that Loango had been a former province of the Kingdom of Kongo, rather insisting that "there is no doubt that this state may well be as old as Kongo itself."[11]

Regardless of its origins, starting in the seventeenth century, the Kingdom of Loango (and its homonymous port) became the dominant state of the Loango Bay. Several European travelers who visited the region described the kingdom's inland capital Mbanza Loango (or Buali), where the *Maloango* resided, as an impressive town. The Dutch referred to its great size, comparing it to Amsterdam.[12] In the seventeenth century, the Kingdom of Ngoyo and the Kingdom of Kakongo formed two smaller polities independent from Loango. Yet the exact moment of their independence is unclear, and the two kingdoms may have continued paying tribute to Loango up to the eighteenth century.[13]

Kakongo was inhabited by the Kotchi and its coast extended over nearly 25 miles, from the Chiloango River in the north to the Lulondo River in the south. Its western frontier formed a curve that met the Congo River at Ponta da Lenha in twenty-first century's Democratic Republic of the Congo, whereas its eastern border curved south, passing Mayombe and the western part of Bungu, and ended at the Congo River near Mboma, today's Boma in the twenty-first century Democratic Republic of the Congo. A few miles distant from the mouth of the Chiloango River was Malembo, Kakongo's main harbor; approximately 28 miles inland was Kinguelé (Europeans called it Banze-Malimbe), the kingdom's capital. At the south, the Kingdom of Ngoyo occupied a territory approximately half the size of Kakongo and one-quarter of the territory of the Kingdom of Loango. Ngoyo's coastline stretched from the mouth of the Lulondo River at the north to the Congo River's estuary at the south; its borders then followed the river's north bank up to the Kakongo border. To the east, the kingdom's territory boarded the rivers Lukala and Kalamu.[14] Ngoyo's capital, Mbanza Ngoyo, was 5 Dutch miles (nearly 18 US miles) from its port, Cabinda.[15] Ngoyo was inhabited by the Woyo people. The Kotchi and the Woyo spoke Kiwoyo, whereas the Vili spoke Kivili.[16]

Historians have written the history of the states of the Loango coast by mainly relying on contemporary written sources produced by European travelers, officers, and merchants, who upon returning to Europe published journals and travelogues, usually illustrated with maps and engravings. As with any other sources, these accounts must be approached with caution. Although several travelers wrote their own travelogues, others were the result of a different process in which an experienced writer composed and published an account based on the traveler's oral observations and written notes. As a specific writing genre, travel accounts use description, narration, and commentary as modes of enunciation. Description aims to offer an allegedly objective point of view of the inhabitants and a picture of the natural world visited by the traveler. Through narration, authors can tell stories of events that took place during their journeys in distant lands. In contrast, passages employing commentary become opportunities to provide judgment and explanations often based on other written sources.[17]

When all these forms of enunciation are employed, travelers end up borrowing elements from other travelogues. As a result, in approaching these sources, historians need to compare these travelogues with other sources, paying attention not only to the possible differences among various editions of the same travel account, but also to different accounts published by various authors who visited the same places in the same periods. Despite the still scarce number of scholarly works focusing on the Loango coast, in the early seventeenth century, several European accounts published in English, Dutch, Portuguese, and French started to describe the West Central African coastal societies north of the Congo River. According to these written reports, the social structure of the three main polities of the Loango coast had similar characteristics.

Loango, Ngoyo, and Kakongo comprised a class structure of nobles, commoners, and slaves. Loango was ruled by the *Maniloango*, Kakongo by the *Manikakongo*, and Ngoyo by the *Maningoyo*. The kings of the three polities exerted their authority over the social, political, and economic spheres of their kingdoms, but their spiritual dimension was crucial. These rulers had strong religious roles and lived very restricted lives. Both the *Maloango* and the *Manikakongo* could not be seen eating or drinking. English traveler and slave trader Andrew Battell, who lived in Loango from 1607 to 1610, recounted this interdiction to Samuel Purchas:

When the King drinketh he hath a cup of wine brought, and he that bringeth it hath a Bell in his hand, and assoone as he hath delivered the cup to the King, hee turneth his face from the King, and ringeth the Bell: and then all that be there fall downe upon their faces, and rise not till the King have drunke ... For it is their Beliefe, that if hee bee seene eating or drinking, hee shall presently dye.[18]

It is hard to determine whether travelers witnessed these events or just heard about these prohibitions. However, Dutch merchant Pieter van den Broecke (1585–1640), who composed his journal upon his return to the Dutch Republic in 1630, nearly seventeen years after the publication of the first version of Battell's account, also corroborated this interdiction: "When this king drinks, no one can watch him, or else forfeit his neck.

When he wants to drink a little bell is rung. Then everyone around him falls on their faces. After he has drunk, it is rung again. Then everyone rises once again."[19]

According to contemporary observers, biased by their Christian views, which led them to portray Africans in a derogatory manner, the subjects of the Loango coast kingdoms perceived their rulers as semidivine figures who held supernatural powers. Van den Broecke, for instance, reported that the "king himself is a great magician and speaks often with the Devil."[20] They were also prohibited from seeing the ocean, consuming foreign goods, and interacting with Europeans.[21] French Abbé Liévin-Bonaventure Proyart corroborated this information in his published account based on observations made by Catholic missionaries who sailed to the Loango coast in 1766. Likewise, French naval officer and slave trader Louis-Marie-Joseph Ohier de Grandpré, who visited the region twice during the same period and published a travel account in the early nineteenth century, underscored that both the *Maloango* and the *Manikakongo* had to follow numerous restrictions.[22] Proyart discussed the origins of these limitations, emphasizing that the "first legislators of the nation may have imposed this law on the sovereigns in order to delay the progress of luxury and to teach the people, by the example of their masters, to do without the foreigner, by seeking remedies in its own industry."[23] Still, he emphasizes that these restrictions were only imposed on the king, while his subjects, including his ministers, trafficked in all kinds of European goods.[24]

The succession to the throne of the three kingdoms on the Loango coast initially followed a matrilineal model. However, choosing a new ruler was a complicated process, and various authors and contemporary observers reported processes that involved elective and hereditary elements. In his early seventeenth-century account, Battell referred to four princes (*Mani Cabango, Mani Salag, Mani Bock*, and *Mani Cay*) of Loango who were the sons of the king's sister; because "the Kings sonnes never come to be Kings."[25] Yet these observations must be nuanced as systems of succession changed over the long period in which the Atlantic slave trade operated in the region. In his eighteenth-century account, Proyart explained that in the Kingdom of Loango, the heir to the throne was selected from among the *Maloango*'s nephews. According to Martin, they usually came from a specific clan, the Kondi (the members of the ruling dynasty).[26]

Other contemporary observers noted that in Kakongo and Ngoyo the throne was not hereditary but elective. In Kakongo, when the ruler died, his brothers became the heirs to the throne, and in the absence of any brothers, the successor was selected from among the sons of his sisters, by order of age. Still, because the successor could only be enthroned after the sovereign's funeral, a regent (*Maboma*) ruled the kingdom during the period of transition.[27] Proyart reported that in the kingdoms where the ruler did not designate his successor before his death or in those where there was an elective process, such as in Ngoyo, the rulers' funerals were followed by battles that could lead to veritable civil wars.[28] Proyart reminded his readers that the ruler of Loango and Ngoyo often delayed for a long time his decision on who was the next in line to occupy the throne "either to not alienate the person he loves enough to want to make him his successor, or to keep all Princes attached to his interests, by letting each of them enjoy the hope of becoming the object of his choice."[29]

In the early seventeenth century, Battell already mentioned four princes of Loango, each of whom was awarded a fief. The fourth of these princes, the *Manikay* (presumably the *Makaya* or *Manicaye*), was "the next to be king."[30] Proyart described the *Mambuku* as a prince whose office was lesser than that of the *Makaya*.[31] According to him, in Loango and Ngoyo, the sovereign designated his successor by awarding a fief (*kaïa*) to the selected candidate.[32] Henceforth, the *Makaya* was prohibited from entering the kingdom's capital until the ruler was dead and interred. As in the Kikongo language, the term *kaya* means, among other things, a remote place, this stance seems to be plausible. Similarly, other French contemporary sources refer to the *Makaya* as the "presumed heir to the crown."[33] In the late eighteenth century, Grandpré explained the commercial activities in Malembo, designating the *Mambuku* and the *Makaya* as two different officials, the former being a wealthy broker and heir to the throne and the latter the prime minister.[34] Some historians refer to the *Mambuku* as being the equivalent of the *Makaya*.[35] But other scholars who examine the social structure of the Kingdom of Ngoyo tend to agree with Proyart and Grandpré by clearly establishing a distinction between the *Mambuku*, described as a governor, heir to the throne, and residing near Cabinda, and the *Makaya*, identified as the *Maningoyo*'s main advisor and prime minister.[36]

1.2 LOANGO'S EXTERNAL TRADE

The Dutch started visiting the Loango Bay in 1593, disrupting the Portuguese commercial monopoly along the coast of West Central Africa.[37] As historian Filipa Ribeiro da Silva explains, these initial commercial exchanges with African societiess involved the combination of long-distance travel and several shorter coastal circuits, which often encompassed several ports in West Africa and West Central Africa. Usually, larger vessels departed from the Dutch Republic followed by a smaller yacht carrying one or two prefabricated sloops. While the main vessel anchored in the port, the yachts and sloops would trade along the coast, collecting goods that were later stored in the main ship.[38]

European observers who traded on the Loango coast recorded information about commercial exchanges in the region. Their early observations indicate that rivalries among European merchants emerged early in the first years of their presence in the coastal area, a few decades before the rise of the slave trade. For example, on board the ship *Neptunnis,* Van den Broecke anchored for the first time in the Loango Bay in April 1608. Upon his arrival, he learned about the antagonistic reactions of Portuguese officials to Dutch competitors; after all, a few years earlier, Portugal had been the only European trading power in the region.[39] Informed about the recent assassination of a Dutch ship master, Van den Broecke soon realized he needed to be vigilant. The tragic event had unfolded before his arrival, when Dutch merchant Pieter Brandt anchored off the Loango coast on board the yacht *Meerminne.* The Portuguese invited Brandt, Pieter Tillmans, and the ship master Augustijn Cornelissen to come on board their ship in the Loango Bay. As Brandt fell ill, only his two men went to the appointment. When they approached the ship, the Portuguese, mistaking Cornelissen for Brandt, "shot [him] dead with a flintlock," captured the other men who were on their boat, and sent them to Luanda.[40] This episode was just one in a series of violent conflicts between European powers that occurred on the Loango coast during the era of the Atlantic slave trade. Although the primary sources rarely refer to violence between European and local populations in the region, these clashes certainly took place.

In 1610, Van den Broecke opened the first Dutch trading post on the Loango coast. The initial commercial and cultural exchanges did not involve the acquisition of enslaved people. Dutch traders purchased from local agents great amounts of ivory from elephant tusks obtained in the interior of the territory. They also acquired *takula* (*tacola* or *tekola*), a red wood comparable to brazilwood found along Brazil's Atlantic coast during the sixteenth century and also used as dye in the textile production.[41] In exchange, they provided local kingdoms with a variety of cloths that had been manufactured in the Dutch Republic.

On his third voyage to the Loango coast in 1611, Van den Broecke reached Cabinda, situated nearly 30 miles north of the Congo River. In an entry from May 1612, the Dutch trader reported that he was "very well received by the natives."[42] However, his journal shows that already in those early days of external trade, it was not just European traders who were in competition; the Kingdom of Loango and the Kingdom of Ngoyo also had conflictual relations. Van den Broecke is not clear on whether he actually met the *Maningoyo* when he visited Ngoyo's capital, Mbanza Ngoyo, as in theory the ruler could not directly interact with European agents. Yet his account described the ruler as an "old and cruel man" who had fought against the Tio Kingdom and the Kingdom of Loango.[43] In his account published in the late seventeenth century, Dapper, who never traveled to Africa, also portrayed the hostilities of the Woyo people of Ngoyo against the Kotchi of Kakongo.[44] By 1631, the Kongo's province of Soyo, located in the coastal area just south of the Congo River, attacked Ngoyo. But one decade later, the Dutch continued to perceive Ngoyo as "the most aggressive of the lands north of the river, with Kakongo as its persistent enemy, but also placed it outside Kongo's control."[45]

Unlike the Portuguese, the Dutch were in a much better position to supply Vili traders with a great variety of their manufactured cloths. In their first contacts with Loango's trade agents, Van den Broecke and the members of his crew purchased elephant's tusks with red *vierlooden*, a heavy cloth "with four lead seals indicating its high quality."[46] Likewise, the *Maloango*'s agents provided the merchant with twenty units of locally made palm cloth, whose unit (*kùtu* or *makutu* or *makuta*) was used as currency on the Loango coast, therefore allowing the Dutch trader to purchase palm wine for his Vili commercial partners.[47] During the seventeenth century, like *takula* red dye, Dutch and Portuguese merchants, as well as the local population, procured palm cloth produced in the polities of the Loango coast.[48] During the 1640s, palm cloth was also the main adopted currency in then Dutch-controlled Luanda.[49] During the eighteenth and nineteenth centuries, visitors to the Loango coast continued to report various uses for *makutu* in the region, including as currency.[50]

The three main kingdoms of the Loango coast entertained exchanges not only among themselves, but also with neighboring states in the hinterland and to the south of the Congo River. In the 1590s, the Portuguese governor of Luanda sent the English trader Andrew Battell to trade in Loango. Battell's cargo included "European manufactured goods" such as blue and red cloths, Irish rugs, a variety of beads, and "looking glasses" (mirrors) with which he purchased elephants' teeth, palm cloth, and elephant tails, commodities that along with copper were the main products exported from the Loango coast states.[51]

The trade connections of the Kingdom of Loango encompassed a wide network spanning from the Gabon estuary in the north to the Pool

Malebo in the south, where the Teke (the inhabitants of the Teke or Tio Kingdom) were established. The Vili also sent caravans to the districts of Sette and Mayumba in the north and to Cango and Kesocuh, two eastern districts of Mayombe, to procure large amounts of ivory that they transported to the coastal area. The Vili also sent convoys to the Niari Basin to procure copper that, since the sixteenth century, they had traded with the Portuguese and then with the Dutch. This area was located between Boko-Songo and Mindouli, east of the kingdoms of Loango and Kakongo and northeast of the Kingdom of Ngoyo, near twenty-first century's southern border of the Republic of the Congo, a region spread over nearly 60 miles.[52] After the smiths mined, smelted, and molded the copper into the form of bars or rings, Vili traders transported it to the coast to feed their commercial transactions in Loango and Kakongo.[53]

As in other societies where slavery existed, in Loango, Kakongo, and Ngoyo, the ownership of enslaved individuals was regarded as a form of wealth.[54] Likewise, a person's position as free or slave depended on the status of his or her mother.[55] In these polities, enslaved people performed a variety of activities. For example, in the Kingdom of Loango, enslaved men cleared the land. They were porters who carried all kinds of commodities and transported people between different places in litters, which they carried upon their shoulders and heads.[56] In addition to extracting ivory, they also obtained *takula* as well as copper, which they transported from the interior to the coast.[57]

1.3 THE TRADE IN PEOPLE ON THE LOANGO COAST

During the seventeenth century, Loango, Kakongo, and Ngoyo gradually started selling enslaved individuals to the Dutch and the Portuguese. The long-existing commercial routes served as the basis for the emerging paths of the Atlantic slave trade, in which enslaved persons increasingly replaced the previously traded commodities. By 1636, Dutch merchants traded in slaves along the coasts of West Central Africa. But until the 1640s, human commerce remained marginal on the Loango coast because its states were unable to provide captives, who were mainly sought by Portuguese merchants and slave traders established south of the Congo River.[58] However, in the 1670s, the demand for captives increased as Dutch, English, and Portuguese merchants procured enslaved Africans for their colonies in the Americas. This new need led to a gradual and steady intensification of slave-trading activities in the region.[59] At the end of the seventeenth century, Dapper was already referring to the commerce in human beings as the most important external trade activity in the Kingdom of Loango, even though ivory, copper, tin, lead, *takula*, and iron continued to be exported in the following years.[60]

According to Proyart, suppliers of captives and traders were not allowed to sell into slavery individuals who had been born in the kingdoms of the Loango coast, except for those who had committed a crime "specified in the law."[61] These customs were similar to those in other regions in West Africa and West Central Africa, where, at least initially, enslaved peoples were outsiders; however, during the eighteenth and nineteenth centuries, this rule was often disregarded.[62] Proyart also emphasized that most enslaved persons sold to the French were individuals who had been captured during raids and wars being waged in the interior of the territory.[63] Martin identifies three main sources for enslaved individuals who were sold in the ports of the Loango coast as part of the Atlantic slave trade. The first included inhabitants of the coastal kingdoms who were being punished for crimes. The second consisted of captives taken during raids led by coastal peoples beyond the borders of their kingdoms. The third comprised individuals enslaved in the interior, who were transported to the coast in caravans along the usual commercial routes. In contrast with Proyart, Martin underscores that only a small number of enslaved individuals purchased at the ports of the Loango coast were obtained through warfare. Although recognizing that obtaining captives "involved ambush, kidnapping, skirmishes, and surprise attacks on villages, rather than full-scale war," she insists that in the eighteenth century most enslaved Africans were acquired through traders who "brought slaves in caravans from the interior."[64]

Relying on European contemporary observers and sociolinguistics sources, Christina Mobley explores the origins of captives who were deported from the Loango coast to the Americas. She emphasizes that Proyart provided a variety of exceptions, ultimately showing that in the kingdoms of the Loango coast only princes and lords who accumulated a large number of dependents were protected from being sold into slavery.[65] Contesting previous conclusions that placed the geographical source of the enslaved Africans traded on the Loango coast either in the Kingdom of Kongo, the inland Pool Malebo, or the upper Congo River, she argues that the peoples of the kingdoms of the Loango coast and the Mayombe forest were not middlemen, as previously assumed, but were rather the very individuals who were sold into slavery. According to Mobley, this shift provoked by the slave trade disrupted traditional political institutions.[66] John K. Thornton disagrees with this interpretation, which explains the transformations in the kingdoms of the Loango coast as provoked by external trade, namely the trade in enslaved Africans. Instead, he explains these changes as the result of rivalries among local lineages seeking to take control of the state, in addition to periodic intervention of Soyo in Ngoyo's and Kakongo's political affairs.[67] More recently, Kathryn de Luna has added new layers to Mobley's interpretation, showing that linguistic evidence suggests that enslaved people could have originated from even further away.[68] However, as we will see in the subsequent chapters, these various interpretations are very probably not exclusive. Internal divisions among powerful clans who sought to control the state were not dissociated from the impact produced by the flow of material resources that was generated by the intensification of the Atlantic slave trade in the eighteenth century.

Regardless of these contrasting interpretations, moments of succession to the throne provoked disputes that led noblemen and noblewomen to be sold into slavery, as in other African societies during the era of the Atlantic slave trade.[69] In the three kingdoms of the Loango coast, succession and inheritance followed matrilineal descent. In his account based on his travel to the region in the late eighteenth century, Grandpré reported the story of Tati, a man from Malembo who was sold into slavery in Cap-Français (also known as Le Cap) in Saint-Domingue, and then brought back home by a French slave trader. Tati was the son of Vaba, the Malembo's *Mfuka*, who married his mother, a Cabinda's princess who was also the sister of the *Maningoyo*. Despite being the son of a woman carrying the title of princess, as explained by Grandpré, his mother was not born a princess, which is why he was not eligible to become king.[70]

As the Atlantic slave trade emerged on the Loango coast during the seventeenth century, the king and the trade's agents established along the coast each had different roles associated with their interaction with European traders and African suppliers. Take the example of the Dutch trader Pieter van den Broecke. It remains uncertain if he met the *Maloango* in person during his three visits to the region. Yet it was clear that he needed the ruler's permission to conduct trade in the Kingdom of Loango. Moreover, obtaining permission to trade involved providing local authorities with valuable presents.[71] Similar to what happened in West African ports such as Ouidah in the Bight of Benin, Anomabu on the Gold Coast, and Benguela and Luanda, rulers of the states of the Loango coast relied on several representatives. Therefore, Dutch traders had many disagreements with Loango's middlemen over these "presents" that had to be paid in addition to the cost of European goods.[72]

1.4 GIFT EXCHANGES AND THE *MFUKA*'S ROLE

Despite disputes between European and African agents, gift exchanges were not new or specific to Atlantic Africa; they had been central to the development of diplomatic interactions since antiquity. Moreover, the practice of giving gifts to initiate trade was not original to the Loango coast. As an instrument to create ties of dependence, gift exchanges had been in place in West Central Africa before the arrival of Europeans in the region and were immediately embraced by the Portuguese in their early contacts with West Central African populations. According to the late Joseph C. Miller (1939–2019), the "[g]ivers initiated transactions to confirm the inferiority of receivers," or in other words, "gifts constituted loans confirming the subordinated borrower's general obligation to repay at some unstated future time and in some other, as yet unspecified, material form."[73] In a much more nuanced way, historian Mariana P. Candido underscores the nature of gifts as tributes when examining the foundation of Benguela in 1617. According to her, the "payment of tributes, or gifts, as the Portuguese officially termed such exchanges, sealed diplomatic relationships and represented the right to settle temporarily in the territory."[74]

A closer examination of gift exchanges on the Loango coast during the era of the Atlantic slave trade shows that gift receivers were not simple borrowers. Moreover, not all gifts were tributes. The practice of giving gifts to obtain advantage in commercial exchanges continued among the agents of the Loango coast kingdoms over the next centuries. When describing Kakongo, Dapper explained that the Portuguese and Dutch traded at its port (Malembo) the same goods they exchanged in Loango, but "are not obliged to give as much presents in order to obtain freedom of commerce."[75] Although not traders, French Catholic missionaries who arrived on the Loango coast in 1768 with the hope of converting its rulers to Catholicism, reported that even a native who wanted to meet the *Maloango* had to offer him a present.[76] Giving gifts to local rulers and agents was also a well-established practice at West African ports on the Guinea Coast, the Bight of Benin, and the Gold Coast.[77] In other words, in the context of these exchanges, these gifts were paid by Europeans to local rulers and agents in order to obtain permission to engage in trade and missions of evangelization.

As in other coastal areas of West Central Africa, the trade with Europeans on the Loango coast operated through an extended network that involved European merchants, ship captains, and their crews, who interacted with a variety of African brokers and traders. These local traders made incursions into the interior, where they obtained goods that were transported by caravans to the coast. Upon their arrival at the coast, European captains paid duties to the *Maloango* in Loango, the *Manikakongo* in Kakongo, and the *Maningoyo* in Ngoyo, which were collected by the *Mfuka*, a sort of minister of commerce.[78] According to a seventeenth-century vocabulary compiled by Catholic missionary Georgius Gelensis, the term *mfuka* means debt, whereas the *mfuku* refers to utility, advantage, profit, and interest.[79] In an early twentieth-century French dictionary of Kikongo-French, several words convey the idea of eating and paying. For example, the verb *dīa* or *dyā* means to eat, have a meal, consume, absorb, gnaw, burn, swallow, finish a dish, devour, serve, and use money. But *dīamfuka* means to go into debt, owe, assume a debt.[80] Likewise the word *dīīka* is the adjective from the verb *dīa* that means feed or give food or something that can be eaten (a goat, for example) as a gift. Therefore *dīīkamfuka* is to give someone the opportunity to get into debt, lend to, prepay, whereas the word *kidīīkamfuka* means creditor.[81] Similarly, the word *kūula* means redeem, pay a debt, deliver, to set free, to free (at the price of money), exonerate, pay the ransom (of a prisoner, of a slave), pay dearly (any price, however high it may be), reward, whereas *kūulamfuka* means to pay, redeem.[82] Perhaps future studies of the word *mfuka* may better illuminate the individual holding the *Mfuka*'s office was in charge of collecting tributes.

Appointed by the king, the *Mfuka* managed the trade with Europeans on the Loango coast. Unlike the rulers of Loango, Kakongo, and Ngoyo whose residences were situated inland, the *Mfuka* resided on the coast where trade occurred. In addition to collecting duties, he set the price of European products, and mediated occasional disputes between European merchants, local brokers, and traders.[83] Moreover, the *Mfuka* was a slave trader, who imposed his captives on local brokers and waived taxes on selected merchants. In return, European merchants gave him gifts and advantages that contributed to his wealth. The *Mfuka* was also a broker, who selected and separated captives brought by slave traders from the interior, therefore acquiring more wealth through the development of his own private trade with Europeans. The *Mfuka* also appointed lesser *Mfukas* in other marginal trading centers situated along rivers and lakes, and in other distant centers where Europeans procured enslaved people.

Despite the *Mfuka*'s significant role, the rulers of Kakongo and Ngoyo also appointed another official, the *Mambuku*, whose role was similar to that of a prime minister (*Makaya*).[84] Yet, starting in the eighteenth century, it may only have been the *Mfuka* who was in charge of collecting duties and organizing the trade with Europeans.[85] The Kingdom of Loango also had a *Mambuku*, but his position was that of a governor who controlled the frontier with Mayombe, an inland region comprising forests and mountains. In contrast, in Kakongo and Ngoyo, the *Mambuku* was a rich man. An important broker, he was usually second in line to occupy the throne. In Kakongo and Ngoyo, the appointment of a second official to negotiate with the Europeans may have indicated a desire to keep control of the trade because these kingdoms' capitals (where the sovereigns resided) were more distant from the coast.[86]

There were also other officers in the three kingdoms of the Loango coast. The *Mangovo za Ngoyo* (or *Mangove*) was a "powerful broker and wealthy man" who oversaw external affairs and introduced foreigners to the court. His aide was the *Mamputu* in charge of the relations with the Europeans.[87] The *Mambele* (or *Manibele* or *Mwelele*) was the king's messenger. In Ngoyo, along with the *Mamboma* and the *Mangovo*, he was a member of the regency committee who ruled the kingdom after the death of the king until the enthronement of the new monarch. The *Makimba* (or *Maquimbe*) was described by Grandpré as an officer responsible for all activity along the coast, including fishing, and whose role was comparable to that of a port captain.[88] Proyart, however, portrayed him as responsible for the forests and waters, and charged with inspecting "all boatmen, fishermen and hunters and it is to him that we send the fish and game that intended to the king."[89] The *Makimba* provided "Europeans with canoes and men to transport goods from ships to factories."[90] There was also the *Mambanza* (or *Manibanze*), a royal treasurer of sorts, who collected taxes and debts owed to the king.[91] The *Matiente* participated in the trade's organization.[92] As Martin emphasizes, all these officials received small amounts of goods and currencies from Europeans. Yet she also underscores that virtually anybody, including nobles, commoners, and servants, could become a broker, in other words, a middleman in the slave trade. Still, the most powerful ones were those holding an official position such as the *Mfuka* and the *Mambuku*.[93] Ultimately, the divine status of the rulers of the three main polities of the Loango coast, and the constraints this entailed, allowed the emergence of several officers who played the role of middlemen in the contacts with European agents trading along the Loango coast. With the intensification of the Atlantic slave trade in the eighteenth century, these individuals acquired an increasing amount of wealth. Through their growing economic power they sought to acquire political authority and to undermine the king's influence, whose mobility and ability to engage in social exchanges was already limited by numerous restrictions.[94]

In the eighteenth century, the rapidly increasing demand for enslaved Africans in European colonies propelled the export of the largest number of enslaved Africans from West Central Africa and West Africa to the Americas. In Brazil, the discovery of gold and diamond reserves contributed to increasing imports of enslaved Africans. During this period, the production of wheat, rice, tobacco, and cotton cultivated by enslaved people consolidated the development of slave societies in the thirteen colonies of North America that at the end of the eighteenth century became the United States of America. More importantly, the ports of the Loango coast, the region that interests us here, were directly impacted by this new context, marked by the consolidation of robust plantation economies in the West Indies that mainly relied on sugar, coffee, and indigo. During the eighteenth century, French slave merchants also started to acquire enslaved Africans in the three ports of the Loango coast in order to provide an enslaved workforce for slave-based sugar production in the French West Indies, especially in Saint-Domingue.[95]

Whereas the slave trade grew on the Loango coast, the *Mfuka*'s wealth also dramatically increased with the intensification of the Atlantic slave trade from the eighteenth century until the middle of the nineteenth century.[96] During this period, the *Mfuka*'s position acquired more importance. In the Kingdom of Loango, the sale of offices became one of the *Maloango*'s main sources of income by the end of the eighteenth century. Thus, only affluent individuals could occupy the *Mfuka*'s position. Moreover, in addition to purchasing the office, the *Mfuka* also paid the ruler an annual fee extracted from the tax he received on the monarch's behalf. Although originally a commoner, the *Mfuka* could marry a princess and obtain the privileges awarded to royalty.[97]

In the early eighteenth century, a series of wars among various western European states disturbed the Atlantic slave trade. These conflicts also impacted the slave trade on the Loango coast, where European powers competed to maintain their access to the ports supplying them with enslaved Africans. From 1703 to 1714, the War of the Spanish Succession fought by France and Spain against Britain and the Dutch Republic, as well as Prussia and Portugal, acquired continental dimensions and ultimately established Britain as an imperial power. Between 1754 and 1764, a war between the British and the French over the control of the center of the North American continent emerged. Despite initial support given to the French by most Amerindian populations, Britain won the conflict and gained control of a growing territory in the west of North America.

Meanwhile, between 1756 and 1763, in what became known as the Seven Years' War (or French Indian War), Britain and France (supported by Spain) were also fighting for the hegemony of the Atlantic region.[98] The war basically paused the slave trade on the Loango coast. After the end of the conflict, as established in the Treaty of Paris of 1763, Britain seized New France and Spanish Florida, and consolidated its presence in the West Indies. With the end of the Seven Years' War, and a few years later with the rise of the American Revolutionary War (1775–1783), France became the dominant power of the Atlantic slave trade on the Loango coast. By this time, the economy of the kingdoms of Loango, Kakongo, and Ngoyo was solidly organized around the Atlantic slave trade.

Despite the growing European presence on the Loango coast during the eighteenth century, and unlike in West African ports such as Ouidah in the Bight of Benin or Cape Coast on the Gold Coast, or West Central African ports such as Benguela and Luanda, local rulers continued to control all dimensions of the Atlantic slave trade in the region. Prevented from constructing forts or other robust permanent settlements along the Loango coast, Europeans still needed to get permission from the *Mfuka* to establish small temporary trading posts to conduct their activities in the coastal area.[99] In the seventeenth century, for instance, the Dutch used *leggers* to trade along the littoral. These vessels have been described as "small yachts or barges … that would stay anchored on the coast for a certain period of time, which could last from a few weeks to a year or longer."[100] Contemporary eighteenth-century accounts reported widespread rumors of ill health, which Europeans feared during their time trading on the coast. Their improvised and temporary outposts, shared by European crew members and their captives, may have contributed to the outbreak of epidemics. Very often, the crews of the slave ships spent the night on board their own vessels, which were transformed into "holding pens," and used the built structures just as warehouses.[101] However, avoiding sleeping in these provisional structures may have been a strategy to prevent possible attacks led by local agents and other European traders, a common occurrence in other ports of West Central Africa.[102]

1.5 RISING TRADE, EMERGING DIVISIONS

Unlike the ports and Portuguese colonies of Luanda and Benguela located south of the Congo River, the ports of Loango, Malembo, and Cabinda were never controlled by Portugal or any other European power.

Likewise, despite several attempts led by Portuguese (and later by French) Catholic missionaries, the rulers of the three polities of the Loango coast never embraced Christianity as did their southern neighbor, the Kingdom of Kongo. Before the arrival of the Europeans in the region, caravans departed from the Loango coast to the interior to procure a variety of commodities, including copper and ivory, which along with palm cloth and other goods used as currencies were traded with their neighbors. In the sixteenth century, the emerging kingdoms of Ngoyo, Kakongo, and Loango continued to rely on these long-existing trade networks for commercial exchanges with Portuguese and Dutch traders. As we have seen in this chapter, the first external trade of these kingdoms included providing goods such as ivory, copper, *takula*, and palm cloth in exchange for European manufactured goods such as textiles, beads, and all kinds of hardware.

As the demand for enslaved men, women, and children increased with the European colonization of the Americas during the seventeenth century, following the track of their neighbors south to the Congo River, the states of the Loango coast started to sell enslaved individuals to the Dutch, the English, the French, and the Portuguese, who after 1807 became along with the Brazilians the dominant presence in the region. As in other African slaving ports, local rulers relied on a variety of official representatives in their dealings with European merchants. However, as the slave trade intensified in Loango, Kakongo, and Ngoyo during the eighteenth century, increasing conflicts emerged among these kingdoms. As we will see in the next chapters, whereas European traders competed among themselves to obtain the best conditions to trade in enslaved Africans, African coastal commercial agents demanded special favors in the form of gifts as the Atlantic slave trade intensified. And as these agents acquired more wealth, they sought to obtain more political power and made attempts to alienate the authority of the kings. As the following chapters show, gifts of prestige increased competition among local brokers and fueled disagreements among European powers trading along the Loango coast. Such internal divisions and dependence on foreign luxury items opened a breach that favored European colonial rule in the region after the end of the Atlantic slave trade.

2

La Rochelle and Atlantic Africa

Slave ships from the French northwestern city of La Rochelle carried a variety of commodities to the various West Central African ports of the Loango coast in the eighteenth century. Using these commodities as currencies, ship captains purchased captive Africans and transported them to the French West Indies, especially to the ports of Cap-Français (Le Cap) and Port-au-Prince in Saint-Domingue (see Map 2). La Rochelle's long slave-trading history and deep connections with slavery in the Americas are imprinted everywhere in the city's streets, houses, wharves, and churches. Most of the city's attentive residents know this history, even though tourists who visit the city today can hardly imagine how this scenic seaport with its preserved medieval towers and early modern buildings could have been connected to the trade in enslaved Africans. But with a quick walk through the streets of the old town, visitors can see a myriad of landmarks that bear witness to the city's long involvement in the Atlantic slave trade.

A tour of the Musée du Nouveau Monde illustrates this atrocious side of the city's history. Housed in the hôtel Fleuriau, the ancient but luxurious residence of shipowner, merchant, and planter Aimé-Benjamin Fleuriau, the museum displays artifacts, artworks, and furniture that bear witness to how the Atlantic slave trade sustained the wealthy lifestyles of La Rochelle's men who traded in human beings. Hanging on one of the museum's walls is the *Portrait de Anne-Marie Grellier avec sa nourrice noire* (portrait of Marie Grellier with her black wetnurse) (Figure 2.1), dated 1718. The oil painting depicts a well-dressed Black woman wearing a gold necklace with a cross pendant. The unnamed woman is sitting on a Louis XIV armchair holding on her knees a young

29

FIGURE 2.1 Anonymous, *Portrait d'Anne Marie-Grellier avec sa nourrice noire* (portrait of Anne-Marie Grellier with her Black wetnurse), 1718, oil on canvas, 52.3 × 40 inches. Musée du Nouveau Monde de La Rochelle. Photograph: Ana Lucia Araujo, 2022.

blonde girl. Like a miniature adult, the little mistress is wearing a red dress with an apron of white lace and black soutache. In the background, the viewer also sees a sophisticated mahogany table covered with a marble plateau. Next to this portrait, hangs the *Portrait of Marie-Jeanne Grellier avec sa négrillone* (portrait of Marie-Jeanne Grellier with her Black girl) (Figure 2.2). Similar to the previous painting, this portrait features the other Grellier sister. The young mistress wearing a hat of sorts on her head is dressed in a floral fabric dress with an apron and white lace sleeves worn over a lilac petticoat. Sitting next to her is an enslaved Black girl. Possibly bare breasted, she is wearing a blue and white striped petticoat, and her hair is covered with a white turban. The legal status of the Black child is clear, as around her neck she is wearing a silver slave collar. Many luxury items displayed in the rich homes of slave merchants and planters of La Rochelle and other slave trading ports were made of silver. But here the slave collar, intended to restrain and mark the legal status of the slave girl, is also made of silver. As in many other museums, this display does not fully explain how the city's wealth is historically associated with the trade in enslaved Africans. Nonetheless, these two portraits along with the building where the museum is housed, and other artworks and objects displayed in the various rooms, offer the museum's visitors visual and material evidence illustrating the links of La Rochelle's eighteenth-century elite with the Atlantic slave trade and slavery.

La Rochelle's slave-trading activities had multiple dimensions. The city's merchants loaded their vessels traveling to the Atlantic coasts of Africa with a variety of commodities and luxury products. These items were not insignificant objects. In various ways they shaped the commercial, social, and cultural exchanges between La Rochelle's merchants and Loango coast local agents during the era of the Atlantic slave trade. Exploring these exchanges can allow us to better understand the positions of La Rochelle's agents Jean-Amable Lessenne, *Le Montyon*'s ship captain, as well as Daniel Garesché, the rich owner of the ship *Le Montyon* who gave the *Mfuka* Andris Pukuta the silver *kimpaba* as a gift following the Cabinda conflict in 1775. Examining these wealthy men's activities also allows us to situate La Rochelle's position in relation to other ports involved in the trade of enslaved Africans, as well as to envision the links between the French port and the Loango coast, and even more specifically its connections with the West Central African ports of Malembo and Cabinda, where the *Mfuka* Andris Pukuta was established.

2.1 A HUB OF THE FRENCH TRADE IN ENSLAVED AFRICANS

Rupella, meaning small rock, was the first form of La Rochelle's name. The settlement emerged as a fishing village on a rocky peninsula in the ninth century. La Rochelle is surrounded by five islands, the biggest being Ré and Oléron. Its medieval harbor was enclosed by walls and was overlooked by two medieval towers built in the thirteenth and fourteenth centuries; these towers are still prominent in the city today. During this period, La Rochelle became an established port by expanding its connections with other ports in northern Europe. Located in the northwest section of twenty-first century's department of Charente-Maritime, La Rochelle was the historic capital of the province of Aunis, one of the twelve French provinces in the eighteenth century.

As France joined the Atlantic slave trade in the second half of the sixteenth century, ships outfitted in La Rochelle gradually entered the trade in African captives. In 1595, the slave ship *L'Espérance* left La Rochelle for Cape Lopez in West Central Africa, from where it acquired and transported enslaved Africans to Brazil. Few traces of La Rochelle's seventeenth-century slave-trading activities have survived in archival records, but evidence about the presence of an ivory turner in the city in 1619 suggests that vessels departing from the French port were trading ivory, leathers, wax, gum, and gold powder on the coasts of Africa.[1] After this early slaving voyage in 1595 French participation in the Atlantic slave trade intensified in the second half of the seventeenth century. At that point, France had secured its position in Québec, establishing the colony of New France in North America, and in the West Indies, through the occupation of Martinique and Guadeloupe in 1635.

French colonies in the Americas required new trading organizations. In 1664, through the initiative of First Minister of State Jean-Baptiste Colbert, France created the Compagnie des Indes orientales (French East India Company) to conduct trade with India via the Indian Ocean and the Pacific Ocean, giving France greater access to the acquisition of Indian textiles, chief products for the Atlantic slave trade. In 1694, France created the Compagnie des Indes occidentales (French West India Company). This state company controlled the trade monopoly of commodities such as sugar, tobacco, and furs, as well as enslaved Africans with the French colonies in the Americas. Because the French West India Company was not able to supply the French West Indies with the necessary number of enslaved Africans, other compagnies such as the Compagnie du Sénégal (Company of Senegal) and the Compagnie de Guinée (Company of Guinea) were created to provide French colonies with African captives during the second half of the seventeenth century. Yet, as noted by Manuel Covo, French colonial agents regularly challenged the regulations imposing colonial monopoly, known as the *exclusif*.[2] In 1697, France occupied the eastern part of Hispaniola that became Saint-Domingue, which during the eighteenth century became the richest French colony in the Americas. La Rochelle played a central role in the colonial trade, with links spanning as far as China. During the Ancien Régime, La Rochelle was not only the first French port trading with Canada, part of the French colony of New France in North America, but was also linked to the French West Indies, especially Saint-Domingue.[3]

In 1716, the French Crown issued an order that ended the previous system of trading monopolies, allowing individual merchants from Rouen, Bordeaux, Nantes, Saint-Malo, and La Rochelle, and later from other ports such as Le Havre and Honfleur, to outfit slave vessels to all regions of Africa and to exempt French-manufactured items from export taxes. Also exempted from exportation fees were foreign items, including cotton textiles imported from India via the French East India Company that remained stored in the company's warehouses in Lorient, which provided items for the cargoes of slave ships sailing to Africa.[4] Moreover, contraband Indian textiles traveling via the Dutch Republic, England, and Switzerland continued during this period.[5] Although the Compagnie d'Occident (Company of Occident) created by the Scottish banker John Law in 1717 held the monopoly of the French slave trade starting in 1722, in 1725 the company resumed selling licenses to private merchants. During this period, La Rochelle's slave-trading activities intensified. Although Nantes outfitted the largest number of French slave ships and transported the largest number of enslaved Africans to the Americas, vessels departing from La Rochelle carried approximately 166,000 African captives, the second largest figure after Nantes. Likewise, nearly 476 slave voyages departed from La Rochelle to acquire enslaved people on the African coasts, a number behind only Bordeaux and Honfleur.[6] La Rochelle's shipowners outfitted slave vessels that sailed to West Africa and West Central Africa, especially to the port of Malembo and Cabinda on the Loango coast. The slave trade from La Rochelle continued during the eighteenth century despite interruptions provoked by international conflicts, including the War of Polish Succession (1733–1735) and the War of the Austrian Succession (1740–1748), and persisted until the late eighteenth century with the rise of the Saint-Domingue Revolution (1791–1804).

French shipowners and merchants who organized and financed slaving expeditions from various French ports including La Rochelle also sponsored other maritime trading ventures, including direct voyages to the French West Indies, voyages to Asia and the Indian Ocean, cabotage navigation along the European Atlantic and the Mediterranean coasts, as well as fishing expeditions.[7] Slave merchants based in La Rochelle conducted other business activities as well. During the 1760s, one merchant traded indigo from Saint Domingue, whale oil from Rotterdam, brandy from the Oléron Island, wheat from Le Havre, furs from New Orleans, and sugar from Martinique.[8] Many merchants also represented companies that insured the vessels transporting commodities from the French West Indies to metropolitan France and enslaved persons from Africa to the Americas. For example, merchants such as Charles-Théodore Sureau, Nicolas et Emmanuel Weis, Louis Fort, and the family Admyrauld represented the Chambre d'assurances générales (Chamber of General

Insurance). Dumoustier et de Jarnac acted for the Compagnie de Rouen
(Company of Rouen), whereas Jean-Ezeschiel Couilladeau represented
the Compagnie d'Assurances de la Rochelle (Insurance Company of La
Rochelle), and Daniel Garesché was the agent of Compagnie du Havre
(Company of Le Havre).[9]

Many of La Rochelle's shipowners and slave merchants were Huguenots, a term referring to individuals who adhered to the Protestant Refor-
mation of 1517. Until the 1620s, nearly 75 percent of the city's residents
fell into this category. But after Cardinal Richelieu captured the city in
1628, this figure declined to 45 percent, and remained steady in the following decades.[10] In 1685, Louis XIV revoked the Edict of Nantes that
gave limited rights to Protestants. Nearly 200,000 Huguenots left France
to settle in other parts of Europe, including the French West Indies. As
the new edict's restrictions prevented Huguenots from engaging in military and public careers, many of them were compelled to join careers
associated with commerce. La Rochelle's Huguenot diaspora fostered
the development of an international commercial system anchored on the
trade in enslaved Africans.[11]

2.2 ATLANTIC TRADING FAMILIES

As the Atlantic slave trade intensified during the eighteenth century, a
growing number of La Rochelle's businessmen joined the commerce in
enslaved Africans, benefiting from a complex network of local individuals
and families. The presence of foreign brokers in the city also facilitated
the supply of commodities to outfit slave ships that sailed to the coasts of
Africa. These international agents, most of whom were from the Dutch
Republic, Ireland, and Switzerland, married women from La Rochelle's
merchant families and contributed to the reinforcement of the Atlantic
connections among these wealthy trading families that directly or indi-
rectly profited from the trade of African captives. Participation in the trade
was not restricted to men. La Rochelle's women such as Marguerite Bouat,
Marie-Madeleine Denis, Marguerite Boucher, and Anne Busquet joined
these trading endeavors, representing important trading companies.[12]

In La Rochelle, as in other European ports that participated in the
Atlantic slave trade, merchant ventures were family businesses; and
Protestantism played a role in intermarriage ties among members of the
merchant class.[13] Merchants passed their companies to their sons, who
also became merchants. The backgrounds of these businessmen were varied. Some merchants were liberal professionals such as medical doctors,

while others were members of the bourgeoisie or belonged to the nobility. Their international networks allowed them to place their children in foreign trading companies in European centers such as Amsterdam and London. Their activities also had ramifications in other French ports such as Bordeaux, Nantes, Honfleur, Le Havre, and Marseille. Like their European counterparts, La Rochelle's merchants initiated their sons into trading activities by employing them as ship pilots and captains. Take the example of Jean-Jacques Proa, born into a rich family of shipowners and merchants. In 1771, when he was just thirteen years old, he boarded as an apprentice ship pilot the corvette *La Sirenne*, which was owned by the rich La Rochelle merchant Louis Admirault and sailed to Asia.[14]

La Rochelle's merchants and ship captains also acquired plantations in the West Indies, especially in Saint-Domingue, where they also sent their sons to acquire trading experience.[15] As was the case in Nantes, Bordeaux, Le Havre, Bristol, and Liverpool, slave merchants and planters maintained luxurious residences in La Rochelle.[16] Surviving postmortem inventories of eighteenth-century slave merchants indicate that nearly 10 percent of their patrimony was composed of furniture, silver items, and cash.[17] For example, a summary of the liquidation of the estate of a very young member of one of these wealthy families shows several silver tableware articles.[18] These families followed the trends of their time by acquiring luxury articles that reflected their high social position in a society that largely relied on the wealth derived from the sugar industry, which totally depended on slave labor. Not only was all sugar produced in the French West Indies to be exported only to the metropole, but also, until 1732, there were successive decrees prohibiting the establishment of sugar refineries in the colonies. Taking advantage of this situation, La Rochelle became a large center for sugar refineries during the eighteenth century, exporting its refined sugar to northern Europe.[19] Still today, the buildings associated with early La Rochelle refineries belonging to the families Creagh and Vivien are visible in rue Chef-de-Ville.

The residences of La Rochelle's merchants and planters displayed sophisticated furniture items made from a variety of tropical woods, especially mahogany, imported from European colonies in the West Indies, Central America, and the Indian Ocean.[20] Hanging on the walls of these rich mansions were portraits of family members painted by French and foreign artists (Figures 2.1 and 2.2), an important marker of distinction for the class of planters, merchants, and slave owners. Decorating the rooms were lavish artifacts such as dinnerware sets, snuffboxes, and cigar trays made of silver, ivory, and porcelain, materials that witnessed the commercial exchanges between La Rochelle and other ports in Europe, Africa, Asia, and the Americas. Bedrooms, living rooms, and libraries were adorned with curtains, tapestries, ottomans, sofas, and divans, upholstered with velvet, damask, and Indian chintz (*indiennes, chittes,* or *toiles peintes* in French, known in English as calicoes and muslins). Often featuring exotic floral designs on a white background, these painted or printed cotton fabrics imported by the French East India Company became very popular in the seventeenth century, not only for home decoration, but also for clothing production. To avoid competition with other textiles produced locally, France prohibited the importation and production of these textiles in 1686. Yet, as we have already noted, from 1716, this ban excluded foreign cotton and silk textiles destined to be used in the Atlantic slave trade that were stored in warehouses waiting to be loaded onto vessels sailing to the African coasts, where they were used to purchase enslaved people.[21] Moreover, manufactures in independent cities such as Marseille and Mulhouse were exempted from the prohibition and started producing painted textiles as well.[22] Eventually, when the ban was lifted in 1759, several French workshops started to produce these cotton fabrics, which then became more widely consumed by wealthy and modest customers.[23] Along with rich textiles, landscape paintings that often evoked the tropical scenery and daily life in the French West Indies also decorated the walls of the residences of La Rochelle's eighteenth-century merchants. Many portraits depict members of these opulent merchant families accompanied by enslaved people, whom they brought from the West Indies to work as domestic servants in their households in metropolitan France. Also visible in these paintings are the lavish interiors of their homes, featuring a variety of luxurious artifacts (Figures 2.1 and 2.2).

The wealth generated by the slave trade allowed La Rochelle's merchants to surround themselves with a sophisticated material culture that shaped their opulent daily lives. In this cycle, slavery and the Atlantic slave trade stimulated the existence of everyday objects designed for the consumption of sugar and beverages such as coffee and hot chocolate, which were produced by enslaved people transported from Africa to the French West Indies and used by enslaved domestic servants who were brought to port cities such as La Rochelle. Likewise, some of the luxury items such as textiles displayed in these rich households were also part of the cargoes of La Rochelle's slave ships that sailed to the coasts of Africa during the eighteenth century. Yet the most opulent fabrics, as well as silver and gold artifacts, were to be found on a smaller scale in

FIGURE 2.2 Chanteloub, *Portrait de Marie Jeanne Grellier avec sa négrillone* (portrait of Marie-Jeanne Grellier with her Black girl), 1718, oil on canvas, 50 × 42.5 inches. Musée du Nouveau Monde de La Rochelle. Photograph: Ana Lucia Araujo, 2022.

the cargoes of French slave ships, as they were only intended to be given as gifts to local African chiefs who controlled the trade in human beings, not necessarily to intermediaries and petty traders.[24]

2.3 OUTFITTING SLAVING VOYAGES

The preparation for slaving voyages from La Rochelle to the Atlantic coasts of Africa had many similarities with the organization of slave expeditions that departed from other French ports such as Nantes, Bordeaux, and Le Havre. Only a few French shipowners and merchants (known as *armateurs* and *négociants*) financed these expensive voyages themselves. Outfitting slave ships took time. To minimize financial risks, merchants formed companies (*sociétés*) that, although not exclusively dedicated to the slave trade, gathered investments from various partners to outfit vessels bound for the coasts of Africa. These investors, who included the shipowner's relatives, associates, and the ship captain, purchased shares in the slave ship. In other words, many individuals came together in different ways to finance the various aspects of a slave ship's voyage to Atlantic Africa.

Once anchored in the selected African port, captains and their crews bought enslaved people to be transported to the French West Indies, a process that could take several months. When the desired number of men, women, and children had been purchased, these vessels sailed to the French West Indies in journeys that could last eight weeks. Many French vessels engaged in bilateral trade, transporting sugar, coffee, and indigo from the French West Indies directly to metropolitan France. Other vessels followed a triangular trade route. Ships engaged in bilateral trade could be adapted to conduct slave voyages as well. When returning from Africa, after disembarking their human cargo in the French West Indies, the same ships transported commodities back to La Rochelle. As we see in Chapter 3, very often we do not know for sure what commodities specific ships transported when they sailed from La Rochelle to the West Central African and West African coasts to acquire enslaved people, as very few slave-trade journals (*journaux de traite*) of slave ships from La Rochelle have survived in private archives.

The volume of commodities transported in slave ships depended on the tonnage of the vessels. In the eighteenth-century French Atlantic slave trade, there were several units of measure that varied over time and among the different regions along the coast, as well as according to various kinds of goods traded. Of course, the existence of multiple local currencies in West Central Africa long predating the exchanges with European agents shaped the development of unities used during the era of the Atlantic slave trade. As put by Jane I. Guyer, these early local exchanges with multiple currencies gave birth to asymmetrical conversions, and the use of specific currencies changed over time it the Congo River's coastal area. Ultimately, "multiple coexisting currencies symbolized, mediated, and were themselves items in the directional orientation of the flow of goods."[25]

Based on records of several of La Rochelle's eighteenth-century slave ships, historian Jean-Michel Deveau has established some parameters to help us understand what these units meant depending on the period of the trade. For example, an *once* corresponded to 55.5 *livres* when the slave ship *La Méduse* traded on the Gold Coast in 1749 and purchased enslaved people for 9 *onces* each.[26] But when the slave ship *Dahomet* traded in Ouidah in 1773, an *once* corresponded to two pieces of *mouchoirs* (cotton cloth or silk tailored for wear and usually measuring about 27 inches square), known in English as handkerchiefs, or one barrel of 30 *livres* of gunpowder, or 3,000 flints, or six muskets without bayonet, or one 1,000-flint buccaneer.[27] Meanwhile, one *barrique*, a unit used to measure brandy, corresponded to between 150 and 160 kilos and approximately 200 *litres*, whereas one *ancre* of brandy corresponded to nearly 50 liters. Another important unit of measure was the *pièce*, which was the equivalent of two *barriques*.[28] In the context of the slave trade between La Rochelle and ports such as Cabinda in West Central Africa, a *pièce* was a unit of measure that evoked the term *peça das Índias* (literally "piece of the Indies"). First used by Portuguese traders in the fifteenth century, this term referred to a piece of cloth employed as currency to purchase enslaved people in West Central Africa, and over time, the term came to directly designate one enslaved person.[29] As the Atlantic slave trade evolved, the *pièce* corresponded to a given set of goods including guns, metals and metallic objects, textiles, alcohol, glass beads, and other items that served to purchase enslaved Africans.[30]

The few existing slave-trading records describing the cargoes of slave ships that left from French ports such as Nantes and La Rochelle during the same period provide an overview of the items that were transported by slave traders to West African and West Central African ports. Consider the example of the slave ship *La Marie-Séraphique* that left Nantes in 1769 for the Loango coast. During this period, 1 *pièce* corresponded to 9 *livres*. Once in the port of Loango, the ship captain Jean-Baptiste Fautrel Gaugy purchased more than 312 enslaved men, women, boys, and girls, whose bodies were represented in dramatic detail in the hold of the slave ship in a series of watercolors today displayed in the Musée d'histoire de Nantes (Nantes History Museum).[31] These renderings of *La Marie-Séraphique* also include a table that lists the goods transported in the ship to acquire these enslaved Africans, comprising casks of brandy, barrels of powder, bags of lead, iron bars, knives, sabers, stoneware cans, as well as dishes in pewter and faience from Nevers, La Rochelle, and Nantes. In addition, the cargo also included muskets, buccaneer rifles, and pistols, usually fabricated in England, the Dutch Republic, or France.[32] The vessel also transported seventeen kinds of textiles. Mostly imported from India, through the French East India Company or by the Dutch, these multiple textiles differed from each other in their thickness and weaving characteristics.[33] Most cloths were white and other solid colors. The *guinées* were blue, one of the most popular colors. Other textiles included the *bajutapeaux* (bajutapauts), a coarse bleached cotton in blue and white

FIGURE 2.3 *Quibangua et intérieur d'un comptoir européen sur la côte d'Angola en Afrique* (quibangua and interior of an European trading post on the Angola coast in Africa) in Louis-Marie-Joseph Ohier de Grandpré, *Voyage a la côte occidentale d'Afrique, fait dans les années 1786 et 1787*. Paris: Dentu, 1801, vol. 1, facing p. 65.

or white, blue, and red, also described as striped, checked, or flowered.[34] Both the *coupis,* a white-striped cotton canvas, and the *tapsel,* a cheap cotton-and-silk textile striped in blue and other colors, were manufactured in Bengal. The *chasselas* and the *néganepeaux* (neganepauts) were blue and white striped and checkered cotton or cotton-silk fabrics, which along with the *liménéas,* a white cloth with flower seedlings, were fabricated on the Coromandel coast in the southeastern coastal area of the Indian subcontinent. Finally, the cargo included *indiennes,* printed cotton, calicoes, and chintz textiles that by this time were produced in several French cities such as Jouy, Nantes, Bolbcc, and Beautiran.[35]

The *quibangua* (Figure 2.3) was a temporary structure erected a few feet above the ground that included an enclosure where African captives were kept. One watercolor representing *La Marie-Séraphique* depicts the activities of French and African traders as well as their agents in Loango.

Whereas lines of chained captives move toward the slave ship, inside the enclosure other groups examine goods carried ashore from slave ships such as rifles, as well as striped textiles in blue and white and red and white.[36] Most of the items were designated for general trade, duties, and consumption. But a number of textile items, in addition to being enumerated in the general trade section, were also listed in the brokerage and gifts section.[37] Yet items such as silk and gauze loincloth, and manufactured clothes such as coats, jackets, and redingotes, fake silver plates and jars, and hunting rifles were listed as gifts.

French slave traders made significant profits, despite the early investments required to outfit slave ships. French mariner Jean-Jacques Proa, the son of a La Rochelle slave merchant, sailed to Ouidah in 1777. His first voyage to Africa was on board *Le Duc de Laval*, a vessel once owned by Daniel Gareshé that had previously sailed to Malembo to purchase enslaved Africans in 1773. But by 1777, Gareshé had already sold the vessel to his brother-in-law, Jacques Carayon, the oldest son of another Jacques Carayon. In his journal, Proa explained that a cargo of 450 enslaved persons was transported, each one purchased for an average of 400 francs.[38] But according to him, once in the French West Indies the average sale price of a "piece" (an enslaved person) was 1,500 francs, the final figure depending on the sex. Therefore, despite the costs, there was always more than 100 percent profit.[39]

Despite being only a sailor, Proa carried with him two *pacotilles*. This term referred to consigned merchandise, often entrusted to an individual, that officers transported in slave vessels allowing them to make additional gains, such as acquiring an enslaved person from the ship's human cargo.[40] For example, Proa's aunt gave him a *pacotille* that included coral. In his journal, the mariner explained that coral was usually acquired in Marseille through the Red Sea and the Mediterranean, and was highly appreciated in Africa where rulers and women used it to make "their ornaments, wearing it in necklaces and bracelets."[41] Nearly a decade later, when Grandpré traded in Malembo and Cabinda, he also observed that coral was appreciated among the Loango coast elites. According to him, coral was to them the "ultimate wealth ... what the diamond is to us."[42] To illustrate this taste for coral, Grandpré also portrayed a "princess-born" of Malembo displaying a long string of coral beads with other strings adorning her neck, arms, wrists, and ankles (Figure 2.4). Eighteenth-century publications and slave-trade journals also emphasized the importance of coral as a luxury product transported in French vessels sailing to Atlantic Africa to purchase enslaved people.[43]

FIGURE 2.4 *Princesse née de Malembo* (princess-born of Malembo) in Louis-Marie-Joseph Ohier de Grandpré, *Voyage a la côte occidentale d'Afrique, fait dans les années 1786 et 1787*. Paris: Dentu, 1801, vol. 1, facing p. 75.

En route to West Africa, with the excuse of repairing damage to *Le Duc de Laval*, the captain sailed to Lisbon where, during a stop of seventeen days, the French traders bought 500 tobacco rolls.[44] On this occasion, Proa mentioned that French traders paid Portuguese kickbacks in the form of presents.[45] One can assume that the French illegally purchased Bahia third-rate tobacco from the Portuguese officials by paying them bribes because first-rate tobacco was imported to Portugal to be sold in the European market. Using the same excuse, several other French slave ships stopped in Lisbon during the last quarter of the eighteenth century to acquire Brazilian tobacco.[46]

Proa also noted that other items were added to the ship's cargo in order to be offered as gifts to African agents, including "a few scarlet pieces, some very shiny, but not very expensive, furniture, such as a large parasol trimmed with a gold or silver fringe all around, a few flasks of brandy and ironmongery."[47] Other French traders also gave presents to African agents to facilitate trade. In the eighteenth century, a Nantes merchant wrote a guide to help Saint-Malo shipowners who wanted to start trading in enslaved Africans, in which he explained that the king of Loango liked to receive gifts such as blue or crimson velvet coats laced with gold. His agents, however, preferred to receive a 6-gallon barrel of brandy.[48]

2.4 THE CLAN GARESCHÉ AND THE ATLANTIC SLAVE TRADE

Like Proa, Daniel Garesché was a member of an important La Rochelle family of slave merchants and owners of slave ships. Born in 1737, he belonged to a Protestant family of merchants, like other shipowners and merchants in the region. His great-great-grandfather, Jean Garesché, born in 1635, was a merchant from the village of Nieulle-sur-Seudre, nearly 30 miles south of La Rochelle. Jean and his wife Marie Gourbelle had five children. Isaac, the third one, had fourteen children from two different marriages. Although converted to Catholicism, he and his wife continued to be Protestants and educated their children as such. Isaac increased his wealth in the maritime trade with Saint-Domingue and Canada in the late seventeenth century. When he died in 1720, he left a great fortune to one of his sons, also named Isaac, who was the first Garesché to travel to Saint-Domingue.[49] His merchant and other business activities occurred during the most intense period of the Atlantic slave trade. Like his father, Isaac (the son) married twice. From his second marriage, he fathered ten children. Of the nine who survived, there were five sons: Daniel Garesché, Jean Garesché du Rocher, Pierre-Isaac Garesché, Pierre Garesché de la Prée, and Etienne-Benjamin Garesché. Isaac raised these men to carry on the family business, by sending all of them to Saint-Domingue at some point.[50]

The Gareschés' wealth relied on the deeds of three generations of merchants and businessmen. In 1763, Pierre-Isaac (often referred to as Pierre Garesché) went to Saint-Domingue to create, with his brother Jean Garesché du Rocher, the Garesché Frères trade company. During the next two decades both men resided in Port-au-Prince.[51] A few years after arriving in Saint-Domingue, Pierre-Isaac became a lieutenant and later captain in one of the French colonial militias in Port-au-Prince.[52] In 1771, the youngest Garesché, Etienne-Benjamin, who was killed in a duel in 1773, participated in the voyage of the slave ship *La Cigogne*, owned by his brother Daniel. [53]

Traces of the Garesché family's involvement in the cruelest dimensions of the Atlantic slave trade and slave ownership in Saint-Domingue are documented in a series of newspaper advertisements reclaiming enslaved people who escaped from bondage in the second half of the eighteenth century.

As early as July 8, 1767, an advertisement in the weekly Saint-Domingue newspaper *Affiches américaines* announced that an enslaved man identified as a *griffe* (a term often referring to a mixed-race Black and indigenous person) had escaped three weeks earlier from the municipality (*quartier*) of Vases in Saint-Domingue.[54] The advertisement does not reveal the name of this bondsman but specifies that the name GARESCHÉ was branded on his body. Born in Guadeloupe, he is described as a cooper, mason, mattress maker, and sailor, who was even able to read a little. As he was born in the French West Indies, the branded name Garesché confirms that the Gareschés were his legal owners. The announcement gave instructions to arrest him and to inform the Garesché brothers in Port-au-Prince.[55] Other fugitive slave advertisements attest that he was not the only enslaved person who escaped bondage to have the name Garesché marked on his body. For example, an advertisement of January 4, 1769, indicates that Joli-Coeur, a bondsman identified as "Congo," was branded "Garesché &" on the left side of his chest. Although the Gareschés are not identified as the enslaved man's owners, the branded name suggests they owned him when he was transported from West Central Africa to Saint-Domingue.

Not all advertisements mentioning the Gareschés described enslaved people branded with their names. From 1767 to 1783, dozens of announcements instructed readers to inform the Garesché brothers of the whereabouts of escaped enslaved men and women such as Amour, Jean-Louis, Louis, Pompée, Antoine, Alexandre, Gaillar, Jean-Jacques, Mathurin, Baptiste, Jacques, Jean-Baptiste, Noël, Atiste, Eugène, Diacoua, Cupidon, Semedard, Jean-Pierre, Couchy, and Joseph.[56] These advertisements suggest that the Garesché brothers were either the owners of these self-emancipated men and women or that they operated as liaison with their owners, some of whom could possibly be absentee planters who resided in France. Another advertisement demanded that people who had ten to fifty slaves born in the country (*têtes de nègres faits au pays*) should address themselves to the Gareschés, who would indicate an individual who was willing to purchase slaves and pay them cash.[57] Likewise, in a letter of October 11, 1780, a slave owner asked the Gareschés to liberate his enslaved man named Gaspard who had escaped and been put behind bars.[58]

In Port-au-Prince, the company led by the Garesché brothers sold the human cargo of newly arrived slave ships as well. For example, on November 30, 1774, the Garesché brothers announced on the pages of *Affiches américaines* they were expecting the arrival of a slave ship from Angola (the French term for Loango coast) carrying "360 captives whose sale they will open three days after the arrival of the said slave ship."[59] Although the advertisement does not provide the vessel's name, the next week the same newspaper announced the forthcoming arrival of *L'Aimable Henriette*, a vessel that had left Le Havre on August 24, 1773, and arrived "from the Angola Coast" in Port-au-Prince on December 3, 1774.[60] Existing records confirm that after a stop at Cap-Français, 362 enslaved Africans purchased on the Loango coast in Port-au-Prince disembarked from the vessel on that day.[61]

In 1777, Pierre-Isaac Garesché formed the company Garesché & Billoteau with Charles Billoteau in Port-au-Prince, replacing the previous Garesché Frères company.[62] Created to operate for a period of five years, Garesché & Billoteau was deeply connected with the wealth generated by the Atlantic slave trade and the ownership of enslaved people. In the company's deed, each partner provided company assets in the form of objects, goods, cash, and enslaved persons. Garesché's enslaved assets included Monte au Ciel, an enslaved barrel maker between seventeen and eighteen years of age, whose price was evaluated at 2,600 *livres*; Marie, a forty-year-old enslaved servant evaluated at 1,200 *livres*; as well as her two sons, Joseph, an enslaved *mulâtre* (mulatto) wigmaker, thirteen or fourteen years of age, evaluated at 2,500 *livres*, and Michel, an enslaved *mulâtre* boy aged between seven and eight years old, evaluated at 1,350 *livres*. Charles Billoteau put up two African-born enslaved persons as company assets: Hector, an enslaved wigmaker of "Tiamba nation," evaluated at 3,000 *livres*, and Alline, an enslaved woman of "Arada" nation, evaluated at 2,500 *livres*, Tiamba and Arada (a reference to the Kingdom of Allada) being labels that identified enslaved peoples who had embarked in the ports of the Bight of Benin.[63]

Even though the Garesché & Billoteau company conducted bilateral trade between La Rochelle and the French West Indies, the vast correspondence with their French business partners discussed commercial transactions involving commodities such as coffee, sugar, cotton, flour, wine, and indigo produced by enslaved people. These exchanges involved other French colonies such as Martinique, Cayenne, and Guadeloupe; ports such as Bordeaux, Nantes, Brest, and Marseille; and British and Dutch colonies such as Jamaica and Curaçao. They also represented other La Rochelle merchants and shipowners such as Jacques Guibert, whose brother Pierre-Isaac Guibert married Marguerite Garesché, a sister of the Garesché brothers.[64] Over time, all the Garesché brothers owned sugarcane plantations in Boucassin, Cap-Français, and Port-au-Prince.[65] Although the company's letters and other records rarely documented the transportation of enslaved people from West Africa and West Central Africa to the French West Indies, various papers referred to the ownership of enslaved men and women whom they sent back and forth from Saint-Domingue to La Rochelle.[66] In 1781, both Jean Garesché du Rocher and Pierre-Isaac Garesché owned seventy enslaved persons in Saint-Domingue.[67]

In 1784, Pierre-Isaac Garesché and Charles Billoteau sold their company to Meynardie & Picard, a firm partially owned by Pierre Meynardie, Garesché's brother-in-law. As part of the transaction, Garesché rented his four domestic enslaved persons (*quatre têtes d'esclaves*), who were listed as capital when he formed his company seven years earlier. This time, the slaves Marie (now described as a laundress) and her two sons Joseph (wigmaker) and Michel are described in the document not only as *mulâtres*, but also as "creoles from Saint-Michel of Azores."[68] The recorded transaction included a series of detailed provisions that indicated the revenue each of these slaves generated through their professional activities. In addition to instructions that the new owners should feed, lodge, clothe, and provide medicines for the four bondspeople, Pierre-Isaac Garesché also stipulated that Meynardie & Picard must put the younger enslaved boy Michel "in apprenticeship to become wigmaker" at their own expense for between fifteen and eighteen months, and among other things keep the right to request that the enslaved wigmaker Joseph should come to France. As we know from other examples, these travels were not uncommon. In 1785, an enslaved domestic servant named Babet, owned by Jean Garesché du Rocher, arrived in La Rochelle from Saint-Domingue.[69] Some lists of passengers of vessels sailing from La Rochelle to Saint-Domingue and vice-versa included enslaved people. Overall, although the provisions regarding his human property may suggest that Pierre-Isaac Garesché cared about his domestic enslaved servants, they more probably illustrate his desire to protect them because of the revenue they generated.

2.5 DANIEL GARESCHÉ AND JEAN-AMABLE LESSENNE

Daniel Garesché was the most prominent member of the Garesché family during the second half of the eighteenth century. He was initiated into maritime commerce by Jacques Carayon, the director of La Rochelle's Chamber of Commerce.[70] Their alliance was reinforced by Garesché's marriage to Carayon's daughter, Marie-Anne-Sara Carayon, with whom he had ten children.[71] In addition to actively participating in the bilateral trade and the trade of enslaved Africans, over a period of twenty-four years Daniel Garesché was the owner of sixteen slave ships that sailed several times from La Rochelle to West Africa and West Central Africa, from where they carried thousands of enslaved Africans to Saint-Domingue. Most probably, *La Cigogne* was Daniel Garesché's first slave ship. In January 1769, the vessel sailed from La Rochelle to Ekpe, a port in the Bight of Benin, east of Lagos, in twenty-first century Nigeria. There, 468 enslaved men, women, and children were brought aboard, but only 399 disembarked alive in Port-au-Prince.[72] Existing records document that *La Cigogne* sailed eight more times to the various ports in the Bight of Benin in West Africa and West Central Africa.[73]

In the twenty-four years that followed *La Cigogne*'s first slave voyage, Garesché acquired fifteen other slave vessels, including *Le Saint-Jacques, Le Duc de Laval, La Bergère, Le Comte d'Hector, L'Iris, Le Comte de Forcalquier, La Comtesse de Puységur, L'Aunis, L'Argus, Le Reverseau, La Fille Unique,* and *Le Prévost de Langristin.* He was also the owner of *Le Montyon* and *L'Hirondelle,* which were involved in the conflict in Cabinda in 1775 that we examine in Chapter 3. These two vessels were not the only to trade in enslaved Africans on the Loango coast. For example, *Le Duc de Laval* left La Rochelle on December 7, 1773, and started trading in the port of Malembo on March 4, 1774, where over nearly seven months the ship's captain Pierre-Ignace-Liévin van Alstein acquired 393 enslaved Africans. On November 11, 1774, the vessel sailed from Malembo and arrived at Cap-Français on January 13, 1775. During the long voyage that lasted more than fifty days, three members of the crew and forty-six African captives perished. Yet on January 21, the first page of Saint-Domingue's newspaper *Affiches américaines* featured the arrival of *Le Duc de Laval,* whose "very beautiful cargo of blacks" would be sold on January 30 by the Mesnier brothers.[74]

International conflicts disturbed the Garesché family businesses in the last quarter of the eighteenth century. The French slave trade was also disrupted from 1775 to 1783, when the thirteen colonies of North America sought independence from Great Britain. After the French were defeated by the British in the Seven Years' War, France provided support to the Continental Army against the British from 1778 during the American War of Independence. Reacting to this alliance, the British Navy seized French vessels, which negatively impacted the French slave trade. La Rochelle's trade was also affected by this alliance, with Garesché complaining about the great losses he was incurring in the trade in enslaved Africans: "The slave trade expeditions are only making victims. ... Captains, agents alone benefit from it, whereas the shipowner is reduced to bearing the loss or growing old without the expectation of profits, this prospect alarms me ... and your remarks are not made to reassure me."[75]

Overall, Garesché's sixteen ships made at least thirty-three slave voyages.[76] Although 16,795 enslaved Africans embarked on these slave vessels in ports of West Africa and West Central Africa, only 14,464 disembarked alive in the French West Indies. Considering the absolute numbers of enslaved people transported in these voyages, the mortality rate was 14 percent. Yet if the mortality toll for each voyage is considered, the average was 36 percent. For example, in 1786, the 203-ton vessel *L'Argus* left West Central Africa carrying 280 African captives, but 70 percent of the men, women, and children on board died during the Middle Passage; therefore only eighty-three enslaved Africans disembarked alive in Port-au-Prince. In 1789, 700 enslaved people embarked upon a much bigger 1,524-ton vessel, *Le Reverseau*, in Porto-Novo in the Bight of Benin and 683 slaves disembarked upon arrival in Cap-Français in Saint-Domingue, a mortality rate of 2 percent.[77]

Considering the thirty-three slaving expeditions undertook by Garesché's slave ships, in thirty-one voyages these vessels departed from Africa transporting on average more than 300 enslaved Africans. On March 31, 1784, for example, the 700-ton vessel *L'Iris* left La Rochelle for Porto-Novo in the Bight of Benin. On December 14, 1784, *L'Iris* left Porto-Novo transporting 966 enslaved Africans. While trading in West Africa, ten sailors and the ship captain Corbie Micheau died. Likewise, 131 enslaved African men, women, and children died on the coast and during the Atlantic crossing. Despite the loss of these lives, 835 enslaved persons disembarked from *L'Iris* in Cap-Français on March 26, 1785.

Between 1775 and 1794, most slave ships that left from French ports such as Saint-Malo, Nantes, Bordeaux, Dunkirk Honfleur, Le Havre, and La Rochelle transported captives from the Bight of Benin and the Loango coast to Port-au-Prince and Cap Français in Saint-Domingue. The voyages of Daniel Garesché's slave ships also followed this general trend. For example, his ship *Le Saint-Jacques* sailed to West Africa five times between 1770 and 1793, and purchased enslaved Africans in ports of the Loango coast such as Malembo and Cabinda, as well as Ouidah and Porto-Novo in the Bight of Benin.[78] In addition, during the same period ships owned by Garesché such as *Le Duc de Laval, Le Montyon, La Fille Unique, Le Prévost de Langristin, Le Comte de Forcalquier,* and *L'Aunis* all sailed to Malembo. These voyages could only succeed because slave merchants such as Garesché nurtured long-lasting alliances with ship captains. As the highest officers on board slave ships, captains came from more privileged upbringings than other crew members. Furthermore, over the years they were able to accumulate wealth derived from the slave trade, not only from wages, but also because several captains invested in slave voyages and personally purchased enslaved Africans to be sold in the Americas.

Jean-Amable Lessenne was among these prosperous ship captains. Unlike Garesché, Lessenne was Catholic. The son of a mariner, he was born in 1739 in Louisbourg, on Île Royale (twenty-first century's Cape Breton Island, Nova Scotia), then part of the French colony of Canada. During the first half of the eighteenth century, the island was connected through maritime trade with Québec, La Rochelle, and the French West Indies. Lessenne's brother, Joseph Lessenne, was also a ship captain. His sister, Marie Jeanne Lessenne was the widow of Antoine Didion, a merchant from Louisbourg, Canada.[79] In July 1758, during the Seven Years War that eventually led France to cede Canada to Britain, Louisbourg capitulated to the British, and some of its residents moved to France. Hence, the Lessennes settled at Saint-Pierre on the Oléron Island, located nearly 18 miles southwest of La Rochelle.[80]

Lessenne remained loyal to Daniel Garesché during his entire career as a ship captain. Before sailing to the coasts of Atlantic Africa, he commanded the vessel *Le Père de famille*, owned by Garesché, which sailed from Marseille to Saint-Domingue in 1767.[81] He was also the captain of five other slave ships owned by Garesché that navigated to the coasts of Africa over nearly fifteen years. His first slave voyage was on board Garesché's slave ship *Le Saint-Jacques* that sailed from La Rochelle to the Loango coast on October 24, 1769. In the ports of Loango and Cabinda, Lessenne and his officers managed to purchase 489 enslaved Africans, including 230 men, 104 women, 31 boys, and 80 girls. After almost nine months, the vessel left Cabinda on October 13, 1770. From Garesché's and Lessenne's points of view the voyage was certainly successful. After more than fifty days crossing the Atlantic Ocean, even though forty-four slaves and five members of the crew died, 445 enslaved people disembarked alive upon arrival in Cap-Français on December 6, 1770.[82]

Garesché started outfitting another slaving voyage for *Le Saint-Jacques* as soon as the vessel returned from Cap-Français, and once again he assigned Lessenne as the new expedition's ship captain. As a result, on June 20, 1772, Lessenne sailed again to the Loango coast as the commander of the slave ship *Le Saint-Jacques*. Existing records do not reveal exactly how long the vessel remained on the Loango coast, but 596 captive Africans boarded the vessel, and upon arrival in Saint-Domingue, 542 enslaved people disembarked alive in Cap-Français on

FIGURE 2.5 *Hôtel* at 18, rue Réaumur, La Rochelle, France once owned by Daniel Garesché. Photograph: Ana Lucia Araujo, 2022.

May 29, 1773, and were put on sale two weeks later.[83] As in the previous voyage, ship logs and journals of these two slave expeditions have not been located, so it is hard to determine if Lessenne purchased captives in Malembo or Cabinda or at both locations. Still, it is safe to assume that after spending several months trading on the Loango coast, Lessenne became very familiar with the region and its various local agents, an experience that largely prepared him to sail to Malembo for the third time as the captain of the slave ship *Le Montyon* in 1775, which we explore in Chapter 3.

The material traces of the fortune made by men such as Garesché and Lessenne are still visible in La Rochelle. Daniel Garesché owned a *hôtel* (private mansion townhouse) on 18, rue Réaumur (Figure 2.5), where several other rich merchants also owned wealthy homes. Like other residences belonging to La Rochelle's merchants, Garesché's sumptuous mansion included a main building with two wings enclosing an inner courtyard surrounded by a wall that included an impressive gate, usually painted in blue. As in other European ports involved in the Atlantic slave trade, wealthy La Rochelle merchants such as Garesché were also deeply active in politics. During the French Revolution, in 1790, Garesché was elected as a member of La Rochelle's municipal chamber. On July 27, 1791, he replaced the city's mayor, Denis-Joseph Goguet, after his resignation, and was elected mayor in November of the same year.[84] Also in 1791, he purchased a coffee plantation in Saint-Domingue for more than 300,000 *livres*.[85]

Like Garesché, ship captain Jean-Amable Lessenne also made an enormous fortune from the trade in human beings. During his lifetime, he became the owner of at least one large plantation in Saint-Domingue. He also owned a sumptuous *hôtel* in La Rochelle. In 1784, as he prepared to retire, he purchased the opulent château La Tourtillière and was appointed the chief treasurer at the finance office of the generality of La Rochelle.[86]

2.6 FRENCH SLAVE TRADERS ON THE LOANGO COAST

The rise of the Saint-Domingue slave rebellion in 1791 threatened the wealth of French planters and merchants. Men such as Garesché and Lessenne lost their plantations and enslaved property. On May 30, 1792, Garesché resigned from his elected office as mayor, and ultimately, the revolution that put an end to slavery and colonial rule in Saint-Domingue provoked a dramatic decline in the French slave trade. La Rochelle's merchants and planters lost estates and human property in Saint-Domingue, the colony to which most captive Africans transported by slave merchants from La Rochelle had been deported. By 1794, three years after the rise of the Saint-Domingue slave revolt, and following the first abolition of slavery in the French colonies, British slave ships started dominating the slave trade in Cabinda and Malembo. After 1804, in the years that followed the end of slavery in Saint-Domingue, the rise of Haiti as the first independent Black country in the Americas led to the end of French participation in the Atlantic slave trade. With the abolition of the British slave trade in 1807, Portuguese and Brazilian merchants ultimately replaced French and British traders on the Loango coast.[87] Yet before this dramatic decline, in the last twenty-five years of the eighteenth century, La Rochelle's captains who sailed to the ports of Malembo and Cabinda on the Loango coast faced fierce competition, not only from other European traders, but also from slave traders from other French ports such as Bordeaux, Le Havre, and Nantes, a dimension explored in detail in Chapter 3.

3

Slave Traders Turned Pirates

During the eighteenth century, ships from Nantes, Bordeaux, Le Havre, Dunkirk La Rochelle, and Saint-Malo sailed to the ports of Loango, Cabinda, and Malembo (Map 2) to purchase enslaved people. Once there, these traders, whose ships were outfitted in different ports, were in competition against each other, seeking to acquire the best captives for the lowest price. To achieve this goal, they not only provided African agents with goods that had local demand, but also attempted to respond to the specific tastes of rulers and brokers, to whom they paid customs, often referred to as presents. But as these arrangements sometimes failed, ship captains did not hesitate to give themselves the upper hand by sabotaging their rivals. On occasion, European traders also physically assaulted even their own compatriots by stealing their cargos of commodities and human beings.

French slave vessels sailed to specific areas of Atlantic Africa. But once ship captains arrived in the selected region, they had the latitude to decide in which port to trade. The selection of a trading port was based on a variety of factors, including European competition and international conflicts. Local disputes and the ability of African rulers and traders to provide the largest number of captives for the lowest price and within the shortest period also mattered.[1] Captains had to consider how the presence of other French and European traders as well as internal conflicts among African states could affect the coastal trade. These factors were particularly important in the context of the slave trade on the Loango coast, to which most slave merchants from La Rochelle sent their ships. At the turn of the eighteenth century, the French started making attempts to get preferential treatment in the region by trying to dominate the slave trade in Cabinda, Malembo, and Loango. As noted by Daniel Domingues da Silva, disputes among European traders were common on the Loango coast, in a context in which the French and the English could provide "commodities such as gunpowder and textiles at cheaper prices than their Portuguese competitors."[2]

French traders from La Rochelle, Bordeaux, Nantes, and Le Havre also fought against each other to obtain the highest number of African captives and the most affordable prices. These quarrels shaped the trading environment of ports such as Cabinda and Malembo, and sometimes led to episodes of robbery and physical violence among European ship captains and crew members. As we will see in this chapter, existing written sources do not explicitly show how Loango coast agents were victimized by European traders. Nonetheless, despite European pressures to monopolize the trade in the region, the rulers of Ngoyo, Kakongo, and Loango kept significant control over their territories during the eighteenth century. However, on some occasions, the Ngoyo's Woyo residents of Cabinda supported the French to fight the Portuguese who also attempted to control the region. Likewise, in some situations, local traders sided with specific French traders to the detriment of others.

3.1 EIGHTEENTH-CENTURY FRENCH SLAVE SHIPS ON THE LOANGO COAST

As discussed in Chapter 1, unlike the West African ports on the Gold Coast and the Bight of Benin, rulers of the kingdoms of Loango, Kakongo, and Ngoyo did not allow European traders to build permanent trade structures along the coast. Despite this interdiction, English slave traders established temporary factories in the region in the late seventeenth century. In 1680, Charles Swan sailed from London to the Loango coast as the captain of the Royal African Company's vessel *Carlyle*. As recorded by officer Will Fry, who kept a journal of the voyage, after paying customs, the English ship crew members established trading factories in Cabinda and Malembo. During this voyage, Swan was able to acquire 489 enslaved Africans. Of this number, 407 disembarked alive in Jamaica.[3]

The French did the same. In his account of the early nineteenth century, Grandpré referred to the annual presence of thirty slave ships in Cabinda, presumably during the last twenty years of the eighteenth century, when he sojourned in the region.[4] In 1701, the wealthy French banker Antoine Crozat obtained the *asiento*. This contract provided the monopoly of the trade in enslaved Africans to the Spanish colonies in the Americas and led Crozat to create the Compagnie de l'Asiento (Company of the Asiento).[5] On July 14, 1702, during the War of the Spanish Succession, in which England and France were opposed, the French vessels *L'Aigle* and *La Badine* left La Rochelle together.[6] Whereas *La Badine* anchored in Ouidah to purchase enslaved Africans to transport them to Cartagena, *L'Aigle* continued sailing to Cabinda where the vessel would purchase African captives to transport them to Buenos Aires in twenty-first century Argentina, an unusual destination for enslaved people from this region.[7] On October 16, while sailing to Cabinda, *L'Aigle* attacked the English vessel *Coventry* and seized commodities sufficient to purchase 200 enslaved Africans. Two days later, after arriving in Cabinda, *L'Aigle* captured the *Don Carlos*, another English ship, from which the officers seized 162 captive Africans.[8] According to an officer account, African men and women were distributed on the spot between the *Coventry* and *L'Aigle*, for fear that in such confusion, "finding everything open by the pillage made by our men, the Negroes would revolt, without us being able to repress them. The precaution was prudent because the crew was so drunk of all sorts of liquors that they no longer knew anyone, not even the captain."[9] Although we do not know more about the African men, women, and children seized by the English, this account shows that disputes among European powers frequently offered captive Africans an opportunity to resist enslavement.

In addition to the slaves seized from the *Don Carlos*, *L'Aigle* along with *L'Opiniâtre*, another French vessel that arrived in Cabinda in 1703, were expected to purchase 1,000 captives.[10] Like other vessels trading in the region, *L'Aigle*'s cargo comprised mainly a variety of textiles, muskets, brandy, gunpowder, mirrors, and knives. Upon arrival, the French representatives went inland to meet the *Maningoyo*, who was assisted by two secretaries, one who spoke Portuguese and another who spoke English.[11] In this cordial initial meeting, the two parties agreed upon the duties to be paid in order to start the trade. But when time to pay the customs arrived, the transaction became more complicated, as Cabinda's *Mfuka* requested one *pièce* of each kind of commodity carried in the vessel, "under the pretext of protecting his [the king's] interests."[12] Eventually, the *Mfuka* accepted the agreed amount, reportedly 118 *pièces*, which allowed *L'Aigle*'s crew members to build a temporary dwelling to house the trading post and to start trading.[13]

According to another report by an officer of the Company of the Asiento, the *Maningoyo* welcomed the French traders. In his view, the port offered great prospects for the trade in enslaved Africans.[14] Whereas the French agreed to "not to put a cannon ashore and to pay the same customs as the English and the Dutch," the *Maningoyo* allegedly promised to prevent these other European powers from trading in his port. Based on this unlikely offer of monopoly, the officer recommended the company to send all its ships to the Loango coast, as Cabinda, Malembo, and Loango would be able to supply "more negroes than they are obliged to carry to the Indies." While specifying other advantages, he also emphasized that these three ports were accessible by land and by water within 25 to 30 *lieues* (roughly 90 miles), making it possible to trade ivory in the Congo River area as well.[15]

In 1705, the French attacked the Portuguese colony of Benguela, south of the Congo River. To some extent, this incident illustrates how early French and other European competitors opposed a Portuguese monopoly over trade in the region.[16] During the eighteenth century, Portuguese agents based in the colonies of Luanda and Benguela recurrently expressed concern about the presence of other European powers, especially the French and the English, on the Loango coast. They feared their competitors would build permanent structures in order to attempt to control the slave trade in the region. Toward the end of the War of the Spanish Succession, the signing of the Treaties of Utrecht, which established peace between Britain and Spain in 1713, allowed the British to obtain the *asiento*, giving British subjects permission to transport enslaved Africans to the Spanish colonies in the Americas. Because of the British *asiento*, in 1721 the Royal African Company obtained permission from the *Maningoyo* to construct a fort in Cabinda. This event confirmed a new European power's attempt to monopolize the trade in enslaved people in the port. On February 4, 1721, the English vessel *Royal Africa* sailed from London to "make a new settlement in Cabinda," and was followed by other vessels such as the *Prince George*, the packet *Royal African*, and the sloops *Accra* and *Congo*.[17]

But the fort was obviously a British attempt to undermine the presence of other European powers in Cabinda. Once the construction was successfully concluded in 1723, the British destroyed a French factory and ordered French traders to leave Cabinda. Too confident of their accomplishment, the English made a big mistake when their vessels refused to pay duties to the Ngoyo ruler and his agents before starting the trade. This affront immediately led the Woyo to attack the newly built fort. Finally, the Portuguese, who did not want any European power permanently settled north of the Congo River, intervened. With the support of the Woyo forces, the Portuguese eventually destroyed the British fort.[18] Likewise, they burned at least one English vessel, the *Royal Africa*, which was still anchored in Cabinda at the time of the incident.[19]

Over the years that followed, similar conflicts continued to emerge. During the Seven Years' War, French and British naval confrontations took place along the Loango coast, even though no documented French slave ships purchased and transported captives from the region to the French West Indies throughout the conflict. In November 1756, the French Navy sent a squadron with two divisions from Brest to the coasts of Africa. One division had three vessels, two frigates, and one corvette, commanded by Captain Kersaint, who sailed first to Senegambia and then to the Gold Coast and the Bight of Benin.[20] The second division, composed of the warship *Saint Michel* commanded by Caumont and the frigate *Améthiste* commanded by Louis Salomon Le Carlier d'Herlye, navigated along the West African coast until the two vessels reached the Loango coast. Along the way to their destinations, the two divisions destroyed several trading posts and British slave ships, seizing their merchandise and capturing enslaved Africans on board the vessels.[21] While in Cabinda, Herlye "gave M. de Caumont the idea of a project to establish a trade on this coast, where there are no forts." As Caumont approved the project, Herlye drew up a "rather informal treaty," which was presumably discussed with Cabinda agents.[22]

On April 7, 1757, Herlye, three other French officers, and Cabinda's *Mfuka* and *Mambuku* signed the eight-article treaty, promising to seal the "friendship and union and to work to establish a trade equally advantageous, lucrative and safe for the two nations."[23] As the treaty was written in French, and both the *Mfuka* and *Mambuku* were illiterate, they signed the document with their "marks." As in any other asymmetric diplomatic transactions of this kind, it is hard to conclude that the *Mfuka* and the *Mambuku* were fully aware of the implications associated with their signatures on the treaty, which stated that "the said French, under the good pleasure of the king, their master, formally undertake to rescue, protect, defend, against any power whatsoever that would like to attack or disturb the conditions set out in the following act." In addition to these conditions, the second article of the treaty awarded "a spacious and convenient land for the establishment of a fort which will be placed in the custody of the French." The third article affirmed that "the said prince, governor, and principal inhabitants of the country engage themselves and promise to supply provisions in exchange for payment or goods, according to the use of the country," whereas the fourth stated that "they will not allow any other power to build forts, nor make any settlement around the said bay." Moreover, the fifth and sixth articles underscored that the abovementioned prince and governor would protect the "French against the insults and attacks of foreign powers who would like to disturb the trade of two nations." For their part, the French were to "use all their forces to protect, defend and support them against the powers from both inside and outside who would come to attack them." The last two articles of the treaty established provisions for the continuation of the Atlantic slave trade. The French committed to send merchants to purchase slaves in Cabinda every year and to provide the prince and governor with all the goods they may need. The final article emphasized that the French officers would do their best to have the present treaty approved "by the king, their master ... and procure them the gifts used in such cases."[24] Although the French fort was never built, the treaty that followed the attacks on British ships was a clear French attempt to monopolize the trade in enslaved Africans in Cabinda.

The treaty of 1757 never took effect, but as well as revealing the French intentions to control the trade in Cabinda, it possibly indicates the willingness of two local rulers, referred to as the *Mfuka* "Classe" and *Mambuku* "governor" Elzina, to accept the deal. More likely, they just pretended to accept the agreement so more French slave traders would come to Cabinda to purchase African captives. These recurrent European attempts to control the slave trade in the port shaped the commercial exchanges between French traders and Cabinda's sovereigns until the final years of the eighteenth century. Although the presence of French slave ships was interrupted during the Seven Years' War, the decade that followed the end of the conflict witnessed the gradual return of French traders to the Loango coast.

In 1763, the vessel *L'Heureux* sailed from Bordeaux to the Loango coast, and 152 captives disembarked in Cap-Français in 1764.[25] Three years later, the competition among French traders in Cabinda had greatly increased to the point that they overtly fought each other.[26] On April 6, 1766, J. Houet, captain of *Le Saint Jean-Baptiste*, sailed from Nantes to the Loango coast, where he traded in Cabinda for several weeks. But on September 9, 1766, the vessels *L'Africain*, *Le Bermudien* (or *Le Vermudien*), *La Marquise de Chateau Renaud*, from Nantes; *L'Uranie*, and *L'Aimable Marie* from Bordeaux also anchored in Cabinda.[27] Worried that the arrival of several other vessels would undermine his ability to purchase more African captives and thereby finish his trade in Cabinda, Houet took the unilateral decision to increase by 5 *pièces* the price for each enslaved African. As a result, instead of paying 22 or 23 *pièces* for one captive, he offered to pay 27 or 28 *pièces*.[28] Aware that this gesture would lead the king and his local agents to direct most captives to Houet, the other French captains who had just anchored in Cabinda protested. They explained to Houet that once his trade was finished, they would have to follow suit and would be forced to pay a higher price for each captive than he had agreed to pay, which would cause them harm. To remedy the situation, the French captains proposed to sell Houet fifty captives they had already purchased for the current price of 22 or 23 *pièces*, but he refused the offer.

After these explanations, on September 23, 1766, the captain of *La Marquise de Chateau Renaud* from Nantes organized a meeting with Costé and the other ship captains in which they decided to reiterate to Houet in writing the observations that had already been made to him. They agreed that if he persisted in his project, they would fiercely oppose it, and to this effect, they would mount guard at his trading post in order to prevent him from purchasing captives for more than the ordinary price. The next day, an officer from *La Marquise de Château Renaud* and a man from each of the other vessels were sent to Houet's trading post to examine the quantity of *pièces* with which he was purchasing captives. On September 25, however, Costé failed to send a man to mount guard at the trading post that only operated on that day. A few days later, new "difficulties and assaults" between Houet and Dubois took place. Once Costé returned to Le Havre, he was accused of these aggressions and sent to prison, from where he addressed a letter to César Gabriel de Choiseul, duke of Praslin, by then the French Secretary of State for the Navy, pleading to be released.

Despite this incident, the captains involved in this conflict managed to acquire hundreds of captive Africans. In Léogane, Saint-Domingue, 565 enslaved Africans disembarked from the vessel *Le Saint Jean-Baptiste* commanded by Houet on January 6, 1767.[29] Likewise on February 7, 1767, and March 16, 1767, from *La Marquise de Château Renaud* and *L'Africain*, respectively, 454 and 378 slaves disembarked in Cayes.[30] Finally, 258 and 364 slaves disembarked from the vessels *Le Bermudien* and *L'Uranie* in Cap-Français on April 14 and April 23, 1767.[31] In 1767, the vessels *Le Duc de Duras*, *La Revanche*, and *Le Glaneur* from Bordeaux purchased dozens of captive Africans in Cabinda, and they were transported to Cap-Français.[32] A similarly intense slave trade activity also existed in Malembo, where according to reports provided by French missionaries, there were four trading posts and 300 French agents in 1768.[33]

3.2 *LE MONTYON* AND *L'HIRONDELLE* SAIL TO THE LOANGO COAST

Many vessels from La Rochelle sailed to the Loango coast in the years that followed the end of the Seven Years War. On June 19, 1775, *Le Montyon*, owned by Daniel Garesché and commanded by Jean-Amable Lessenne, sailed from La Rochelle harbor to the Loango coast.[34] During the previous six months of that year, *Le Marquis de Narbonne* and *La Nancy* had also departed from La Rochelle to the coasts of Africa, but *Le Montyon* was the only one that left La Rochelle to trade in the ports of the Loango coast. Garesché owned and outfitted the 300-ton vessel whose crew was composed of sixty men, most of them from La Rochelle and its environs. As in other slave ships, these men were assigned several roles. Among those with the rank of naval officers were the captain, Lessenne, the second captain, Pierre Ménager, and Jacques Cousse, the first lieutenant.[35] The crew also included the first surgeon Louis Chaslon, an experienced officer who in 1761 signed a three-year indenture contract with Pierre Neau and François Leleu to board the vessel *L'Aigle* and spend three years in Saint-Domingue.[36] Other members of the crew included several petty officers and non-petty officers, such as a gunsmith, a cook, and a baker, in addition to sailors, novices, and cabin crew members. As usual, several cabin crew and novices were very young men on their first expedition to the coasts of Africa.[37] Although the names of all crew members are recorded in existing naval records, invoices and slave-trade journals specifying the cargoes of these ships have not survived to this day.

Yet one La Rochelle "invoice for goods forming a cargo to purchase 500 negroes" in "Angola" dated 1775 is perhaps that of *Le Montyon*.[38] This hypothesis is plausible because all other vessels that sailed from La Rochelle to Africa in 1775 went to the Bight of Benin, except for *Le Marquis de Narbonne*, which sailed to the Guinea coast, and *Le Baron de Montmorency*, which headed to the "coast of Angola". Admittedly, the specific destination ports of these two vessels were not recorded, but each one carried 310 and 385 enslaved Africans, respectively, numbers much smaller than the 500 indicated in the invoice. Even if this surviving invoice does not list the goods purchased to outfit *Le Montyon*, it certainly accurately illustrates the typical goods transported to the Loango coast to acquire captive Africans in 1775.

According to the invoice, most of the cargo consisted of items also found in vessels such as the Nantes's vessel *La Marie Séraphique*, discussed in Chapter 2. Among the cargo were cloths imported from India, such as *guinées, indiennes, liménéas,* and *chasselas.* The invoice also included a great variety of other cotton and silk textiles such as *bajutapeaux, néganepeaux, boulanges* (wools), *romals, nicanees,* and *tapsels* fabricated in India and Rouen. Other items listed included muskets, gunpowder, brandy, iron bars, knives, as well as gifts such as Bombay textiles, cotton and silk cloths, coats, and jackets, no doubt intended for the ruler and his higher representatives in the ports of the Loango coast such as the *Mambuku* and the *Mfuka.*

Jean-Amable Lessenne was an experienced captain who had already traveled to the Loango coast twice, in 1769 and 1772. As with other vessels that left from La Rochelle and other French ports to trade on the Loango coast, we can assume that Lessenne received written instructions from Daniel Garesché before departing to the coasts of Africa, indicating which route to take, how to manage the vessel's supplies, where to conduct trade, how to pay customs, how many enslaved individuals to purchase, and possibly bonuses associated with the sale of enslaved Africans. *Le Montyon*'s exact itinerary is unknown, but unless allowances had to be made for adverse weather or mechanical problems, slave ships leaving from La Rochelle to the Loango coast all basically followed the same path.

Like other vessels sailing from the North Atlantic, *Le Montyon* benefited from the Guinea Current that propelled vessels counterclockwise southward and then eastward.[39] Therefore, after leaving La Rochelle's port, slave ships passed the Oléron Island. Sailing south along the European Atlantic coast, they successively reached the Madeira Islands, the Canary Islands, and the Cape Verde archipelago. After arriving on the West African coast, vessels navigated eastward. At this stage, they often stopped either at the port of Anomabu on the Gold Coast or at the São Tomé and Príncipe islands, where captains could acquire new supplies such as manioc flour and beans before finally reaching the Loango coast, where they selected which port to anchor in and trade with.[40]

When *Le Montyon* reached the coast of West Central Africa, the configuration of European trade activity on the Loango coast had changed. In 1775, the Dutch presence in the region had declined in comparison with the state of affairs in the seventeenth century. In contrast, the number of British and French merchants purchasing enslaved Africans in the ports of Loango, Malembo, and Cabinda had increased.[41] Lessenne was certainly not surprised when, upon arriving in Malembo, he once again heard rumors of conflicts among European traders that had been ongoing for several decades. Proyart, whose account draws from correspondence with French missionaries in the region during the second half of the eighteenth century, explained that in Malembo and Cabinda (respectively, the ports of the kingdoms of Kakongo and Ngoyo), the measure used to trade enslaved people was the *marchandise* (commodity), which by the time of his visit to the region corresponded to a piece of cotton cloth or *indienne* of 10 to 14 *aunes* (the equivalent of 3 feet); therefore, the *marchandise* was equal to 30 to 42 feet of these textiles. According to Proyart, in addition to these commodities slave traders paid an extra amount for each purchased African captive. This payment consisted of three or four muskets, an equivalent number of sabers, fifteen jars of brandy, 15 pounds of gunpowder, and a few dozen knives, and if there was a shortage of any of these goods they could be replaced with other items.[42]

In the port of Loango, the currency was the *pièce*, which as discussed in Chapter 2 and as described by Proyart in the late eighteenth century, corresponded to a set of goods including cloths.[43] Despite making a distinction between *marchandise* and *pièce* as currencies, the amounts paid in the three ports of the Loango coast for African captives were basically the same, according to Proyart. Regardless of local practices, cloth was an important commodity and currency on the Loango coast and in Angola. As historian Phyllis Martin explains, locally produced raffia cloth called *libongo* (plural *mbongo*) made from palm tree leaves was employed as a currency in commercial exchanges in the region and had various uses in burial ceremonies, such as wrapping the deceased body. It was also used to create bags, as well as bed and floor coverings.[44] With the rise of the Atlantic slave trade, textiles imported from Europe and India became coveted commodities among the region's ruling groups. Although various kinds of imported cloth were consumed by commoners as early as the seventeenth century, West Central African elites developed preferences for fabrics and colors, such as white and blue, that conveyed their symbolic, political, economic, and religious power.[45] As a result, items listed as gifts in slave ship cargos sailing to the Loango coast included the most sophisticated textiles.

Once *Le Montyon* anchored in Malembo, Lessene and his experienced crew members knew they would spend several months stationed on the coast. First, they had to start the usually long procedures to purchase dozens of men, women, and children to be transported to Saint-Domingue. As noted in Chapter 1, in the ports of Loango, Cabinda, and Malembo, the *Mfuka* was the king's highest agent in charge of the commercial exchanges with European traders. He collected customs, established the prices of commodities, and also arbitrated occasional disagreements among European traders and local agents.

It was customary that European travelers, traders, and missionaries visiting the Loango coast provided their hosts with gifts. Thus, to proceed with the trade, in addition to paying duties, ship captains also offered the *Mfuka* and other lesser agents a variety of gifts that echoed their tastes. Eighteenth-century traders noted how nobles, local commercial agents such as the *Mfuka*, and ordinary people appreciated the manufactured apparel items that European agents gave them. Grandpré, for example, observed that on the Loango coast, local agents "strut proudly under a rich jacket, or under an embroidered coat, old scraps of thrift we give them." While admitting that clothing items given to these agents were very often second-hand, eighteenth-century French traders seemed surprised about Africans' taste for novelty, as they also noted how they got tired of these items and passed them down to other individuals until "so full of vermin, so dirty, so greasy, so soaked in sweat that you can no longer recognize either the color or the embroidery."[46] Despite suggesting that Loango coast agents only cared for the "enjoyment of the moment," French traders knew that African agents developed tastes, expected specific presents, and were able to recognize secondhand clothes fabricated with lesser materials, which is probably why they quickly got rid of them. A similar kind of economy around manufactured items was created by the Atlantic slave trade in the Americas. Numerous nineteenth-century visual images illustrating European travel accounts show how slave owners paraded in the streets followed by their slaves dressed in their owners' used clothes. Other visual representations show enslaved people wearing old hats, shirts, and coats (Figure 3.1) that white people passed on to them.

Based on the cargos of previous slave vessels such as *La Marie Séraphique* and an unnamed slave ship that, respectively, sailed from La Rochelle to the Loango coast in 1769 and 1775, presents included various types of textiles from India and Europe, muskets, gunpowder, brandy, iron bars, knives, coats, redingotes (a man's double-breasted, short-waisted topcoat with a full skirt), and jackets, as well as fake silver pots and plates.[47] Other European visitors to the region also had to provide local rulers and agents with gifts. Proyart, who went to the Loango coast in the second half of the eighteenth century, corroborated these descriptions by explaining that gifts included coral, silver cutlery, rugs, and more or less valuable furniture items.[48] Evidently, in addition to making these exchanges, the trade depended on crewmen, porters, and boatmen transporting the commodities from a vessel to the trading

FIGURE 3.1 *Les barbiers ambulants* (traveling Barbers) in Jean-Baptiste Debret, *Voyage pittoresque et historique au Brésil*. Paris: Firmin Didot Frères; 1834–1839; second part, plate 11.

post. On the Loango coast, as no European nation was ever successful in establishing permanent structures such as fortresses, slave traders stored the commodities in trading posts named *quibanguas*, as explained in Chapter 2. Constructed by their crewmen or leased from local agents, these provisional stilt houses were surrounded by dwellings and located in an elevated area some 100 feet from the seashore, where goods could be more safely stored (Figure 2.3).

3.3 CABINDA: A PORT ALWAYS IN CABAL

On August 26, 1775, *Le Montyon* arrived on the Loango coast and anchored between Malembo and Cabinda.[49] The vessel was joined by the corvette *L'Hirondelle*, a vessel from La Rochelle also owned by Daniel Garesché. It remains unclear when the corvette left La Rochelle and what its original destination was. However, according to a memorandum (*mémoire*) written by the ship captain Lessenne and presented to La Rochelle's Chamber of Commerce, the shipowner Daniel Garesché, in order "to make the most" of the trade, associated the corvette

L'Hirondelle with the expedition, providing it with a "particular role and passport."[50] According to existing records, up to 1775 *L'Hirondelle* may have been only conducting the bilateral trade between La Rochelle and Saint-Domingue, rather than sailing to Africa.[51] Later in 1781, the same *L'Hirondelle*, described as a 200-ton vessel, owned by Garesché and commanded by Paul Hardy, sailed from La Rochelle to Saint-Domingue; it is recorded as having arrived back in La Rochelle on April 11, 1782.[52] Records show that *L'Hirondelle* also sailed from La Rochelle to Ouidah, in the Bight of Benin, in March 1783.[53]

What happened next was not very different from other transactions between French and African agents on the Loango coast. Like other slave vessels, *Le Montyon* carried small boats to conduct the trade along the coast. Lessenne sent two of these vessels to Malembo and Cabinda to get to know how the slave-trading business was developing. When the canoes returned to the *L'Hirondelle*, several "country's chiefs" took the opportunity to come on board to request the slave vessel's captain to anchor in Cabinda. But Lessenne refused this offer because he learned from the French captains Antoine Babinot, Jacques-Thomas Barbel, and Jean-Baptiste Barbé, whose vessels were anchored on the coast, that Cabinda was *toujours en cabale* ("always in cabal).[54] Despite this rumor, which was a direct warning from these captains, Andris Pukuta, Cabinda's *Mfuka*, was determined to change Lessenne's mind and promised him he would stop the conflicts.[55] Eventually, as Lessenne maintained his decision to trade in Malembo, Cabinda's *Mfuka* committed to deliver him 200 African captives for 198 *pièces* in three months in order to attract him to the port. As has already been discussed, in the context of the slave trade between La Rochelle and Cabinda and in this specific context, a *pièce* was an unity used to purchase enslaved people that varied over time, and corresponded to a set of goods that served as currencies.[56]

After sealing the deal and discussing the payment of customs, the *Mfuka* informed the king (presumably the *Maningoyo*) of Lessenne's presence. After receiving permission to trade in Cabinda and being assured he would receive protection from the king and his agents, Lessenne remained anchored in Malembo. While waiting, the corvette *L'Hirondelle* was set up and supplied with food and equipment, Lessenne sent his officer Jacques Cousse and five other crewmen to Cabinda on board his big canoe to transport six packages of merchandise. Once in Cabinda, Cousse conducted the trade, but when he was about to finish the dealings and return to his vessel, he spotted by the sea twenty-four men on board three chaloupes commanded by Babinot, Barbel, and Barbé, the three French captains who had warned Lessenne about the "cabals" upon his arrival. The three captains certainly knew what they were talking about. Armed with guns, sabers, and cutlasses, they seized Cousse's canoe, took the captives and commodities on board, and threatened to kill him. Forced to escape to land, Cousse and five of his men took refuge in the *Mfuka*'s house, where they were forced to spend two nights and to face the biggest fear of slave merchants in the region – sleeping in land where they were "exposed to perish by diseases to which few Europeans resist in these countries."[57]

When Lessenne learned about this "act of violence," he sent his officer Martin Dubouscoua to Cabinda on a second canoe to tell Cousse to show Babinot, Barbel, and Barbé the passport that had been issued by the Admiralty of La Rochelle in order to prove he was an "officer in the vessel *Le Montyon* and captain of the corvette *L'Hirondelle,* attached to the expedition, trading with part of its crew and his canoe while waiting the corvette to get there."[58] But when Cousse and four of his men went on board the ship *Nairac* (commanded by Babinot) to show his passport, the three captains, who knew exactly what they were doing, did not recognize their alleged misconduct. Instead, they aggravated the situation. This time, not only did they state his passport was false, but they also warned him that if the corvette *L'Hirondelle* came to trade in Cabinda, she would meet the same fate as the canoe.

Following these failed conversations, Lessenne dispatched a letter to the captains requesting the canoe's restitution. This was in vain. His men had to abandon it, "along with the Negroes, merchandises, and effects, which were in the canoe at the time of the abduction."[59] Despite these obstacles, Lessenne did not give up. He sent Cousse once again to trade in Cabinda, using a chaloupe borrowed from Gaudence Bloyet, the captain of the vessel *Le Saint-Charles* from Nantes, which was also trading in Loango and Malembo.[60] Then, "not daring to renew their piracy," the three rogue captains suggested that the *Mfuka* Andris Pukuta had signed two letters preventing Lessene from trading in Cabinda; even tough this was impossible because as these events were unfolding, Captain Cousse was dealing with the same *Mfuka* in Cabinda. When the *Mfuka* learned about "this trickery," he sent Lessenne "a Negro" to take his corvette and gave him orders to wait for the vessel if it was not ready and then take it to Cabinda, also making sure there were already ten captives to be sent on board when Lessenne deemed it appropriate.[61] In the conclusion of a memorandum addressed to the Chamber of Commerce of La Rochelle, Lessenne finally stated that he would leave to Garesché "the care of reclaiming the damages and to assert the rights that his minutes certified by my crew give him." He also emphasized that his expedition would have been lost had he not acted with moderation and prudence.[62]

Surviving documents do not allow us to know much more about what happened in Cabinda. Moreover, the existing sources only provide us Lessenne's and Garesché's points of view. Still, as we will see in Chapter 4, evidence suggests that Cabinda's *Mfuka* effectively protected Cousse and his men from the assault led by Babinot, Barbel, and Barbé. Yet several elements remain unclear regarding the motives that led the French traders to attack Cousse's canoe and seize his enslaved human cargo and commodities. The obvious answer is that they were attempting to prevent Cousse and his corvette *L'Hirondelle* from trading in Cabinda. But this motive alone does not seem to be strong enough to justify this degree of violence. There were always other French ships trading in the port, and as we will see, mutual attacks by vessels under the same flag on the Loango coast were less common than French rivalries with other European powers, especially the Portuguese.

Despite these interrogations, Lessenne's request to the Chamber of Commerce of La Rochelle offers some possible clues to explain these hostilities. The captain states that *L'Hirondelle* had joined *Le Montyon* with a special role and passport to trade in Cabinda. Unfortunately, neither this passport nor any outfitting records for *L'Hirondelle*'s voyage seems to have been preserved to offer an explanation as to what this special role and passport were and why the vessel was trading in Cabinda. Although Daniel Garesché owned *L'Hirondelle*, the first time the vessel appears conducting a slave voyage in available maritime records is during the Cabinda incident in August 1775. Moreover, several questions remain unanswered. Why is Jacques Cousse listed as an officer in *Le Montyon*'s armament and disarmament papers while he was the captain of *L'Hirondelle*? Perhaps the vessel's original captain died and Cousse had to replace him? This seems unlikely because deaths were usually recorded, and even appeared in the notices announcing the arrival of slave ships in Saint-Domingue that were published in the newspaper *Affiches américaines*. How and why did *L'Hirondelle* sail to Cabinda? Was it possible that the vessel changed its route after departing for the French West Indies or while it was performing cabotage navigation along the French coasts? If the corvette did not have permission to sail to the Loango coast, the French captains' statement about Cousse's fake passport and their attacks on Cousse's canoe and his men would be more understandable. Or was the corvette simply a tender of *Le Montyon*, perhaps explaining why no records of its voyage to Cabinda were left behind?[63]

3.4 GARESCHÉ SEEKS RESTITUTION

Daniel Garesché and other merchants presented Lessenne's memorandum of July 18, 1776, to the Chamber of Commerce of La Rochelle. In this letter, the ship captain narrated the Cabinda conflict. On July 23, 1776, the chamber's director, Furcy Legrix, referred to the case in a letter addressed to the Navy minister, Antoine de Sartine (Count of Alby). Legrix indicated that Garesché pleaded with the courts to be granted an indemnity, and stated that he was confident that "the judgment which will intervene will pecuniarily punish the infraction of the laws and will forbid them [Babinot, Barbel, and Barbé] from recidivism" for the sake of trade's good order and safety, and to prevent similar occurrences from happening to other traders. The director then begged the minister "to take into consideration the complaints of these merchants and to give the necessary orders in the various ports sending ships to the African coast, so that all captains are forbidden to assault or use violence when they find themselves dealing concurrently on the said coast."[64]

But the director's support had no visible effect. In a letter dated August 27, 1776, addressed to the directors and syndics of the Chamber of Commerce of Aunis (La Rochelle), several prominent slave merchants based in the city, including Daniel Garesché himself and his brother-in-law Jacques Carayon (the eldest son of Jacques Carayon), complained that the Navy minister and the Chamber of Commerce's director and syndics were remaining silent about Lessenne's written request:

We have already placed before your eyes the memorandum of Sr. Lessenne concerning the piracy exerted on the coast of Angola in Guinea against the vessel *Le Montyon* of this port by captains Babinot of Bordeaux and Barbel and Barbés of Le Havre, with the request to inform the Navy Minister and claim his authority against such brigandage.

Your silence, gentlemen, is no doubt a result of that of the Minister. We see with astonishment that such an act of unpunished violence will give rise to others. However, here we are at the moment of outfitting, should we do it? Prudence forbids it or advises us to oppose force with force; to what risks then are we exposed by our expeditions? What a position for shipowners who already have too many obvious risks against them, inseparable from this trade!

Deign gentlemen to renew your entreaties to the enlightened Minister who today governs the colonies. He is the friend of Commerce and the Protector of Those engaged in it. He would doubtless regret being obliged one day to punish his captains who, independently of the rivalries of the slave trade, would still have the resentment of outrage and unpunished thefts; Finally, it is easy to prevent the violence that French ships would exert on each other if they could imagine that justice would be demanded in vain against violators of order and peace.[65]

Two months later, the director of the Chamber of Commerce of La Rochelle sent a shorter letter, requesting the Navy minister to give orders to prevent further acts of violence among French captains, thus suggesting that preventive measures had not been taken and that no warning had been issued to the slave traders who had attacked Cousse and his canoe in Cabinda the previous year.[66]

Although the complaints of La Rochelle's slave merchants were met with silence, and despite the attack on Cousse's canoe in Cabinda, the voyages of *Le Montyon* and *L'Hirondelle* were profitable. After less than five months anchored in Malembo, Lessenne was able to purchase 599 enslaved men, women, and children. On January 20, 1776, the newspaper *Affiches américaines* announced that on January 17, *Le Montyon* from La Rochelle, commanded by Captain Lessenne coming from Malembo, on the Angola coast, had arrived at Cap-Français "with a cargo of 545 beautiful Blacks [*Noirs*]" who would be on sale at Mesnier brothers on January 27.[67] We do not know for how long *L'Hirondelle* remained in Cabinda, as there is no paper trail for this vessel. Yet one week after advertising the arrival of *Le Montyon*, the *Affiches américaines* of January 27, 1776, announced that *L'Hirondelle*, commanded by captain Cousse, had arrived in Cap-Français, not from Cabinda or Malembo (usually referred to as the coast of Angola), but from the Gold Coast (Côte d'or), a term used by the French to refer to the Bight of Benin which encompassed the ports of Ouidah (Map 2), Porto-Novo, as well as Badagry.[68] Although one can assume the wrong place of purchase in Africa was listed by mistake, errors of this kind were actually rather uncommon in the announcements made by the Saint-Domingue's newspaper. As a result, many question marks persist regarding the voyage of the *L'Hirondelle*.

The vessels commanded by the French captains turned pirates also succeeded in purchasing, transporting, and delivering alive nearly 1,000 enslaved Africans in Cap-Français, Saint-Domingue. The vessel *L'Apollon*, owned by the company Mouchel & Beaufils from Le Havre and commanded by Barbé, left Cabinda on October 13, 1775, and arrived in Cap-Français on December 15, 1775, carrying 338 "beautiful *Noirs.*" These men, women, and children were put on sale one week later at Lory, Plombard & Compagnie.[69] The vessel *Le Comte de Colbert*, owned by the Le Havre company Baudry & Bologne, and whose captain was Jacques Thomas Barbel, left Cabinda on November 15, 1775, carrying 229 enslaved Africans. On January 20, 1776, the *Affiches américaines* announced that the vessel had arrived in Cap-Français on January 13 with "200 *Nègres,*" who were put on sale at Blanchardon & Bellot on

January 23.[70] Finally, *Le Nairac*, commanded by Antoine Babinot and owned by Bordeaux's shipowner Paul Nairac (the family's eldest son), took on board 527 African captives in Cabinda. Despite the loss of more than 40 captives of his human cargo during the Middle Passage, 480 enslaved Africans disembarked alive in Cap-Français on April 2, 1776.[71] Unfortunately, we do not know the fate of these men, women, and children, who remained nameless in these records.

3.5 ANOTHER INFAMOUS CABINDA AFFAIR

After the conflict in Cabinda, although *L'Hirondelle* apparently did not return to trade on the Loango coast, as we see in Chapter 4, Garesché's vessel *Le Montyon*, once again commanded by Lessenne, sailed to Malembo in 1777. Meanwhile, nothing suggests that Barbé, Babinot, and Barbel were ever punished for their violent actions against Cousse and his men. On the contrary, all three captains led new voyages to Atlantic Africa just a few months after their return to Le Havre and Bordeaux, including in the final year of the American War of Independence, 1783, when a growing number of French ships sailed to Africa. These voyages were not uneventful. Barbel, at least, faced problems in his next two slaving voyages. On April 3, 1783, he navigated to the Loango coast as the captain of *L'Homme Instruit*, which left Le Havre along with *L'Apollon*, commanded by Barbé, with whom he had been in Malembo five years earlier. Once on the Loango coast, Barbel sailed his vessel to Cabinda, but this time he was not able to purchase enslaved people in that port. The Portuguese captain Antonio Januario do Valle stopped his ship and told him he could not anchor in Cabinda; if he did, he would be considered an "aggressor of an attack committed in the royal domains of your majesty."[72]

Valle's warning to the French ship captain relied on an old Portuguese claim over the territory of the Loango coast. Unlike Barbel, Valle was not a slave trader, but rather the commander of an operation that intended to build a Portuguese fort in Cabinda, giving origin to an episode known in the historiography of the Atlantic slave trade as the Cabinda affair. As we already know, the Portuguese monopolized the trade south of the Congo River, where the two major West Central African slaving-trading ports of Luanda and Benguela were located. Yet the Dutch, the French, and the British constantly challenged this monopoly.[73] As the Portuguese never succeeded in controlling the trade in the ports of the Loango coast, in order to prevent other European powers from doing so, they put into practice the plan of building a fortress in Cabinda, a feat that both the British and the French had unsuccessfully struggled to accomplish.

On July 13, 1783, Antonio Januario do Valle sailed from Luanda to Cabinda as the captain of the frigate *Nossa Senhora da Graça*, along with the frigate *Loanda Nossa Senhora Monte do Carmo*, and the three corvettes *Invencível Nossa Senhora da Conceição, São José*, and *Sararoca*. The crew of 1,000 individuals included officers, soldiers, sailors, artisans, workers, and enslaved men and boys owned by the officers. Transporting foodstuffs and instruments before reaching Cabinda, the vessels anchored at the mouth of the Dande River to load other effects such as lime, firewood, wood, and charcoal, which they needed to construct the fortress. According to the Portuguese report, upon arriving in Cabinda, the expedition disembarked quickly and marked the site where they intended to build their fort without giving time for the "Blacks to attempt neither to prevent, nor to delay" the construction work, an observation that reveals the Portuguese fear of local opposition to the invasion.[74]

The fortress's site was an elevated area nearly 130 feet from the beach, encompassing the place where the English built their fortress in 1723, described by the Portuguese officials as a location less subject to sudden assault and more advantageous for dominating the port, preventing losses and smuggling in the future.[75] Although fearing attacks from other European powers, the Portuguese officials were concerned about placating local rulers, agents, and commoners in a "way that makes them conceive peaceful ideas of commerce and security."[76] Before their departure from Lisbon, the minister for Portugal's colonies, Martinho de Melo e Castro, advised the governor of Angola, José Gonçalo da Câmara, to provide the Ngoyo's ruler with "presents which were to be mainly made of sufficient quantities of *cachaça* [Brazilian sugarcane brandy]."[77] However, Portuguese officers were also advised to "severely punish all people who insult the Blacks or do the least violence to them, as this can result in great detriment to the royal service, especially as long as the Portuguese Dominion is not well rooted there."[78] These paternalistic views of Ngoyo's subjects were not part of any benevolent plan but rather a strategy to contain Cabinda's residents. Thus, it is not surprising that the Portuguese also admitted that if by any chance they were not able to persuade the ruler of Ngoyo and his agents about the advantages the Portuguese had to offer, they were given permission to impose their presence by force. But according to them, as the locals were "naturally ambitious and needy, it is probable that, treating them well, and making them known by experience, that they can obtain abundance and gifts from our neighborhood, they will prefer us to foreigners, who dislike them, offend them and sometimes steal."[79] These positive and optimistic views of the local population did not last long.

After the Portuguese invaded and settled in Cabinda, the Woyo gave the invaders exclusive rights to trade in the port, and construction of the fort started.[80] But after the agreement was sealed, it was not surprising that the *Mambuku* (also referred to as governor or prince) changed his mind, as until that date no European power had succeeded in building a fortress or monopolizing trade in any of the ports of the Loango coast. The *Mambuku*'s response met the French interests, as a Portuguese monopoly would undermine their intense slave trading activities in the region. Led by the *Mambuku*, the Woyo allied themselves with the Kotchi of Kakongo to resist the Portuguese. Quickly, the Portuguese invasion became a war against Cabinda's people and their allies in Malembo.[81]

French officials naturally contested Portugal's claim of territorial rights over the region, as since the Portuguese had settled south of the Congo River in Luanda and Benguela, they had never controlled any of the ports of the Loango coast.[82] As the French investigated the events unfolding in Cabinda, a memorandum of April 2, 1784, concluded that "the coasts of Congo and Angola have always been common to the different nations of Europe and that they [the French] traded there, particularly in Cabinda, without any claim, which excludes any idea of ownership on the part of the Portuguese."[83] Although Portugal declared that there was no intention to prevent other nations from trading in the region, the French feared that remaining silent regarding Portuguese claims about Cabinda's ownership would mean not only recognizing their right, but also allowing them to prevent the French from trading in the region in the future. According to the French official, "saying one is the country's owner but has no intention of hindering the commerce of another nation means neither to renounce to use property rights one day nor to recognize France's acquired freedom to trade in the areas that gave rise to the difficulty. The terms in which the response from the Lisbon's court is conceived are remarkable and it would be dangerous to misunderstand their true meaning."[84] Although this memorandum advised that preventing the construction of the fortress would not be possible, it naively suggested the French could also construct a fort in Cabinda.

Two months later the French assessment had changed. On June 17, 1784, a French squadron composed of one frigate and two barges commanded by Gaspard de Bernard de Marigny anchored in Cabinda. The next day, the French met two delegates of the "Black Prince residing one *lieue* [approximately 3 miles] from Cabinda," presumably including the *Mambuku*, who promised to support the operation against the Portuguese fort.[85] Next, Marigny sent a letter to inform the French captains anchored in Malembo of his arrival and also emphasize that he had received orders from the king to "support and protect Europeans' freedom of commerce on the coast of Angola."[86] Meanwhile, upon approaching the Cabinda fort, still unfinished, the French found nearly 600 men, "few of whom were white, many black soldiers, wearing uniforms and the rest black workers or slaves."[87] In a letter confirming their support of Marigny's operation, the French, British, and Dutch captains anchored in Malembo complained about the Portuguese, who fired cannons at their vessels, expelled them from Cabinda, and forced them to anchor in Malembo, a crowded port where there were nearly eighteen vessels. They decried that this competition increased the price of the captives, forcing them to extend their stay on the coast, thus increasing their costs and giving them higher expenses. For these ship captains, the Portuguese intentions were clear: "As long as the Portuguese have a fort, they will be masters of the country."[88]

Relying on a total of 331 men, including thirty-one grenadiers and 300 riflemen, in addition to 1,200 armed Africans, Marigny sent a missive to the Portuguese commanding officer telling him "to take down his fort whose purpose could not be against the natives of the country and to promise to open the port of Cabinda to all nations, otherwise he would attack it."[89] Eventually, the Portuguese capitulated, and their commanders consented to raze the fort to the ground and to withdraw with his garrison, effects, and men to Luanda.[90] As the French officers demolished the fort, they sent to Malembo most of the Portuguese who could not board the available vessels and put them on board French slave ships until additional vessels came to transport them to Luanda.[91]

But in their official correspondence, the Portuguese officers provided a different version of the events, in which they appeared as victims. They accused the Woyo of Cabinda and their Kotchi allies in Malembo of killing those Portuguese who had deserted the fortress. Moreover, they blamed these local African agents of selling to the French traders in Malembo the Black sailors and workers (enslaved and free) who were helping to build the fort. According to this correspondence, Portuguese captains found several of their "Black mariners and workers, either slaves or free" sold into slavery on board the French slave vessels anchored in Malembo, though the correspondence emphasized that only slave ship captain Gayot, who commanded the corvette *La Rosalie*, agreed to exchange the captives.[92] Although it is hard to corroborate the Portuguese version, it is possible to confirm that during the conflict in Cabinda, there were two vessels named *La Rosalie* anchored in Malembo. *La Rosalie*, commanded by Henry Gayot, left Nantes in March 1783, passed through La Rochelle on April 2, 1783, and arrived in Malembo on July 3, 1783, where it remained anchored until September 1, 1783, before Marigny's arrival, and then transported 557 enslaved Africans to Cap-Français.[93] When Marigny's expedition arrived in Cabinda in June 1784, *La Rosalie* anchored in Malembo was a vessel from Le Havre, commanded by Michel Duval, one of the ship captains who wrote to Marigny denouncing the actions led by the Portuguese when he attempted to anchor in Cabinda in May 1784.[94]

The Cabinda conflict illuminates Woyo's and Kotchi's ideas of sovereignty. On the one hand, without African men willing to fight to take down the fort, Marigny's expedition would never have succeeded in forcing the Portuguese capitulation. On the other hand, the Portuguese knew that African forces, supported by French vessels and ammunition, outnumbered their 1,000 men. This complex event also shows how far European nations such as Portugal and France were willing to go to hold onto their ability to trade in Cabinda and Malembo. Whereas the Portuguese claimed territorial rights and consequently the power to control Cabinda's trade in enslaved people, the French fought to keep the port open in order to protect their own commercial interests. As we see in Chapter 5, the Cabinda conflict reshaped Franco-Portuguese relations not only on the Loango coast, but also in the Bight of Benin, where one French trader from La Rochelle started advocating for the construction of a fortress in Porto-Novo. This newly emerging slave-trading port was nearly 48 miles from Ouidah, the slave port controlled by the Kingdom of Dahomey, where there was a French fortress.

According to Grandpré, the destruction of the Portuguese fort by the French Navy in 1784 impacted Cabinda's elite clothing trends. Grandpré amusingly noted that after Cabinda's residents saw the naval officers who participated in the French intervention of 1784, they "wanted nothing else than uniforms and epaulettes." Therefore, ship captains "constrained to adhere themselves to this fashion, and to bring them uniforms of all colors, adorned with epaulettes." Hence, Cabinda agents received the French traders with cargoes of enslaved people and kept their prices very high, imagining they had great importance, "because they were clothed in a habit for which they had seen that people had deference." Yet Grandpré concluded that the new fashion passed very fast because the captains only brought fake items, both in gold and silver, and "these ornaments became so black that they soon grew disgusted with them."[95]

3.6 COMPETING FRENCH SLAVE TRADERS

Following the conflict in Cabinda, a convention held in Madrid reinstated free trade on the Loango coast.[96] We do not know exactly what happened to Barbé's vessel after the encounter with Valle's frigate during the war in Cabinda in 1783, but certainly both *L'Homme Instruit* and *L'Appolon* went to trade in Malembo and left the region before Marigny's arrival. On February 10, 1784, *L'Apollon* landed in Cap-Français. Two weeks later, the 380 enslaved men, women, and children who had been transported in the vessel were put on sale in Port-au-Prince.[97] On May 31, 1784, *L'Homme Instruit*, commanded by Barbel, landed 178 enslaved Africans in Cap-Français.[98] A few months later, on October 2, 1784, when the Cabinda incident had been resolved, Barbé sailed again from Le Havre to Malembo as captain of *L'Apollon*. Almost one year later, on September 15, 1785, his vessel brought 191 enslaved Africans to Cap-Français.[99] After the Cabinda incident, Babinot also sailed from Bordeaux to Malembo twice more, in 1786 as the captain of the vessel *L'Aigle* and in 1788 as the captain of *L'Emilie*. Together these two slave ships transported more than 700 enslaved Africans to Cap-Français.[100]

After the voyage of 1783, Barbel also returned to the coasts of Africa twice more. On September 19, 1785, he sailed from Le Havre to the "Gold Coast" (meaning to the Bight of Benin) as the captain of the *L'Aimable Ninette*; this vessel arrived in Cap-Français carrying 504 slaves on April 1, 1786.[101] Finally, Barbel left from Le Havre to the Loango coast as the captain of the slave ship *Le Patrocle* on August 16, 1787. The outcome of this voyage was tragic, as the vessel ran aground when approaching the Loango coast on December 17, 1787.[102] Barbel died in Malembo. Eight different vessels that were trading along the coast at the time rescued and took on board the vessel's crew members. Ironically, one of these vessels was *Le Comte de Forcalquier*, owned by Daniel Garesché, the same shipowner who twelve years earlier had one of his men and cargo attacked by Barbel, Barbé, and Babinot in Cabinda.[103] Despite his captains having been assaulted by three French captains, Garesché sent his vessel *Le Montyon* once again to Cabinda. As we see in Chapter 4, this time, the vessel's mission was not only to purchase enslaved Africans, but also to thank Cabinda's *Mfuka*.

4

Deciphering the Gift

After the 1775 Cabinda conflict, when French slave ship captains became pirates and attacked the slave trade expedition outfitted by Daniel Gareské, slave ship captain Jean-Amable Lessenne and his officer, Jacques Cousse, sailed on board *Le Montyon* and *L'Hirondelle* to Saint-Domingue and from there back to La Rochelle.[1] We do not know when *L'Hirondelle* arrived in La Rochelle, but *Le Montyon*, commanded by Lessenne, anchored in the French port on June 19, 1776.[2] Despite the attack by Barbel, Barbé, and Babinot, as soon as Garesché's vessel landed in La Rochelle, the shipowner started preparing it for a new voyage to the Loango coast.

The quick preparation of a new expedition confirms that despite the incident in Cabinda, the trade in enslaved Africans in that region had generated profits, and thus it was worth taking the risk to sail to the region one more time.[3] Commanded once again by Lessenne, *Le Montyon* left La Rochelle to the Loango coast during the winter, on January 26, 1777, with sixty-four officers and crew members on board.[4] Although we do not know the composition of the cargo of this voyage, it is possible to imagine that most items were the same as previous slave expeditions from La Rochelle to Loango, Malembo, and Cabinda. Yet it is very likely that during this voyage Lessenne carried with him a gift for Cabinda's *Mfuka* who two years earlier had protected Jacques Cousse and his men when three rogue French captains and their crews attacked them. This object was not a tribute or an ordinary present, but rather a special gift: a silver ceremonial sword engraved (Figure 4.1) with the words "Andris Macaye Mafouque le juste de Cabinde" (Andris Makaya Mfuka The Just of Cabinda).[5] This chapter explains how the eighteenth-century silver ceremonial sword embodies the complex interactions between French male slave traders and Cabinda's male authorities.

FIGURE 4.1 *Kimpaba*, silver, 20,2 inches, Musée du Nouveau Monde
de La Rochelle. Photograph: Max Roy. Courtesy: Musée du Nouveau
Monde de La Rochelle.

4.1 CONCEIVING THE GIFT

Beyond the Loango coast, in the broader region of the Kingdom of Kongo, metal swords, usually made in iron, were insignias of political power that conveyed the symbolic importance of their owners.[6] Like other swords, the silver gift is a gendered object, an object of power usually carried by male rulers. Unlike swords locally made in the kingdoms of the Loango coast, swords named *kimpaba* (plural *bimpaba*) and also designated as *ximpaba, cimpaba, chimpaba, chimpava, tshimpaba*, and *tshimpaaba*, the French version was made of silver, a precious and valued metal in Atlantic Africa during the era of the Atlantic slave trade.

The handle of the silver *kimpaba* and the engraved ornaments decorating its false blade carry several features of late eighteenth-century European silverware. However, the artifact contrasts with existing eighteenth-century French silver swords. Whereas generally evoking other West African and West Central African ceremonial swords, knives, and scepters, the French silver version more specifically reproduces the formal elements of a *kimpaba*. According to the typology established by Tristan Arbousse Bastide when examining African weapons, the *kimpaba* corresponds to the wider category of chopping knives. Mostly found in West Central Africa, these "short-bladed weapons" with very peculiar shapes measure between 14 and 28 inches, their blades are wider than those of cutlasses, and they are used as both symbolical and practical weapons.[7]

Part of the regalia of Woyo rulers, the *kimpaba* is described in contemporary sources as a "proverb sword," because the versions produced on the Loango coast contain geometrical figures symbolizing local epigrams. Through its multiple layers, this object embodies the cross-cultural exchanges between Africans and Europeans and specifically between the Woyo and the French. Given as a gift to *Mfuka* Andris Pukuta, the French silver *kimpaba* was gradually transformed into a sacred object, an artifact of power, and an object of prestige. Exploring its various layers allows us to better understand the uses and meanings of this object and other similar swords for the rulers and peoples of Loango coast's polities in general and Cabinda in particular. Ultimately, the creation, exchange, and circulation of objects of prestige such as this sword shaped the development of the trade in enslaved Africans and European colonialism in Africa.

A few years after their arrival in the Kingdom of Kongo in the late fifteenth century, the Portuguese ruler Dom Manuel sent to the region scholars and missionaries with a variety of gifts, such as luxurious textiles as well as silver crosses, cups, and censers to allow the newly converted

FIGURE 4.2 *Commandant d'escadron, 1er régiment de dragons* (commander of
squadron, 1st regiment of dragons), engraving, 1797.
Source: Gallica: Bibliothèque Nationale de France, Paris, France.

local rulers to perform Catholic services.[8] Presents continued to be central elements in the transactions between European captains and African
rulers and agents on the coasts of Africa during the entire era of the
Atlantic slave trade. Still, surviving written records of slave ship cargoes
do not allow us to identify any special gifts.

More often than not, items listed as gifts in ship records were luxurious textiles, specific kinds of guns, silver cutlery, and other manufactured
items. On September 1, 1769, the Nantes vessel *Le Pompée*, commanded
by Pierre-Ignace-Liévin van Alstein, anchored in Loango. As established,
he gave presents to the main Loango agents. To the *Maloango* he offered a
"dragon officer brass helmet covered with tiger fur," which was probably
similar to the helmet represented in an eighteenth-century French engraving (Figure 4.2).[9] Van Alstein also gave a rug to the *Mfuka* and two other
rugs to two other agents. Likewise, Grandpré described the presence of
European furniture and luxury items in the residence of Kakongo's *Mambuku*. According to him, the *Mambuku* lived in a European fashioned

quibangua "perfectly furnished with seats, beds, sofas, rugs, tapestries ... almost everything is velvet." Also according to Grandpré, the French had made very fine silverware for him; this included "two large silver fountains each having four taps, for the use of the four separate compartments; he filled them with various liquors and placed them on the two ends of his table, where they served drinks to his guests."[10]

After the Cabinda conflict in 1775, Garesché and Lessenne likely concluded that an ordinary gift would not suffice to thank the *Mfuka* and continue to obtain advantages in the trade of enslaved Africans in Cabinda. Andris Pukuta was an experienced slave-trading agent, and according to Dutch records he had held the office of *Mfuka* since at least 1768.[11] Also, as discussed in Chapter 1, although the *Mfuka* was originally a commoner, the social position of local agents gradually changed as the Atlantic slave trade expanded. Hence, the *Mfuka* could be related to noblemen and noblewomen, and, like other commoners, he could marry a princess. For example, in his account published in 1776, Proyart mentioned that the *Manikakongo* (king of Kakongo) was a man named "Poukouta ... aged 126 years."[12] Therefore, it is plausible that the *Mfuka* Andris Pukuta was related to the ruler of the neighboring Kingdom of Kakongo. Moreover, according to the silver sword's dedication (see Figure 4.1) Pukuta may also have been the Kingdom of Ngoyo's *Makaya* ("macaye") a prime minister of sorts.

One can imagine that following the quarrel with the French traders turned pirates in 1775, Lessenne oversaw the purchase of captive Africans. He heard their laments and cries in the hold of *Le Montyon* during the weeks he spent between Cabinda and Malembo. Lessenne may have started to think about offering a special present to Cabinda's *Mfuka* during the long Middle Passage between the Loango coast and Saint-Domingue. While stationed on the coast, Lessenne and especially Cousse and his officers, who spent at least one night in the *Mfuka*'s house, learned about his tastes, how he dressed, the objects and gifts he cared about and kept in his home, as well as his regalia; in other words, the clothing and artifacts that represented his official power in the region. We do not know the emblems of Cabinda's *Mfuka* when the incident with the French captains took place in the late eighteenth century, but according to Grandpré's account a cap (*bonnet*) was one of his insignias.[13]

One can assume that Lessenne, Cousse, or one of their officers saw a *kimpaba* somewhere during one of their stays in Malembo and Cabinda and that they drew the object on a sheet of paper. Or perhaps they acquired one of these swords and transported it to La Rochelle with the idea of reproducing it and taking it as a gift for Cabinda's *Mfuka*. Neither action was unheard of. Many seamen who participated in the Atlantic slave trade wrote and published journals of their voyages that included descriptions of local objects and African royal insignias. For example, one mariner on board the French slave ship vessel *Le Diligent* left a detailed and richly illustrated journal of his vessel's voyage from the port of Vannes in northeast France to purchase enslaved Africans in Jakin in the Bight of Benin.[14] European traders, missionaries, and visitors also depicted in detail artifacts they observed while on the African coasts.[15] Several others brought home African items that were gradually incorporated into the emerging European museums during the eighteenth century. Yet swords of prestige from this period are rather rare in museum collections, as most artifacts of this type were brought to Europe during the nineteenth and twentieth centuries, as we will see in Chapters 5 and 6.[16] Regardless of all these questions, because Garesché almost immediately started to outfit the vessel for a new voyage to the Loango coast, he may have commissioned the sword from a silversmith as soon as *Le Montyon* entered the port of La Rochelle.

We can speculate that after returning from the Loango coast in 1776, Garesché, Lessenne, or whoever commissioned the silver sword went to the workshop of one of the twelve silversmiths active in La Rochelle.[17] The silversmith was provided with an actual *kimpaba* brought from Cabinda, a drawing depicting this kind of ceremonial sword, or perhaps only an oral description.[18] In contrast with West Central African blacksmiths who produced *bimpaba* and European artisans who created many other items, craftsmen who produced eighteenth-century silver artifacts did not remain anonymous. During the Ancien Régime, the profession of silversmith was regulated in the Kingdom of France, which controlled the production of silver and gold items to insure the collection of taxes. As master artisans, silversmiths belonged to guilds (*jurandes* or *communautés de métiers*), as did other artisans and professionals such as carpenters, surgeons, and shoemakers. Following social and technical regulations, guilds exerted disciplinary power over their members, who were organized according to a hierarchical structure composed of *maîtres* (masters), *compagnons* (workers), and *apprentis* (apprentices). As compulsory organizations, guilds were regulated by public law and had a legal personality. Only silversmiths who belonged to these associations were authorized to produce silver items in France, which is why European silver items carried hallmarks of charge and discharge that provide information about their context of production.[19]

The silver sword (see Figure 4.1) bears one crowned "H," identifying the jurisdiction of La Rochelle; another crowned "H" along with the letter date

"R," situating the artifact's manufacture between February 1775 and February 1777; and the discharge mark in the form of a squirrel, attesting that the silversmith had paid his duties and so could sell the finished product.[20] These marks and the dedication written in French connect the object to the incident that occurred just after the arrival of *Le Montyon* and *L'Hirondelle* in Malembo around the end of August 1775. But despite these several details, there is no hallmark identifying the master silversmith. However, because the sword's handle carries features similar to a silver oiler manufactured in 1775 and attributed to Jean (or Jean-Baptiste) Chaslon (or Chalon), the most important silversmith active at La Rochelle at the time, experts believe that he may have manufactured the silver sword.[21]

4.2 THE SILVERSMITH

Jean Chaslon was the son of Jacques Chaslon, and was born in Marans, near La Rochelle, on March 11, 1735.[22] Jean became an apprentice silversmith in the workshop of Jean-Baptiste Troquet in 1747, when he was probably twelve years old.[23] In the 1770s, Chaslon was a very well-established master silversmith who resided at Rue du Palais in the Saint-Barthélemy parish, near hôtel Fleuriau where the Musée du Nouveau Monde is located today and where the silver *kimpaba* (Figure 4.1) is on display. Several merchants involved in the trade of enslaved Africans also resided in this part of the city during the eighteenth century, including Daniel Garesché, the owner of the slave ships *Le Montyon* and *L'Hirondelle*; it is also where the ship captain Jean-Amable Lessenne purchased a sumptuous house (*hôtel*) years later.[24]

A notarial record of March 15, 1777 shows that Jean Chaslon took his own eleven-year-old son, François Chaslon, as a silversmith apprentice. In this document, Chaslon, the father, appears as *marchand et maître orfèvre* (merchant and silversmith master). This term indicates that, in addition to creating and producing silver items, he could sell silver artifacts manufactured by other masters.[25] But the similarities of the silver sword's handle with other silver articles attributed to Jean Chaslon are not the only elements that lead us to believe he created and produced the sword gifted to Cabinda's *Mfuka*. Indeed, Jean Chaslon had a very personal connection with the Cabinda incident because his brother, Louis Chaslon, sailed to the Loango coast as the first surgeon on board *Le Montyon* in 1775.[26] Perhaps Louis himself was one of the officers who was attacked by the three rogue ship captains and therefore had to spend the night in the *Mfuka*'s house in Cabinda. As members of the guilds of silversmiths and surgeons, the Chaslon brothers had a visible position in La Rochelle. They could have been Catholics like the ship captain Lessenne or Protestants like shipowner Garesché, who belonged to an old and prominent Protestant family of merchants. In addition, there is evidence attesting that both Chaslon brothers were Freemasons, members of the lodge *L'Union parfaite*.[27]

After several months spent on the coasts of Africa, when Louis Chaslon returned to La Rochelle in 1776, he certainly met his brother Jean and told him the stories of his slaving voyage to Cabinda and Malembo. As an officer, the most important of these stories was not the dreadful transportation of hundreds of enslaved men, women, and children to Saint-Domingue, which apparently occurred with no major incidents, but rather the Cabinda incident, in which other French slave traders attacked and threatened to kill his crew members, and perhaps even himself. As we have noted, few silversmiths were active in La Rochelle in 1776, so it is logical to conclude that once Garesché or Lessenne decided to commission the silver ceremonial sword as a gift to thank Cabinda's *Mfuka*, the ship surgeon's brother quickly became the preferred candidate for the commission. We assume Garesché paid for this exquisite gift, even though it is not impossible that ship captain Jean-Amable Lessenne could have ordered the silver sword. Although Louis Chaslon himself could have given a personal gift to Cabinda's *Mfuka*, in the context of a slave voyage in which he played an official role as first surgeon this hypothesis is rather unlikely. Thus, Chaslon remains the closest link between the silver sword and the *Mfuka*. Not only was he the brother of the silversmith who created and manufactured the silver sword, but he also sailed again to Malembo as the *Le Montyon*'s first surgeon on January 26, 1777, just a few months after returning from the Loango coast, after the Cabinda incident.[28]

We do not know the month and day of *Le Montyon*'s arrival in Malembo, but the voyage from La Rochelle to the Loango coast could last up to ninety days. We can assume that by the end of April 1777, Lessene and his crew anchored in Malembo and offered the silver ceremonial sword as a gift to Andris Pukuta. The sword's blade (Figure 4.1) measures nearly 15 inches by 3 inches, with a gadrooned (or notched) handle measuring approximately 5 inches. The spine of the ceremonial sword is reinforced with a riveted silver rod and eleven openwork geometric elements, which may have been added after it was originally created. Both sides of the sword's blade contain the same elements. A flower garland is engraved along the false edge. The tip of the knife has a wider recess measuring approximately 5 inches, and a cross shape is perforated in its rounded, unsharpened point. Engraved on the edge, the dedication to the *Mfuka* suggests the silver *kimpaba* was no ordinary present. Rather than a personal gift, the silver sword can rather be interpreted as an official gift. By expressing his gratitude with a significant present, Garesché, the owner and outfitter of the *Le Montyon* and the *L'Hirondelle*, as well as Lessenne, reinforced the message that, by having defended La Rochelle's slave traders, Cabinda's *Mfuka* Andris Pukuta chose the morally correct side in the immoral and inhuman trade in human beings.

Not only did Garesché wish to continue sending his vessels to purchase enslaved Africans in Cabinda, but he also wanted his captains to enjoy advantages in these commercial exchanges. Therefore, a special gift could ensure access to the best captives. But how to assess the importance of a present in the context of the Atlantic slave trade? Ultimately, its significance could be measured in several ways. The agents based on the Loango coast and other regions of Atlantic Africa who exchanged and interacted with European merchants greatly appreciated objects that carried monetary value. But this gift was not a tribute. As we have already discussed, items allocated for the payment of customs in slave ship cargoes were basically the same items that were used to purchase enslaved Africans. Presents were typically carried in smaller quantities than items intended for the payment of customs, and usually included wines and spirits, cutlery, firearms, and a few pieces of luxurious textiles. The silver *kimpaba* did not fit the category of ordinary presents included in nearly all cargoes of slave ships. In other words, the silver sword was a unique object, exclusively manufactured for its receiver.

Therefore, when Garesché commissioned Chaslon to produce a sword to be given as a gift to Cabinda's *Mfuka*, the choice of silver mattered. Silver had been highly valued in various regions of Europe, Asia, and the Americas since antiquity. Likewise, silver objects were luxury items on the African coasts, where coined silver had been in use since at least the medieval times as one of the several existing currencies.[29] Global access to silver began to increase from the late fifteenth century, when Spanish conquerors and colonizers took possession of the world's largest silver mines, located in Potosí, in the then viceroyalty of Peru, twenty-first century Bolivia, and also the reserves situated in the viceroyalty of Mexico, a region that became the largest producer of silver during the eighteenth century.

With the rise of the Atlantic slave trade, European agents increasingly introduced silver articles to West Africa and West Central Africa. As early as in the sixteenth century Portuguese traders transported enslaved Africans from Luanda to Buenos Aires, from where they illegally carried silver from Potosí, back to the coasts of West Central Africa and then to China.[30] In West Central Africa, like iron, copper, and gold, silver was a metal of prestige. On the one hand, as Eugenia W. Herbert noted, unlike iron and copper, silver deposits were rare in Africa, which is why its local use was much more limited until the rise of European conquest and colonization in the nineteenth century. On the other hand, silver "was too soft for utilitarian purposes."[31] As Toby Green explained, whereas copper and iron became "soft currencies" during the seventeenth century, following the rise of the Atlantic slave trade, silver along with gold, retained their value across time and space, and therefore became hard currencies.[32] In this context, whereas gold was usually exported by West African societies, especially on the Gold Coast, most African states imported silver. To local populations of the Loango coast, and West Central Africa more broadly, silver was a rare foreign metal of prestige, only accessible to members of the elite.

As early as the seventeenth century, European traders carried luxurious silver artifacts produced in Potosí across the Atlantic Ocean to be offered as gifts to African rulers, who also reciprocated by offering Europeans silver presents. In 1642, for example, as part of the exchanges associated with the trade in enslaved Africans from Angola to Brazil, the king of Kongo Nkanga a Lukeni a Nzenze a Ntumba (King Garcia II) gave a richly decorated deep silver basin as a gift to Johan Maurits van Nassau-Siegen, the governor of the Brazilian captaincy of Pernambuco, which between 1630 and 1654 was under Dutch domination.[33]

During the era of the Atlantic slave trade, silver was a valued metal in Atlantic Africa and also highly in demand in Europe and China. Whereas enslaved Africans composed the largest workforce that mined, smelted, and refined silver in Potosí, Native Americans who were either enslaved or submitted to other forms of forced labor constituted the workforce in the Mexican silver industry.[34] At the height of the Atlantic slave trade in the eighteenth century, coined silver was a currency widely employed in the three continents involved in the Atlantic slave trade and the trade in the Indian Ocean.[35] Silver coins circulated in great numbers following the same European, African, and American pathways taken by slave traders.[36]

In this context, for both French traders and Cabinda's royal and commercial elites, silver was a valuable currency and a metal associated with rare foreign objects that were not intended for daily use. Whereas silver was consumed by West Central African coastal elites in contact with European traders, during the eighteenth century, African artisans used silver to create objects of prestige and adornment that conveyed social, economic, political, and symbolic status. Grandpré, who visited Cabinda

Pangou, courtier de Loangue.

FIGURE 4.3 *Pangou, courtier de Loangue* (Pangou, broker in Loango) in Louis-Marie-Joseph Ohier de Grandpré, *Voyage a la côte occidentale d'Afrique, fait dans les années 1786 et 1787*. Paris: Dentu, 1801, vol. 1, 70.

the same year the *Mfuka* received the *kimpaba*, observed in his travel account that wealthy residents of the Loango coast appreciated silver, by emphasizing that "rich people wear a long silver chain, which wraps eight or ten turns around the waist" (Figure 4.3), as observed in one of the engravings illustrating his account.[37]

We do not know the origin of the silver used by La Rochelle's silversmith to produce the sword we are discussing. During the eighteenth century, France imported precious metals from Spain through the port of Cadiz, where French trading companies purchased silver coins (*piastres*) made of Mexican silver, as well as silver ingots and bars.[38] Indeed, since the Middle Ages and still during the eighteenth century, silver plates were reserves of precious metals that could be melted and transformed into coins at any time. Moreover, as fashions changed, it was common that owners of silver plates, including members of the French royal court, decided to melt sets of silver items to produce new ones according to the tastes of the moment.[39]

Regardless of these considerations, the work of a silversmith consisted of manually transforming a silver sheet into an object. One litho-
graphic plate (Figure 4.4) from the *Encyclopédie* by Denis Diderot
and Jean le Rond d'Alembert represents a silversmith's workshop in
eighteenth-century France. The engraving shows the master, apprentices,
and journeymen at work.[40] As displayed on the left side of the image,
the central structure in the workshop was the forge where the silver was
melted. To transform silver into artifacts of various sizes and shapes, the
silversmith employed many dozens of different kinds of hammers and
chasing tools, as represented in detail in several other plates included
in the encyclopedia. To fabricate the sword's relatively thin blade, one
of the workers began by pouring the liquid silver in an ingot mold that
had the form of a Woyo *kimpaba*.[41]

Once the molded metal was solid, the item was soaked in pickle, a
solution of sulfuric acid that cleaned the silver and also made it more
malleable. The silver was then scraped to remove any remaining debris.
Using hammers and anvils, the silversmiths, apprentices, and journeymen

FIGURE 4.4 Print, *Orfevrerie Grossier, Ouvrages*, Plate I from *Encyclopédie
ou Dictionnaire Raisonné des Sciences, des Arts et des Métiers*. Designed
by J. R. Lucotte (French, 1750–1784); edited by Denis Diderot (French,
1713–1784); printmaker: Robert Bénard; France; engraving on paper; gift of
Mrs. George A. Kubler; 1949-152-2. Courtesy: Cooper Hewitt, Smithsonian
Design Museum. New York, United States.

worked the silver blade to even its surface, occasionally heating the piece to restore its flexibility. After this process was concluded, the artisans may have carved the Latin cross on the blade's wide tip, even though, as we see in Chapter 6, the cross could have been added after the sword reached Africa. Once the blade had been polished and adjusted several times, the silversmith used very delicate chisels to engrave the flower garland and the dedication along the blade's false edge. Meanwhile, the artisans produced the sword's handle separately by following the same process used to create the blade, with chasing tools being used to ornament the gadrooned handle. Following Louis XVI style, the handle evokes the form of a classic column, featuring a curbed shaft surrounded by hollow flutes of two alternated lengths and a chapiter ornated with convex indentations.

The silver sword bears formal elements found in other eighteenth-century French silverware items. The handle emulating a classic column is decorated with shapes that follow the formal repertory found in other silver articles, including the eighteenth-century oiler produced by Chaslon. The flower garland engraved on the false edge is a formal element used in various cultures to honor specific individuals. Represented in drawings and paintings and on sculptures, monuments, and buildings, flower garlands and wreaths also evoke a connection to classical antiquity. Used to frame written visual representations, garlands, leaves, and foliage can symbolize purity, beauty, peace, love, and passion, but especially victory. Although it is hard to envision the connection between these emotions and the atrocious trade in human beings, one eighteenth-century watercolor representing the French slave ship *La Marie-Séraphique* and a *quibangua* on the Loango coast (discussed in Chapter 2) features an elaborate garland of flowers and leaves framing the slave vessel and the French trading post (Figure 2.3), suggesting that as in other contexts, slave merchants and traders used depictions of garlands to represent successful slave voyages.

4.3 VALUE AND SIGNIFICANCE

In silver alone, the sword could be valued today at more than $5,000. But even if silver is a very malleable metal that can be easily melted, amended, and transformed into another object, the sword was not a simple silver bar. Its special status derived in part from the fact it was commissioned and produced in the workshop of one of the most important silversmiths active in La Rochelle. More importantly, at its conception, the French-manufactured silver sword was a cross-cultural object carrying French and West Central African features. As we have already

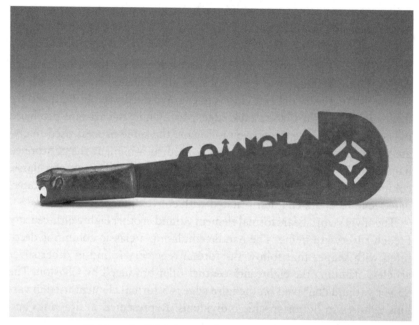

FIGURE 4.5 *Tshimpaba* (Chief's sword), iron, lead, Democratic Republic of
Congo and Cabinda, Angola, Woyo Region, h. 16¼ × w. 4½ inches. Courtesy:
Virginia Museum of Fine Arts, Richmond, Virginia, United States, Kathleen
Boone Samuels Memorial Fund, 97.130.

discussed, during the era of the Atlantic slave trade, rulers in Atlantic Africa highly appreciated foreign items. But as the silver sword's
format evoked locally produced swords of prestige, the object certainly impressed the *Mfuka* Andris Pukuta's dependents, and therefore
acquired additional symbolic power.

In the form of a large cutlass, the silver sword (Figure 4.1) emulates
a West Central African *kimpaba*, also designated as a *kimpabala*. One
of these Woyo swords displayed at the Virginia Museum of Fine Arts
(Figure 4.5) is made of iron and lead, its grip representing a leopard
that symbolizes Ngoyo royalty. In addition, the center of the tip's blade
includes a cutout in the shape of the Kongo ideographic expression or
cosmogram *dikenga*, a four-pointed star surrounded by four bars that
evokes the cycle of life. This diagram in its various versions embodies several metaphors associated with Kongo cosmology, evoking the realm of
the living and the dead, north and south, and the cycles of the sun.[42] As
we see in Chapter 6, this symbol is also in dialogue with the cosmology
of the Fon peoples of the West African Kingdom of Dahomey.

In Kikongo the term *ki-mpa* is defined as a "story game, entertainment, trick, enigma, mystery."[43] Anthropologist Carlos Serrano also suggests that the term *kimpaba* possibly derives from the verb *kimpakubala*, which in Kikongo means "power or faculty of becoming invisible."[44] According to Serrano, this invisibility may have been associated with the fact that the holder of the insignia did not need to be present to give orders or solve problems, but could send a messenger carrying the *kimpaba* that symbolized the ruler.[45] A *kimpaba* was conceived as an object of prestige in the kingdoms of Kongo, Loango, Kakongo, and Ngoyo. Emulating the sword carried by the Ngoyo ruler, the *Maningoyo*, these swords or scepters were part of the royal regalia and embodied the power of its holder. Yet the very existence of *bimpaba* (the plural of *kimpaba*) that may have served as models for the fabrication of the silver *kimpaba* suggests that as early as the late eighteenth century other Woyo regalia included this kind of sword.[46] Like other objects of prestige owned and displayed by rulers in West Central Africa and West Africa, such as swords, cloths, sandals, thrones, parasols, and scepters, Woyo rulers also had several royal symbols such as a drum (*ndungu ilu*), three elephant tusks (*zimpungi*), double bells (*ngongie*), the skin of *ngola-nhundu* (an otter of sorts), leopard skin (*ngó*), cat skin (*sinzi*), and a royal cap (*nzita*). Each of these royal items were associated with different proverbs, with the *kimpaba* being an insignia intended to assert and show the special status of these dignitaries.[47]

The French silver *kimpaba*, as we see in Chapter 6, shares many formal and symbolic elements with other scepters and ceremonial swords of prestige in use by other West Central African and West African peoples, including the Fon of Dahomey and the Akan of the Gold Coast. These swords such as the Fon *gubasa* and the Akan ceremonial swords *afena*, often had similar sizes and were made of various materials, including wood, iron, ivory, brass, and copper. According to Grandpré, who sojourned on the Loango coast, before and after Gareschè's agent gifted the *kimpaba* to Cabinda's *Mfuka*, the *Manibele* (an agent of the Loango's ruler, the *Maloango*) displayed as his symbol a ceremonial knife made in copper, a metal largely available in the Mayombe region, north of the Congo River. Grandpré described "a silver knife, 16 or 18 inches long, and 5 or 6 wide, with a round tip, pierced and scalloped, without a cutting edge. This knife was made of copper before the arrival of the Europeans, who then made it in silver. I don't know why they call this instrument a knife, it has nothing to do with those we call that way; but as they designate it as *belé*, I had to translate it as knife."[48] Grandpré also noted that the coastline between

Malembo and Cabinda was referred to as Bele banks, as its format evokes that of a knife (*bele*), very similar to that of a *kimpaba*.[49] In the Kingdom of Ngoyo, there was also a *Mambele*, the ruler's messenger, who also carried a ceremonial knife named *mbele*.[50] As Zdenka Volavka explains, the term *mbele* refers to a variety of "profane and ceremonial knives, daggers, and swords of various sizes and shapes."[51]

Portuguese Catholic priest José Martins Vaz, who lived and worked as a missionary in the archdiocese of Luanda for a decade in the twentieth century, stated that the *mbele lusimbu* (chief's knife) was used in death sentences and has always been a symbol and instrument of a chief's discretionary power.[52] However, he also emphasized that by the eighteenth century, these swords with false edges were no longer used for capital executions but only to symbolize the king's absolute power. Probably drawing on Grandpré, Vaz underscored that during the era of the Atlantic slave trade these knives were replaced with *bimpaba*, and he also noted that slave traders even gave heavy versions made of silver to local chiefs.

Likewise, Belgian curator Julien Volper associates the *bimpaba* with these medium-sized, curved, single-edged swords of prestige found among the Kikongo-speaking peoples and known as *mbele a Ne Kongo* or *mbele a lulendo*. He emphasizes that the handles of these swords were usually shaped into zoomorphic figures such as crocodiles and lions with anthropomorphic attributes such as human heads and hands.[53] The blades and handles of *bimpaba* were originally made of iron, copper, wood, and lead. Despite Grandpré's statement about silver having replaced copper, it was more probably the greater presence of European traders (especially French) on the Loango coast during the second half of the eighteenth century that led to the introduction of imported silver-made *mbele* and *bimpaba*. Still, existing locally made swords of prestige preserved in museum collections today confirm that Woyo artisans continued to use copper and iron to fabricate these artifacts. Therefore, except for the sword created in La Rochelle, all surviving silver *bimpaba* housed in museum and private collections date from the nineteenth and twentieth centuries, after the period when Grandpré traded on the Loango coast. As a result, when he referred to silver ceremonial knives offered by the European traders to local agents, perhaps he had in mind the very silver *kimpaba* given as a gift to Cabinda's *Mfuka* Andris Pukuta.

Contemporary sources described *bimpaba* as "proverb swords."[54] Proverbs are instruments of control in traditional societies. As popular, short, and generic precepts that draw on daily events, they provide advice or a moral lesson by often using analogy and humor. Among the Woyo, proverbs were memorized and passed down from generation to generation. Characterized by their metaphorical dimension, these proverbs were employed to address judicial matters, conduct debates, and determine sentences in village and family assemblies.⁵⁵ By displaying a *kimpaba* during these meetings that were intended to apply justice, Ngoyo's rulers and clan chiefs asserted their power as mediators of conflicts among community members.

Like other West Central swords, the false edges of the versions produced on the Loango coast contain openwork consisting of geometrical figures. However, there is a crucial distinction. In *bimpaba* produced in West Central Africa, including the Loango coast, the openwork is cut out from the false blade. In the silver *kimpaba* gifted to Cabinda's *Mfuka* this ornamental work was added to the edge of the false blade. It remains unclear if the French version's openwork was part of the original artifact when it was fabricated in La Rochelle. However, it is worth addressing the hypothesis that the geometrical forms were part of the original silver item, before exploring the second and more likely possibility that the openwork was added to the sword only after it reached the Loango coast or Dahomey in Chapter 5.

Although Jesuit missionaries produced a catechism written in Kikongo in the early sixteenth century, only a few elite members of local communities could read and write this West Central African language. Hence, oral language and visual arts representing ideas through figurative and abstract forms (pictograms) prevailed as forms of communication among the populations of the Loango coast such as the Woyo of Ngoyo. From the eighteenth century until the twentieth century, Woyo swords included cutout pictograms forming epigrams or proverbs associated with the chiefs of lineages who carried them (Figure 4.5). A writing system of sorts among the Woyo, the combination of pictograms formed proverbs conveying messages intended to be memorized and passed down among the members of a particular family and lineage.⁵⁶ In this context, Woyo *bimpaba* incorporated local epigrams also featured in other items such as bead bracelets, baskets, calabashes, scepters, woven mats, house walls, and wooden pot lids (Figure 4.6). As for the proverbs featured on these other items, the pictograms could be combined and interpreted in multiple ways that changed over time.⁵⁷

Upon reaching Cabinda, the French silver *kimpaba* was not a simple reproduction of West Central African *bimpaba*. The sword already embodied elements from the various cultures involved in the Atlantic commercial and cultural exchanges, including symbols that had

FIGURE 4.6 Kakongo and Cabinda pot lids. Museu de Etnologia de Lisboa, Lisbon, Portugal. Photograph: Ana Lucia Araujo, 2018.

cross-cultural significance. One of the most visible symbols carved in the sword's wide tip is the sign of the Latin cross, which was perhaps part of the original artifact that was fabricated in La Rochelle. Although the cross preexisted Christianity, it was embraced by Christians to symbolize Jesus of Nazareth's crucifixion. When the Portuguese reached the Loango coast, the cross was known to West Central African populations, for whom the cross evoked the cycles of life. As Cécile Fromont reminds us, the cross was also a "predominant motif of central African art [that] appeared in rock paintings, textiles, and engravings—in their simplest expression as two intersecting lines as well as in elaborate geometric derivations."[58] Fromont also argues that, starting in the late fifteenth century, other artifacts and objects of prestige produced in the Kingdom of Kongo included the cross, which by this time had become a correlation between Christianity and Kongo religions.[59] Even though the kingdoms of Loango, Kakongo, and Ngoyo never embraced Christianity as the Kingdom of Kongo did in the late fifteenth century, the cross and its derivations were popular among the populations living on the Loango coast. Therefore, for Garesché, Lessenne, and Chaslon, who commissioned, created, produced, and offered the silver *kimpaba*, the cross was a Christian emblem, while for Andris Pukuta, who received the gift, it was also a meaningful symbol.

4.4 SPEAKING IN MANY TONGUES

Like other Loango *bimpaba*, the French silver version includes an openwork consisting of eleven geometrical figures. The eleven symbols are a jagged semicircle followed by a set of two equilateral triangles whose tips point to one another, an equilateral triangle, another jagged semicircle, a circle, and a right angled triangle, followed by a space, then another set of two equilateral triangles whose tips point to one another and a jagged semicircle, followed by a space, then a straight vertical line, which is probably the surviving edge of a right-angled triangle, a circle, and a final set of two equilateral triangles whose tips point to one another. On other swords, similar symbols that are raised from the blade function as "abstract representations of people, houses, plants and shells," offering a "vocabulary to the chief, who would interpret them with proverbs, according to the needs of the moment."[60] Evidently, these symbols are in dialogue with the openwork of the silver *kimpaba* as it stands today. But very likely these geometrical figures were added to the sword after it left Cabinda, as we see in Chapter 6.

In locally made *bimpaba*, the geometric symbols were intended to underscore the political and supernatural powers of the *kimpaba*'s holder. Yet any specific interpretation of a particular *kimpaba*'s signs would require to consider the context in which the sword was used. Although *bimpaba*'s uses and meanings have changed over time, existing studies of Woyo symbolism can provide us some clues to the possible meanings of the geometrical shapes decorating these swords. According to priest Joaquim Martins, the jagged semicircle evokes the sun (*Ntangu*). Among the Woyo, this symbol refers to a commoner who "presented himself everyday as the sun usually does," because nobles such as the *Maningoyo* hide "from others' sight and from contact with the commoners."[61] Thus, the presence of a sun symbol in the openwork of a *kimpaba* suggests that its holder was a commoner. As a result, if the *kimpaba* was once a *Maningoyo*'s insignia, during the eighteenth century, and especially in the nineteenth century, it became part of the *Mfuka*'s regalia, even though this agent was a man who lacked royal status. This transformation seems to be in line with the fact that with the growth of the Atlantic slave trade, more Woyo agents were playing the role of intermediaries between the king and European traders during this period. Consequently, through their in-between positions, they were led to acquire more wealth and political power. In Cabinda, several proverbs were associated with *bimpaba*. Martins collected some of these proverbs. For example, the proverb "*Kimpaba: Ono ubika Kiau, fumu nene*" means "Kimpaba: who leaves it as an inheritance is a sign of having been great Lord." Other proverbs stated "*Ono ubá kimpaba: Fumu nene*" meaning "Who has '*kimpaba*' is a great lord" and "*Kimpaba: Mbembo fumu*" or "*Kimpaba*: it's the king's voice," as when the sword appeared, the king's orders arrived.[62]

During the era of the Atlantic slave trade all Woyo clan chiefs owned a *kimpaba* and "kept it as their most precious property."[63] Complicating the interpretation of the epigrams featured on these swords, other items such as Woyo pot lids belonging to clan chiefs could also display the image of a *kimpaba* (Figure 4.7), creating a metanarrative of sorts.[64] For example, one pot lid displaying a *kimpaba*'s depiction was interpreted as meaning "the *kimpaba*, knife of pride" and also "the one that we see with it is the chief of the village or the chief of the clan."[65] In both interpretations, a chief who holds a *kimpaba* is affirming his power. Over time, despite the king's absence, any delegation or embassy carrying a *kimpaba* inspired respect among the local population and foreign visitors, confirming the sword's status as an object of prestige.

FIGURE 4.7 Woyo pot lid, Cabinda, Angola, wood, h. 2.9 × d. 10 inches. Twentieth century. Photographer: António Rento. Photography Archive, Museu Nacional de Etnologia, Lisbon, Portugal. Courtesy: Museu Nacional de Etnologia.

Although *bimpaba* were conceived as elite objects carried by a few powerful West Central African individuals, European traders started offering a growing number of these silver swords to local chiefs as the slave trade increased in the eighteenth century. Along with the Atlantic slave trade, the rise of European colonialism in the region also contributed to the incorporation of European languages such as French, English, and Portuguese and a multiplication of the messages communicated by these swords. During the nineteenth and twentieth centuries, European agents, especially the Portuguese, started offering *bimpaba* displaying the names of their owners, a trend also apparent in locally made swords.[66]

As swords of prestige and objects of power, since their inception *bimpaba* were conceived of as speaking objects that "addressed a reader outside themselves."[67] These swords convey a narrative composed of geometric symbols that were used to communicate existing proverbs that are usually associated with a particular clan or village. Although originally there may not have been any geometric symbols on the eighteenth-century

FIGURE 4.8 Fountain and cooling vessel, Alger Mensma (attributed to), 1731, silver, h. 9 × w. 43.4 × d. 35.7 inches. Courtesy: Rijksmuseum, Amsterdam, Netherlands.

silver *kimpaba* gifted to Andris Pukuta, the article stands out as probably the oldest surviving silver sword of this kind manufactured in France and sent to West Central Africa. Moreover, the French *kimpaba* was already a speaking object when it reached Cabinda in 1777, as at that point it contained its engraved dedication. Written in French, the sentence praising the *Mfuka*'s qualities as a righteous man added to his importance and political prestige. Admittedly, in the eighteenth century, Woyo people, and very probably even the *Mfuka*, could not read the French dedication, but European agents and slave merchants trading in Cabinda certainly could. Moreover, the *kimpaba*'s large size and the prestige metal in which it was made were elements sufficiently impressive to attract respect for its holder whenever the object was displayed in public.

Other European silver diplomatic presents exchanged during the seventeenth and eighteenth centuries worked as speaking objects as well. Some of these items bear written engraved dedications to their receivers. For example, a silver wine fountain and cooler attributed to Alger Mensma, manufactured in 1731 (Figure 4.8), was offered by the Admiralty of Amsterdam to the Dutch naval officer Cornelis Schrijver. The Dutch Republic and North Africa's Regency of Algiers had been at war most of the seventeenth century and signed a peace treaty in 1726. In 1730, Schrijver sailed to Algiers to pay a ransom to redeem dozens of Dutch slaves. From a list including the names of 256 captives, he was initially successful in repurchasing sixty-six Dutchmen. Therefore, the silver gift was intended to thank him for his heroic naval feats associated with the Dutch naval conflicts in North Africa and the Mediterranean slave trade.[68] Today housed at the Rijksmuseum in Amsterdam, the Netherlands, the richly decorated silver bowl measuring 17 by 14 inches, 9 inches in height, and weighing 1 pound, features the Dutch Republic lion coat of arms surrounded by ornate representations of fishes, shells, and sea gods. Celebrating the captain, below the coat of arms the engraved inscription reads: "*Dit Koelvat is door het Collegie ter Admiraliteyt te Amsterdam residerende aan den Capiteyn Cornelis Schryver vereerd, in erkentenisse van de veroveringe van het Zaleese Roofschip, op den 10 Augustus 1730,*" which translates, "This cooling bowl by the College of the Admiralty of Amsterdam honors the Captain Cornelis Schryver in recognition for the capture of a pirate ship from Salé [present-day Morocco], on the 10th of August 1730." More than a simple gift, this present was intended to speak to all those unaware of Schryver's feats; therefore, it became a landmark item commemorating the release of Dutch captives in North Africa.

The silver French *kimpaba* also worked as a reminder of the heroic role of Cabinda's *Mfuka*. But more importantly it matched the transformations occurring on the Loango coast where the office of *Mfuka* had been gaining importance during the eighteenth century as the Atlantic slave trade intensified in the region.[69] The silver *kimpaba* was not the only expression of the *Mfuka*'s growing political importance and economic power in the region, a transformation emphasized by previous historians.[70] To please the main king's commercial agent upon their arrival on the Loango coast, slave merchants started to name their vessels *Mfuka*.[71] As early as 1752, Bordeaux shipowner Pierre Feydieu named his slave vessel *Le Mafouque* and sent it to trade on the Loango coast.[72] In the following years, at least three other ships paying homage to the royal agent *Mfuka* sailed to the Loango coast. In 1768, *Le Grand Mafouque* owned by Bordeaux shipowner Raymond Lassus, in 1773 the *Mafougue* owned by Nantes shipowner Jacques Gruel, and in 1784, also from Nantes, another vessel named *Mafouque* sailed to the ports of the Loango coast as well.[73] Likewise, the name of the Liverpool slave ship *Mampookata* (*Madam Pookata*), owned by James Penny, which sailed to Cabinda probably for the first time in 1783 and then again eight other

times to Ambriz and the Loango coast, was perhaps a homage to one of
the wives of *Mfuka* Andris Pukuta.[74]

4.5 CHANGING *BIMPABA*

Even though in the Kingdom of Ngoyo the *Mfuka* lacked royal status,
as we mention in Chapter 1, with the intensification of the slave trade
in all three kingdoms of the Loango coast, the office of *Mfuka* became
increasingly closer to royalty. The *Mfuka* could marry women of royal
lineage and acquire royal privileges. Several *Mfukas* became very wealthy
individuals. Especially during the eighteenth century, the power of the
Mfuka dramatically increased to the point of obscuring the authority
of the *Maningoyo*, who, as previously noted, lived inland and could not
directly interact with European agents. The *Mfuka* and *Makaya* were
central representatives of their communities during the era of the Atlantic
slave trade and later during European colonial rule. This shift perhaps
partly explains how the *kimpaba* embodied the *Mfuka*'s new power. By
carrying it, a royal insignia whose magical properties could originally
make one invisible, the *Mfuka* became more than the commercial representative of the *Maningoyo* who could not be seen in public. Being made
"invisible" meant he could assign other lesser *Mfukas* to represent him in
the active commercial exchanges with European agents.

Exchanges between African and European traders were bilateral. As
the *Mfukas* became wealthy, they also sent their children to France. In
1774, the French slave ship *Saint-Guillaume* transported from France
to Malembo a twenty-year-old African man named François Guillamba,
who identified as Kongo and was the son of one of the local "princes."[75]
On October 13, 1788, the vessel *Sainte-Anne* sailed from Nantes, transporting a man named Qinlouamba, identified as the son of the *Mfuka*
Pangoust, back to Cabinda.[76] Like many other children of African rulers
and agents who traveled to cities in France, Portugal, Britain, the Dutch
Republic, and Brazil, the *Mfuka*'s son went to Nantes to receive education and strengthen the French slave trade along the Loango coast.

Despite these late interactions, as we will see in Chapter 5, the French
slave trade dramatically declined in the 1790s with the Saint-Domingue
Revolution that gave birth to Haiti in 1804. By 1786, the gift receiver
Mfuka Andris Pukuta was already dead. Grandpré described his funeral
in his illustrated travel account *Voyage à la côte occidentale d'Afrique*
published in 1801. Neither a new nor a naïve contemporary observer,
Grandpré, who was born in 1761 (see Chapter 5), was fifteen years old

FIGURE 4.9 *Vue de la montagne de Cabende prise au midi* et *Deuil du mafouc, Andris Poucouta, macaye* (view from the Cabinda's mountain taken at noon and mourning of *Mfuka*, Andris Poucouta, *macaye*) in Louis-Marie-Joseph Ohier de Grandpré, *Voyage a la côte occidentale d'Afrique, fait dans les années 1786 et 1787.* Paris: Dentu, 1801, vol. 1, 143.

when he sailed from the French port of Saint-Malo to Cabinda on board the slave ship *Le Sevère* in 1776; his second voyage was in 1785 on *Le Mesny*, whose captain was his experienced father, Louis-Athanase Ohier, who traveled to the Loango coast to purchase enslaved Africans multiple times during the eighteenth century.[77]

Grandpré witnessed Pukuta's burial during his stay in Cabinda, and even though the French slave trader did not provide an exact date in his account, he arrived on the Loango coast in early 1787 and left some six months later. As Grandpré noted in his illustrated account (Figure 4.9), the body was only buried nearly a year after Pukuta's death, so the funeral occurred no later than September 1787. Grandpré explained that the mourners laid the *Mfuka*'s dead body on a "bed of honor, placed in the middle of a courtyard, under a roof supported by columns ... [and] covered the interior with deceased's best goods."[78] It may be assumed that the silver *kimpaba* was displayed among Andris Pukuta's most precious goods. Grandpré continued by noting that once this structure was ready, the deceased's wives surrounded the corpse and cried, and then hired women mourners continued the ritual by crying, dancing, and singing praise-names. A detailed account of how after these initial rituals the body was emptied of its organs, parched, and coated with a thick layer of red earth is also provided by Grandpré. The deceased's precious belongings were added to his corpse and then wrapped in a bundle (the size of this mass being proportional to the wealth and the importance of the deceased), composed of numerous layers of different kinds of cloth, before the body was permanently buried.[79]

Confirming Pukuta's importance, Grandpré added that the mortuary rituals included wrapping the corpse to form a giant bundle. According to his description in words and visual images, the roll of an impressive size measured "at least 20 feet long, 14 high, and 8 deep; it was surmounted by a little head which designated that of the dead. A year had been spent in packing and mourning him."[80] Grandpré's account is attested by earlier contemporary accounts. Proyart, for example, explained that a deceased's body was smoked and then wrapped with local and foreign cloths until a massive package was formed. The bundle's size and the length of the period the corpse was displayed in public view were proportional to the importance of the dead person. As a result, someone who was prominent would be wrapped into a very large cloth package and the funeral could last one entire year.[81] Once the lengthy ceremonies ended, the mourners interred the body in a deep grave. According to Proyart, the rich clans interred their dead along with their "favorite jewelry, some pieces of coral or silver."[82]

Later explorers and scholars also described the preparation of rulers' corpses on the Loango coast as following two steps – first drying the body and then wrapping it in several layers of cloth to create a massive roll, on the top of which was placed a small head.[83] Although the *Mfuka* was not a noble, the description of the treatment given to his corpse is very similar to that given to the body of the deceased *Maloango*, described by the German naturalist Moritz Eduard Pechuël-Loesche, who accompanied Paul Güssfeldt in the Loango expedition between 1873 and 1876. According to Pechuël-Loesche, the giant bundle of cloth wrapping the ruler's remains looked like "an enormous chrysalis, larger than an elephant."[84]

Because of its huge weight, European carpenters from the slave ships anchored in Cabinda, built a wheeled vehicle to transport the giant package of Pukuta's remains (Figure 4.10). The ship captains anchored in the area lent the *Mfuka*'s heir heavy ropes that were attached to the dolly pulled by a group of 500 boys, who took four days to transport the bundle to the burial site and eventually lower it into the grave.[85] The tomb was decorated with two giant elephant tusks fixed on the ground on which the carpenter from Grandpré's vessel had engraved the words "Mafouc,

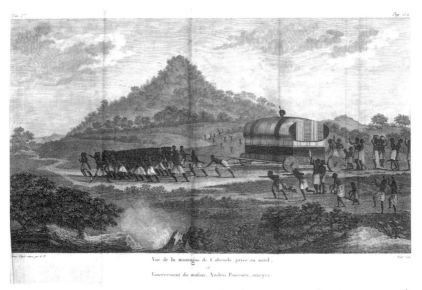

FIGURE 4.10 *Vue de la montagne de Cabende prise au nord et Enterrement du mafouc, Andris Poucouta, macaye* (view from the Cabinda's mountain taken from the north and burial of *Mfuka*, Andris Poucouta, macaye) in Louis-Marie-Joseph Ohier de Grandpré, *Voyage a la côte occidentale d'Afrique, fait dans les années 1786 et 1787*. Paris: Dentu, 1801, vol. 1, 152.

Andriz Poucouta, Macaye." Like the engraved dedication on the silver *kimpaba*, the tomb's inscription, confirms Pukuta's authority not only as a *Mfuka*, but also as a *Makaya*, or prime minister. According to Grandpré, the monument was still visible in Cabinda when he wrote his account.[86]

4.6 A CROSS-CULTURAL SPEAKING OBJECT

This chapter has shown that the silver *kimpaba* gifted to Andris Pukuta was conceived by Jean Chaslon in his La Rochelle workshop to commemorate the *Mfuka*'s gesture that protected Jacques Cousse and his crewmen from the attack by French traders turned pirates on Cabinda's shores. A valuable and symbolic gift, the *kimpaba* also guaranteed new slave-trading ventures in a port where a growing number of French traders were competing to obtain the best African captives for the lowest price. An object that spoke to a Woyo dignitary, Cabinda's population, and to European traders, the *kimpaba* also confirmed the increasing power of Andris Pukuta. In many ways, the silver sword embodied the growing power acquired by the *Mfuka* to the detriment of the ruler of Ngoyo, whose powers were decreasing with the intensification of the slave trade. Grandpré noted that upon his demise Andris Pukuta was a very rich man.[87] Following the local tradition, his fortune was inherited by his brother Andris Nsambo (or Sambo or Samba) who three years earlier, in 1783, had already been identified as an established slave trader who sold one captive to Daniel Deslandes, captain of the Saint-Malo slave ship *Le Baron de Binder*.[88] Just as La Rochelle's traders did, other European traders commissioned imitations of West Central African artifacts to give them as gifts to local agents. Yet the French-made *kimpaba* is not an ordinary replica of a Woyo *kimpaba*. Rather, it is a cross-cultural speaking object of prestige that, in the context of the Atlantic slave trade, also became an African diaspora object witnessing the history of the trade in human beings and the rise of colonial rule in West Africa. As we see in Chapter 5, Grandpré's account and the competing context of the French slave trade on the Loango coast and the Bight of Benin provide essential clues to understand the itinerary of Pukuta's silver *kimpaba*.

5

A Displaced Gift

Historians have approached the Loango coast and the Bight of Benin as two separate regions during the period of the Atlantic slave trade. But the tortuous trajectory of the silver *kimpaba* examined in this chapter shows how these two regions were closely connected during the eighteenth and the nineteenth centuries. After the funeral of Cabinda's *Mfuka* Andris Pukuta in 1786, we ask ourselves what happened to the precious silver *kimpaba* that La Rochelle's slave traders gave him as a gift in 1777. As in other parts of West Africa and West Central Africa, Ngoyo rulers may have owned stools used as boxes and seats used as chests that were "both containers and treasuries" and were therefore a place where they kept their possessions.[1] Traditionally, following the ruler's death, his corpse was dried, and his empty chest was filled with his nails and hair. Grand-pré explained that the dried corpse was covered with goods, "first with its coral and of all most precious things he has," as these things "must perish with him."[2] Eventually, the body was wrapped in several layers of *makutu* (palm-cloth used as currency), then the deceased's own cloth, including European cloth such as blue cotton fabrics, *indiennes*, and silks, forming a giant bundle that would be placed in a huge sarcophagus (*lukatu*) to be interred in the sepulture, as discussed in Chapter 4.

According to Grandpré, who witnessed *Mfuka* Andris Pukuta's funeral, the corpse could not be interred before the mortuary rituals had been completed, which took nearly a year. In theory the *Mfuka* was not a royal, but his funeral was evidence that by the 1780s he was treated as a member of the royalty. When the *Maningoyo* died, this long waiting period was justified because the ruler could only be interred after his successor was selected. In the *Mfuka*'s case, as confirmed by Grandpré, the rituals also lasted a year, which leads us to infer that Andris Pukuta received the same treatment as the Ngoyo's ruler. As a central figure in the commercial exchanges on the coast, he needed a successor, which makes it plausible that his body would be interred only after his successor's selection.

Since the *Mfuka*'s body was buried in a huge bundle of cloth, including his most precious possessions, the valuable silver *kimpaba* could have been interred with him. Grandpré questioned why the *Mfuka*'s heir would agree to lose all these precious possessions, but he concluded that their religious beliefs likely prevailed.[3] Although burial traditions changed over place and time, some existing accounts of royal funerals in the Kingdom of Kongo and the Kingdom of Loango show that the rulers' insignias such as their stool or throne were buried with them, whereas successors were provided with a new seat after the interment. However, other accounts state that although the chest (that often also served as a seat) containing the dead ruler's possessions was buried with the sovereign, another "ancestral basket" outlived the deceased king.[4] In addition, we should also consider the fact that the French *kimpaba* was not originally fabricated as a Woyo object of power. Thus, it is likely that Pukuta had his own locally created *kimpaba*. Still, the French silver *kimpaba* became an object of power in the context of the commercial exchanges between the Woyo and the French in the late eighteenth century, which is why it would not be surprising if despite being an imported royal insignia, it was passed down to his successor.

5.1 INSIGNIAS AND THE DEAD

The incorporation of European items offered as gifts with the regalia of West Central African royal courts dates back to the fifteenth century during the first official interactions between Portuguese explorers and the rulers of the Kingdom of Kongo. As described by John K. Thornton, Portuguese ambassadors who visited Kongo's capital city of Mbanza Kongo in 1491 noticed that the *Manikongo* Nimi a Mpanzu (King Alvaro III) was seated on his ivory throne surrounded by his insignias, his lower body covered with a damask loincloth that Portuguese explorer Diogo Cão had given to him as a gift.[5] Likewise, the Dutch merchant Pieter van den Broecke reported in 1608 that the *Manisoyo* (king of Soyo) sat on a "Spanish chair with a red velvet covering and covered with gold stacks."[6] We do not know if this throne was actually fabricated in Spain or if it was modeled after a Spanish throne; but whichever is the case, its existence shows that European regalia and local regalia modeled after European insignias were part of the material culture of West Central African royal courts. Also in the seventeenth century, during the coronation ceremony of Nkanga a Mvika (King Pedro II) in 1622, in addition to his usual royal insignias, the ritual included placing around his neck "a bag of brocade with [a] silk strap commonly called the 'Santissimo Sacramento' ... [that] was said to contain a great many papal indulgences" given to Nkumbi a Mpudi (King Diogo I) to be "worn around the kings' necks as a sign of their being very religious."[7]

But probably the most impressive foreign item in the king of Kongo's regalia was a "crown of gold-plated silver blessed by the pope" given to King Garcia II in 1651.[8] Fromont notes that "the combination of local and foreign elements in the regalia and sartorial practices of the Kongo endured in its main traits over the centuries."[9] Thus, when French traders gave the silver *kimpaba* as a gift to Andris Pukuta, two centuries after the events described in Kongo, several rulers and royal agents in West Central Africa had already integrated European-made gifts into their sets of royal insignias. As discussed in Chapter 4, Grandpré described a scepter knife carried by the king's messenger, which although traditionally made in copper, by the late eighteenth century could also be found in silver. Therefore, it is reasonable to assume that the *Mfuka*'s French-made *kimpaba* not only remained with the other gifts decorating his house, but was also embraced as his insignia and displayed by him during public events gathering locals, as well as during meetings with European traders and other foreign visitors.

Examining the roles of these insignias helps us imagine what might have happened to Pukuta's silver *kimpaba* after his death. If the silver sword became the *Mfuka*'s insignia, it is rather unlikely that this object of symbolic and material value was interred inside the bundle wrapping his body. And even if we take seriously the unlikely possibility that the ceremonial sword was interred with him, whoever recovered the object would have had to violate his tomb. Considering the *Mfuka*'s stature and the sacred dimension of West Central African burial grounds, it is hard to imagine that any Woyo individuals would dare to desecrate a dignitary's grave. In his account, Grandpré explains that the peoples living in Loango coast societies believed the deities watched tombs to prevent them from being desecrated, and that when people passed a tomb they looked away, as they believed that the deity (*nkisi*) killed those who approached a burial ground.[10] More likely, the silver *kimpaba* was transformed into the *Mfuka*'s insignia, outlived him, and was transmitted to his successor and brother, Andris Nsambo, as was done with other insignias belonging to Ngoyo's rulers such as the royal scepter and the royal cap that were passed down to the ruler's successor.[11] According to Grandpré, Sambo was very rich and powerful. As "he owned seven hundred boys, he was reputed to be unconquerable, and the king treated him like a man who could do anything, for or against him."[12]

As described by ethnologist and missionary Joseph Cornet, who conducted fieldwork among the Woyo during the second half of the twentieth century, the emblems of Ngoyo's rulers such as the *kimpaba* were very often represented on wooden pot lids. Cornet also mentions that one year after a chief's death, his objects of power were gathered and either brought to the cemetery where he was laid to rest or to his village where a ceremony was held, and then during three consecutive nights "a spokesperson told the life of the deceased, his habits, his virtues, his exploits, placing them in the history of the tribe, the village and the clan." Such ceremonies confirm the role of *bimpaba* as speaking objects that after the death of their holders also became objects of collective memory that were used to remember the dead. Moreover, the ethnologist noted that the various "speeches were punctuated by proverbs, interspersed with songs, animated by the masks."[13] Cornet observed these ceremonies almost two centuries after the *Mfuka*'s demise but as the regalia of Woyo chiefs remained central elements symbolizing their authority during the twentieth century, these more recent rites can certainly illuminate some dimensions of past rituals associated with the dead.

We will probably never know what exactly happened to the silver *kimpaba* after Pukuta's death. But between 1786 and the second half of the nineteenth century, the ceremonial sword left Cabinda and was taken to Dahomey, where it remained stored in Abomey's royal palaces. When the French forces invaded Dahomey and removed King Béhanzin from power during the second Franco-Dahomean war between 1892 and 1894, they looted the silver item along with many other artifacts and artworks. Despite this fact, two questions remain unanswered: What events allowed for the removal of the French-manufactured, eighteenth-century silver *kimpaba* from Cabinda? Who did transport it to the capital of the Kingdom of Dahomey? There is no definitive answer to either question. Made of silver, in addition to its symbolic value, the French-made *kimpaba* was certainly perceived as a rare power object, an object of prestige, and was incorporated into the royal collections of the king of Dahomey. To explore several hypotheses, it is necessary to consider the changing landscape of the Atlantic slave trade in the late eighteenth century on the Loango coast and the Bight of Benin, a region that included the ports of Ouidah (Map 2) and, moving east, Porto-Novo, as well as Badagry, as seen previously in Chapter 3.

As discussed in Chapter 4, Andris Pukuta died probably in 1786, as Grandpré witnessed the ceremonies surrounding his funeral. Three years later, the French Revolution erupted in France; and then enslaved people who had been resisting slavery in multiple ways for several decades led a major slave rebellion in Saint-Domingue in 1791.[14] These two developments negatively impacted the French slave trade for several reasons. First, because Saint-Domingue was France's richest colony. Second, because French slave traders transported most of the enslaved Africans they purchased on the Loango coast, including the port of Cabinda, and in the Bight of Benin, especially in Ouidah (referred to as Juda in French sources), to Saint-Domingue (Map 2). Whereas we know the French were never able to construct a permanent structure to trade in African captives in any of the Loango coast ports, they built a fortress in Ouidah in 1704. But following the quick decrease of the slave trade and the rise of the Saint-Domingue revolution, the fortress was abandoned in 1797, and only reoccupied from 1842, by the Maison Régis. This French commercial firm had been established in Marseille to trade with West Africa and West Central Africa between the period of the decline of the trade in enslaved Africans and the intensification of "legitimate" trade in which palm oil became one of the main products of export in Atlantic Africa, especially in Dahomey.[15] In 1908, already during the period of French colonization, the fort was demolished, possibly to erase the material traces of French participation in the trade in enslaved Africans in the region.[16]

Several factors must be considered to understand what possibly happened to the French silver *kimpaba* after the *Mfuka*'s death. Because no written record revealing how the *kimpaba* was transferred to Dahomey has yet emerged, historians may be tempted to find relevant information by looking far afield. But another way to proceed is to look at the very historical actors related to the production of the silver *kimpaba*, who either interacted with *Mfuka* Andris Pukuta when he was alive or who were in Cabinda and Malembo at the time of his death and during the year of his funeral, between 1786 and 1787. But to examine the connections between the Loango coast and the Bight of Benin, we need to revisit in more detail two moments of this long story: first, 1777, the year when Lessene gave the silver *kimpaba* as a gift to Cabinda's *Mfuka*, and second, the immediate years that followed the *Mfuka*'s funeral. As we will see, these connections evolved because of the actions of specific traders. Many of these men were French, and several of them came from La Rochelle.

5.2 GRANDPRÉ, THE SLAVE TRADER

Lessenne arrived in Malembo on board *Le Montyon* carrying the silver *kimpaba* in April 1777, as discussed in Chapter 4. Unlike the previous voyage, which gave rise to the conflict in Cabinda, this slave-trading expedition seems to have taken place without major incident. But it is worth emphasizing that during the weeks Lessenne spent in Malembo, Louis-Athanase Ohier, a prominent French slave ship captain from Saint-Malo, was also anchored in Malembo. Older than Lessenne, Ohier was the nephew of the French ship captain Louis Ohier, who sailed at least three times from Saint-Malo to the Loango coast on board *Le Vigilant* in 1740, *Le Grand Vigilant* in 1744, and *La Mignonne* in 1751. Like his uncle, Louis-Athanase Ohier sailed several times to the Loango coast. He was the captain of the vessels *L'Heureux* in 1764, *Le Sévère* in 1766, 1769, and 1771, the newly built *Le Sévère* in 1777, and *Le Mesny* in 1785.[17] Ohier was not only a prosperous ship captain, but he was also the father of Louis Marie Joseph Ohier de Grandpré, the only eyewitness who provided a written account describing Andris Pukuta's funeral.

On board the ship *Le Sévère*, Louis-Athanase Ohier sailed from Saint-Malo in November 1776 and likely reached the Loango coast in January or February 1777, a few weeks before Lessene's *Le Montyon* anchored in Malembo. Although both Ohier and Lessenne had traded in the region before, they had seemingly never crossed paths on the Loango coast. But this time they certainly met because both ship captains traded in Malembo between approximately April and July 1777. As related in Chapter 3, Malembo and Cabinda were separated by no more than 12 miles. Ship captains circulated between the two ports, acquiring African captives, and many slave vessels transported African captives acquired in both ports. Likewise, Ohier's son, Louis Marie Joseph Ohier, who adopted his family's honorific name "de Grandpré" as his pen name, accompanied his father during this slave-trading expedition to the coasts of West Central Africa. A young man aged nearly sixteen at the time, he boarded *Le Sévère* as an unpaid volunteer. More importantly, in his travel account, published in 1801, Grandpré reported that he met Captain Lessenne along with four priests from La Rochelle, who went to Malembo and Cabinda in 1777.[18]

As we note in Chapter 4, Grandpré described existing ceremonial knives (*mbele*) as originally fabricated in copper, but also mentioned that Europeans started offering silver swords to local agents. Still, his observation is at least intriguing, because during the period of Grandpré's travels to the Loango coast in the last quarter of the eighteenth century, nearly all slave ships trading in the region were French and the only silver eighteenth-century silver *kimpaba* that has survived to this day is the one fabricated in La Rochelle and offered as a gift to the *Mfuka* Andris Pukuta. Undeniably, still today the silver *kimpaba* is visually unique for its large size and noble metal, which combines geometric forms with delicate ornaments. It is logical to infer that the artifact greatly impressed eighteenth-century African and European agents. Hence, because of its beauty, as well as significant monetary and symbolic value, Grandpré certainly heard about the precious gift or even saw it with his own eyes during his stay in the region, where French ship captains all knew about each other's presence in Malembo and Cabinda. In other words, in all likelihood, whoever seized the *kimpaba* in Cabinda either took it himself to the Bight of Benin or had connections with someone who knew it existed.

In addition to being in Cabinda in 1777, Ohier and Grandpré were also in the region between 1786 and 1787, including the period of the *Mfuka's* yearlong funeral. Ohier sailed from the French port of Saint-Malo to the Loango coast as the captain of *Le Mesny* in September 1785. It may be assumed the captain traded in Malembo and Cabinda for several months in 1786, then traveled to Saint-Domingue by the end of the year and arrived in Léogane in February 1787 with a cargo of 500 enslaved men, women, and children.[19] But this time it is unlikely that his son, Grandpré, was on board *Le Mesny*. In his account, Grandpré stated that he commanded the vessel *Le Comte d'Estaing*.[20] But although this slave ship effectively departed from La Rochelle in July 1786, Grandpré is neither listed as the captain nor as a crew member on this ship. However, he boarded *Le Comte d'Estaing*, which first sailed from Saint-Malo to La Rochelle, from where it would sail to the Loango coast along with two other ships, *Le Plutus* and *Le Railleur*. Eventually, both *Le Plutus* and *Le Comte d'Estaing* left La Rochelle for Malembo on July 14 and July 21, 1786, respectively. *Le Railleur* only sailed from La Rochelle to Malembo on November 3, 1786. Grandpré had no official role on any of these vessels, but probably, because he financially contributed to outfitting their voyages, Grandpré may have boarded *Le Railleur* as a supercargo, a representative of the interests of the shipowner and outfitters, which is why his name is absent from the crew list.[21] In his travel account, he stated that he traded 300 elephant tusks and 1,500 enslaved Africans in the Loango coast over six months in 1787, a number that roughly corresponds to the number of men, women, and children transported by the three vessels to Saint-Domingue that same year.[22]

Despite Grandpré's account inaccuracies and gaps, we can place both him and *Le Mesny*, the ship commanded by his father, in Malembo between 1786 and 1787. Consequently, although at different moments, both father and son witnessed Pukuta's funeral ceremonies. Of the four ships, only *Le Comte d'Estaing* is recorded as having sailed back from Saint-Domingue to La Rochelle. Could Grandpré or one of his men have carried the *Mfuka*'s silver *kimpaba* to La Rochelle after his death? Despite no written evidence, this hypothesis is plausible, because there is solid proof that Grandpré met Lessenne in 1777, when the *Mfuka* received the gift and he can be placed in Cabinda in the year of his funeral as well. Could father or son have been responsible for transferring the *kimpaba* to Abomey? In theory, yes, as both traders were in Cabinda when the *kimpaba* was given to Pukuta and when his funeral took place. Yet neither Ohier nor Grandpré seems to have sailed to the Bight of Benin after Pukuta's death. Still, because it is likely both father and son knew about the silver item, one of them could have carried the silver *kimpaba* back to France, allowing it to be transported later by other agents to the Bight of Benin, where the French were still actively purchasing enslaved Africans until 1793.

Despite these convergent leads, there are also other hypotheses to be considered. Some ship captains from La Rochelle traded in enslaved Africans on the Loango coast and then led other voyages to the Bight of Benin, including during the three years that followed Pukuta's death. Lessenne himself was in Cabinda as the captain of Garesché's slave vessel *La Fille Unique* during the first half of 1786. Like Ohier and Grandpré, he certainly witnessed part of the yearlong funeral of *Mfuka* Andris Pukuta, the man who ten years earlier had saved the life of his crewmembers. More than anyone Lessenne knew about the valuable silver *kimpaba* and could have taken it back to La Rochelle. Still, because Lessenne's voyage to Malembo as the captain of *La Fille Unique* in 1786 and then back to La Rochelle in February 1787 was his last recorded voyage to Africa, he could not have carried the *kimpaba* to the Bight of Benin himself.[23] Could Lessenne have entrusted the item to another La Rochelle captain? It is not impossible, but because the silver *kimpaba* was almost certainly commissioned by Garesché, it would be even more probable that if Lessenne recovered the silver *kimpaba*, he entrusted the item to a ship captain who also worked for the La Rochelle shipowner. However, this possibility raises another problem. If the person who removed the silver *kimpaba* from Cabinda made a calculated decision to give it to another agent in a different African region, why did he keep the short dedication identifying the original owner as Andris Pukuta, "the just of Cabinda"? If the sword had been brought back to La Rochelle to be given as a gift to another African ruler, it would be reasonable to ask Jean Chaslon or another silversmith to remove the engraved dedication to Andris Pukuta. Thus, more probably, whoever took the *kimpaba* from Cabinda either stole it or simply "took it back," neither daring nor brave enough to take it to a French silversmith to have the short, engraved inscription removed. Although no records indicate that Lessenne sailed to West Africa after 1786, as we shall see, several other La Rochelle ship captains did.

5.3 FRENCH SLAVE TRADERS IN THE BIGHT OF BENIN

Conflicts among European powers on the Loango coast as well as in the Bight of Benin marked the six years that followed *Mfuka* Andris Pukuta's death and the period surrounding the transfer of the silver *kimpaba* from Cabinda to Abomey. Nearly two years before the *Mfuka*'s death, the French destroyed the Portuguese fort in Cabinda. Despite this attack, Portuguese slave merchants (as well as merchants from Brazil, their colony in the Americas) remained well established in Ouidah, where the French were actively sending slave ships to purchase enslaved Africans. The Portuguese had already built Fort São João Batista in 1721. Before the Portuguese, the French had established a trading post in Ouidah in 1671, which was later abandoned and then destroyed during a local war in 1692. The French rebuilt a new fort in Ouidah by 1704 and named it Fort Saint-Louis de Grégoy.[24] As explained by historian Robin Law, the French fort remained under the authority of several trading companies, but the French Crown controlled it from 1767 until 1797, when it was again abandoned, only being reoccupied in 1842. The English also built a fortress in Ouidah in 1684. Known as William's Fort, the building was located east of the French fortress.[25] Ultimately, in the context of the eighteenth-century Atlantic slave trade, the French and the Portuguese were competing both on the Loango Coast and the Bight of Benin.

Over the last quarter of the eighteenth century, several French slave ships traded both in Ouidah and Porto-Novo. Ouidah was the seaport of the Kingdom of Hueda, which had been conquered by Dahomey in 1727.[26] After Dahomey conquered the Kingdom of Allada (or Ardra) in 1724, the defeated kingdom's royal family refugees formed the state of Porto-Novo between the 1720s and the 1730s. Because of this connection with Allada, French eighteenth-century sources continued to designate Porto-Novo as "Ardres." Porto-Novo (literally "new port" in Portuguese) was locally designated as Hogbonu, and its capital was located east of Ouidah, on the northern bank of Lake Nokoué, in what is the modern town and capital of the Republic of Benin, Porto-Novo. Facing the Atlantic Ocean, and controlled by the kingdom of Porto-Novo, was a coastal village, also referred to as Porto-Novo (twenty-first century Semé), which soon became a busy slave-trading port. Ouidah and Porto-Novo were not as close as Cabinda and Malembo, but the distance of nearly 33 miles between the two ports still allowed slave traders to purchase enslaved Africans in both locations. For example, *Le Sauveur* sailed from Saint-Malo to the Bight of Benin in July 1763 and traded mainly in Ouidah. Yet the captain sent a canoe eastward to Porto-Novo, Ekpe, and Badagry to check how commercial transactions were evolving in these three ports.[27] In 1775, the vessel *La Nancy* sailed from La Rochelle to the Bight of Benin. Although the place where *La Nancy*'s ship captain purchased African captives remains uncertain, when the slave ship stopped at São Tomé and Príncipe, existing records indicate it came from Porto-Novo. When it arrived in Cap-Français in Saint-Domingue, though, the recorded provenance was Ouidah.[28]

Likewise, *Le Colibry* sailed from Le Havre to Ouidah in December 1776. But upon arrival in São Tomé and Príncipe and then Cap-Français, the declared port of provenance was Porto-Novo, and not Ouidah as originally reported. Moreover, other records indicate that one sailor died in Porto-Novo and a second one perished in the sea in Badagry. Therefore, we can only assume that *Le Colibry* traded in these three different locations.[29] One year later, in July 1777, La Rochelle vessel *Le Hoogwerff* set anchor in Porto-Novo, but upon arrival in Cap-Français, the declared port of origin was Ouidah.[30] Despite these cases, there were instances in which the two slave-trading ports were clearly indicated. The slave ship *Le Caraïbe*, for example, also from La Rochelle, traded both in Ouidah and Porto-Novo between December 1784 and March 1785.[31] Similarly, the vessel *Le Bon Français* that sailed from La Rochelle to the Bight of Benin in 1787 purchased slaves in Ouidah, Porto-Novo, and Onim (Lagos), in present-day Nigeria. Furthermore, *L'Alexandrine*, which departed from Nantes in October 1788, also traded in Ouidah and Porto-Novo.[32] These various examples indicate that French slave ships operated in several ports of the Bight of Benin, including Ouidah and Porto-Novo, during the same slave-trading expeditions.

During the late 1780s, local wars disrupted the trade in enslaved Africans in the Bight of Benin. Dahomey sought to attract European traders to Ouidah and therefore attacked neighboring ports such as Porto-Novo, Badagry, and Lagos, which were controlled by other states. Although

France had a fort in Ouidah, as early as the 1770s French officials reported the unfair competition with other European nations such as the English. In 1774, the director of the French fort met Kpengla, the recently enthroned king of Dahomey, who reported to him that the English offered him many more presents, such as *eau-de-vie* (brandy), than the French.[33] Ten years later, the competition was even greater. In 1784, the Marquis of Castries, Charles Eugène Gabriel de La Croix de Castries, then the Minister of the Navy and Secretary of State, informed the members of the Chamber of Commerce of La Rochelle about the considerable competition with the Portuguese, as well as the exorbitant prices of captives – who were also increasingly scarce in Ouidah.[34] Meanwhile, several other slave-trading ports east of Ouidah such as Porto-Novo, Badagry, and Lagos were emerging competitors. As a result, in 1786, La Rochelle ship captain Paul Hardy not only complained to the director of the French fortress in Ouidah about the horrible conditions of trade in these ports, but also forwarded a copy of his letter to the Chamber of Commerce of La Rochelle. He described the ports of the Bight of Benin as sites where "pestilential exhalations devour and consume them incessantly and where [Europeans] are plundered, stolen, molested."[35] These adverse conditions led Hardy to argue that the French should trade in these areas only after the kingdoms had allowed the construction of forts.[36] Eventually, Hardy's efforts paid off. The secretary of the king of Porto-Novo, a "clever, cunning and enterprising" man known as Pierre who had been raised in France, served as intermediary in the negotiations.[37] In a letter dated August 27, 1786, he informed the Marquis of Castries that the king had given permission to the French to build a fortress in Ekpe and another one in Porto-Novo, along the kingdom's coast. In exchange, however, he demanded the French to offer protection, because once the fortress is built "I will make myself enemies and will need to be protected."[38]

5.4 THE RISE OF PORTO-NOVO

Records documenting slave voyages in the Bight of Benin between 1786 and 1788 note the region's unstable conditions. Dahomey's army often attacked Porto-Novo's harbor by plundering European slave traders, kidnapping slave ship crewmembers, and stealing the goods with which they acquired enslaved people. For example, *Le Bonhomme Richard* sailed from La Rochelle to the Bight of Benin in October 1786.[39] After stopping for a few weeks in Lisbon to obtain Brazilian tobacco, greatly appreciated by African agents in the Bight of Benin, it sailed to Porto-Novo, where it started trading in February 1787. Likewise, *Le Désiré*, which left La Rochelle on December 31, 1786, stopped as usual in Lisbon on January 10, 1787, and then sailed to the Bight of Benin. The vessel *La Victoire*, also from La Rochelle, sailed to the Bight of Benin in January 1787.[40]

On the night of June 5, 1787, Dahomey soldiers attacked the barracks where the crewmembers from La Rochelle were lodged. They stole goods from *Le Désiré*, *Le Bonhomme Richard*, and *La Victoire*. Whereas some of the officers and other people who occupied the barracks sought refuge on board the ships anchored on the coast, the attackers captured several crewmembers and African boatmen (*piroguiers nègres*) from the three slave vessels and brought them as hostages to Abomey (see Map 1). From *Le Désiré*, the attackers seized dozens of pieces of cotton cloths (such as *siamoises* and *mouchoirs*), many pounds of cowries, rolls of tobacco, trade rifles, iron bars, and thirty-six *ancres* (barrels) of *eau-de-vie*. In addition, the Dahomean army also kidnapped three crewmembers of *Le Désiré* identified as "whites" as well as three boatmen. In the attack on *Le Bonhomme Richard*, the Dahomean army also kidnapped one officer, one sailor, and three boatmen in addition to trading goods.[41] From *La Victoire*, they abducted crewmembers and stole several goods, including textiles, pipes, cowries, *eau-de-vie*, rifles, and tobacco rolls. In addition, the attackers also took with them eighteen enslaved Africans acquired on the coast who were waiting to be taken on board the vessel, two whites, and six boatmen.[42]

As a result of this single attack, the captains of the three slave ships had to send Pierre Simon Gourg, the director of Ouidah's French fortress, to Abomey to rescue the hostages. They were supposed to provide him with commodities to be used as ransom to get the officers, sailors, and boatmen back. The ship captain of *Le Désiré* delivered to Gourg goods such as *eau-de-vie*, cowries, textiles, gunpowder, and rifles.[43] Likewise, the ship captain of *La Victoire* provided the director with a significant amount of goods to pay the ransom.[44] But the captain of *Le Bonhomme Richard* had to borrow from the Nantes ship *Jeune Thérèse* a variety of items, especially textiles, tobacco, and gunpowder, in order to redeem the officers, sailors, and African boatmen made prisoners in Abomey.[45]

Finally, the vessel *La Nouvelle Betsy*, outfitted by the society Pierre-Jean van Horgwerff & Fils, whose captain was originally André Begaud, sailed from La Rochelle to the Bight of Benin on February 19, 1787, and anchored in Porto-Novo to purchase enslaved Africans between early June and September that same year.[46] As with the three other La Rochelle ships, the Dahomean army attacked the crew of *La Nouvelle Betsy* and seized a variety of goods, such as pieces of *mouchoir*, *eau-de-vie*, gunpowder, tobacco rolls, pipes, and rifles. But more importantly, they took as hostages one crewmember (*patron*) and "*trois canotiers de nègres libres attachés au service du navire*" (three free African boatmen at the service of the ship), and as happened with *Le Bonhomme Richard*, the captain had to pay a ransom to free these individuals. Therefore, once again he provided the director of the French fortress with cowries, textiles such as *platilles, mouchoirs, coutils,* and *siamoises,* as well as twenty-four barrels of *eau-de-vie* to be paid to the king of Dahomey.[47] According to the account of the items stolen and used to pay the ransom, goods such as cowries, *eau-de-vie,* textiles, robes, and hats "embroidered with faux gold" were stolen by the "naturals of the country" during the transportation from the coast to Abomey.

But despite providing the ransom, the transaction did not go well. According to the report, the director of the French fort returned the barrels of *eau-de-vie* to *La Nouvelle Betsy* "on the pretext that it was not good, although the ship had done all the trade with *eau-de-vie* of the same quality."[48] Because the ship captain had no better *eau-de-vie* to provide and because he ended the trade and was on the eve of sailing to Saint-Domingue, he wrote from Porto-Novo to the French fortress's director on October 12, 1787, telling him that he would ask the ship captain Jean Dubosque of the ship *L'Aimable Suzanne* "belonging to the same shipowners to pay him these 24 barrels of pure eau-de-vie and following the advice given by him to his shipowners they loaded on board the said ship *L'Aimable Suzanne* departed by March 3, 1788 under the mark B, 24 anchors and a half of the best *eau-de-vie* of this country to be delivered accordingly to Mr. Gourg in Judah [Ouidah] for the balance of the above ransom."[49] *L'Aimable Suzanne* effectively sailed to the Bight of Benin in March 1788, and we can assume that the ship captain delivered the promised barrels of *eau-de-vie.*[50]

Other attacks by the Dahomean army against vessels anchored in Porto-Novo occurred in July 1787. Written records of the ship *Le Bon Français* from La Rochelle, which traded in Ouidah between July 16 and 18, then in Porto-Novo between July 18 and 23, and finally in Onim (Lagos) from July 24, 1787, also reported "frightening movements of war and robberies" during the trade in Porto-Novo.[51] Despite these repeated incidents, Dahomean attacks on European vessels were nothing new. In the four previous decades, several Portuguese subjects were taken hostage in Abomey, including João Basílio, the director of the Portuguese fort, imprisoned in Abomey in 1741.[52] Unlike the French, the Portuguese would not pay ransoms to rescue ordinary sailors.[53] As expected, payments to redeem French captives did not solve the conflicts provoked by the competition among European traders and between African states seeking to attract buyers to the ports they controlled. As ransoms were paid, French officers in Ouidah accused Gourg of having encouraged the king of Dahomey to attack Porto-Novo, while also dissuading French traders from trading in Ouidah. Other French captains in Ouidah blamed Gourg for having disbursed too much in ransom. In his defense, Gourg explained that French ship captains redeemed the prisoners with merchandise of inferior quality.[54] In a detailed memoir written in 1791, four years after the kidnapping, Gourg continued to provide a different version of the story, emphasizing that the French slave traders never paid him the full amount of the ransom due to the king of Dahomey, which is why he was himself abducted later on:

...forced to buy back officers, merchants, sailors, and negro boatmen kidnapped by the Dahomets in Porto-Novo. The trading captains were to provide me with the merchandise which I agreed to supply; but none of them fulfilled their obligation. By redeeming all these people, I have given my gratitude to the negroes, and the fort has replied. I invite the director to ask that the goods which are lacking to complete the payments be provided to him, and he must insist on this point all the more because I warn him that he must expect a great deal of inconvenience if he does not satisfy this debt and that the default, I have found myself facing, is partly the cause of my abduction.[55]

In addition to the regular trade in enslaved Africans, the dynamics of the slave trade in the Bight of Benin continued to generate multiple instances in which European luxury goods were transferred to Abomey. For example, when King Agonglo was enthroned after the death of his father, King Kpengla, Gourg along with the directors of the other European forts, traveled to Abomey in May 1789, taking presents to the new ruler.[56] Consequently, if we assume that a French agent took the silver *kimpaba* from Cabinda after the death of Andris Pukuta, there were multiple situations in which Dahomean agents could have seized the silver item and in which French traders and officers could have given it as a gift to the king of Dahomey.

5.5 BETWEEN THE LOANGO COAST
AND THE BIGHT OF BENIN

Despite the adverse context for trade in the Bight of Benin, French slave ships continued sailing to the region until the early 1790s. Among these French vessels, there were several ships owned by Daniel Garesché. Hence, the silver *kimpaba* could also have been transferred to Dahomey by one of Garesché's agents, who may well had carried it from Cabinda and then during a different voyage transported the item to Ouidah, Porto-Novo, or Badagry, from where the silver item could have reached Abomey. As we know, Garesché continued sending his vessels to trade in Cabinda and Malembo during the time of the *Mfuka*'s funeral and until 1792. Moreover, sometimes the same ship or the same captain that took the route to the Loango coast went on a subsequent voyage to the Bight of Benin, which is why Garesché and his captains remain among the closest agents connecting the silver *kimpaba*, the port of Cabinda, and the ports of the Bight of Benin that were linked to Abomey.

Following the *Mfuka*'s funeral in 1786, six slave vessels owned by Daniel Garesché sailed from La Rochelle to the Loango coast: *La Fille Unique*, *L'Argus*, *Le Prevost de Langristin*, and *L'Aunis* traded in Malembo in 1786. *Le Comte de Forcalquier* also purchased enslaved Africans in Malembo between 1787 and 1788, and *Le Reverseau* conducted trade in one or more ports of the Loango coast in 1791. Meanwhile, Garesché's slave ships also left from La Rochelle to sail to the Bight of Benin. For example, *La Comtesse de Puységur* and *Le Reverseau* (also spelled *Le Reverseaux*) arrived in Porto-Novo in 1787 and 1789 respectively. Likewise, *Le Comte de Forcalquier* (which traded in Malembo three years earlier) and *Le Saint-Jacques* anchored in Porto-Novo in 1790, while *La Cigogne* traded in that same port in 1791. Finally, Garesché's slave ships *Le Comte d'Hector*, *La Cigogne* and *Le Prévôt* traded in the Bight of Benin, in 1788, 1789, and 1791 respectively, even though the ports where they purchased enslaved Africans are not specified in the existing records.

Because Garesché's slave ships took both the sea route to the Loango coast and to the Bight of Benin, it is plausible to consider the possibility that one of his ship captains or crewmembers, or perhaps a ship captain from another French port connected to him, stole, purchased, or was given the silver *kimpaba* in Cabinda and transported it to one of the ports of the Bight of Benin, from where it was taken to Abomey. Take the example of Jean Frémont (referred to also as Jean Frémon or Jean Frémond). After 1786, he was the only ship captain who worked for Garesché and sailed from La Rochelle both to Cabinda and then from La Rochelle to the Bight of Benin. In the early 1780s, Frémont was already an established ship captain. In 1754, he sailed from La Rochelle to Saint-Domingue as the captain of the vessel *Le Comte de Pontchartrain*.[57] On August 28, 1782, his son Jean-Étienne Frémont, also a ship captain, married Marie-Marguerite Chadavoine, whose father was Laurent Robert Beltremieux, a prosperous La Rochelle merchant (*négociant*).[58] As discussed in Chapter 2, Atlantic slave trade was a business that connected members of many prominent families in La Rochelle, who sought to marry within these networks.

One of the members of the trade company Beltremieux et veuve Odet, Beltremieux purchased indigo from Saint-Domingue, whale oil from Rotterdam, brandy from the Oléron Island, wheat from Le Havre, furs from New Orleans, and sugar from Martinique.[59] Three years after his son's wedding, on September 28, 1785, Frémont served as the captain of the 200-ton corvette *L'Argus* that sailed from La Rochelle to the Loango coast as part of a slaving expedition aimed at transporting nearly 1,800 enslaved Africans to Saint-Domingue. Originally, 280 enslaved persons boarded *L'Argus*. But mortality spread in the other vessels that were part of the expedition and *L'Argus* became the expedition's hospital.[60] Eventually, when the ship arrived in Port-au-Prince on December 5, 1786, there were eighty-five enslaved men, women, and children on board.[61] Several weeks later, *L'Argus* sailed back to La Rochelle, where it arrived on June 26, 1787.[62]

On December 31, 1788, Frémont sailed again from La Rochelle to the Bight of Benin, this time as the ship captain of *Le Reverseaux*.[63] The vessel stopped in Lisbon between January 14 and February 3, 1789, and eventually arrived in Porto-Novo on March 15, 1789. The trade was profitable, and unlike his previous voyage to the Loango coast, except for the death of one sailor on the coast and another one being drowned at Cap-Français, no major incidents were recorded. Only three months later, on June 14, 1789, *Le Reverseaux* sailed to Saint-Domingue, transporting the impressive number of nearly 700 enslaved Africans. The ship eventually anchored at Cap-Français on July 22, 1789, and then weeks later sailed back to La Rochelle, where it arrived on November 13, 1789.[64] Because Frémont is the only captain who traded on the Loango coast (assumedly in Malembo and Cabinda) during the year of the *Mfuka*'s funeral and three years later also traded in Porto-Novo as the captain of Garesché's slave vessel, he is among the possible candidates for having transported the silver *kimpaba* to the Bight of Benin, where it reached Abomey.

Admittedly, existing sources do not reveal exactly where Frémont purchased the men, women, and children who boarded *Le Reverseaux* in 1789. However, it is reasonable to assume that it may have been difficult to load the vessel with 700 captives in one single port. Although existing written records do not specify if any smaller boats were carried on board *Le Reverseaux* or if the ship itself sailed to Ouidah to purchase African captives, as already noted, this kind of movement had been recorded before and after the vessel's voyage to the Bight of Benin. For example, in 1792, Daniel Garesché sent his last slave ship to the coasts of Africa. *Le Saint-Jacques* sailed from La Rochelle followed by a *goélette* (schooner) and a *corvette*. Like other ships that went to the Bight of Benin, the vessel stopped for several weeks in Lisbon to get tobacco, before anchoring in Ouidah.[65] Whereas *Le Saint-Jacques* traded in Ouidah, the two small vessels went to trade in Porto-Novo. *Le Saint-Jacques*'s trade shows once again how Ouidah and Porto-Novo were close, a geographical position that allowed slave ships to purchase enslaved Africans in both locations during the same voyage.

But the outcome of this final voyage was negative for Garesché because as these events unfolded, the War of the First Coalition (1792–1797), which followed the French Revolution, continued to evolve in Europe, and Britain declared war on France. As the bad news arrived at the Bight of Benin, *Le Saint-Jacques* left from Ouidah to the island of São Tomé and Príncipe, where slave ships usually stopped to fetch supplies before sailing to the Americas.[66] Meanwhile, the two smaller vessels as well as *Le Saint-Jacques*'s captain were left behind on the coast and were expected to join *Le Saint-Jacques* later. But the plans went wrong, as the English captured the two boats, though they eventually released them. Upon arriving on São Tomé and Príncipe, *Le Saint-Jacques*'s crew sold the African captives on board for the lowest possible price. But the English captured the vessel, which was eventually seized by the Portuguese army.

Written records document ordinary goods and crewmen on board slave ships, but not the silver *kimpaba*'s arrival and departure from Cabinda. Nevertheless, silver artifacts (if not melted) often outlived the other goods that circulated between La Rochelle, Cabinda, Porto-Novo, Ouidah, Abomey, and Cap-Français, and even the people who undertook the same journeys. Despite the lack of written records attesting the dates of the *kimpaba*'s movement, the dedication to Andris Pukuta that made it a speaking object allows us to retrace the object's itinerary, even though discovering the exact dates of its movement is an impossible task. A special and valuable gift, the *kimpaba* was not transported with the ordinary cargo but was very likely transported in the ship captain's cabin, not only when it left La Rochelle for Cabinda, but also when it was transferred from Cabinda to Porto-Novo or Ouidah, before being carried to Abomey.

5.6 THE END OF THE FRENCH SLAVE TRADE

French vessels almost completely stopped sailing to African ports between 1794, when slavery was first abolished in revolutionary France, and 1802, when Napoleon Bonaparte reinstated slavery in the French colonies. As the Saint-Domingue slave revolt continued to expand until 1804, when the colony abolished slavery and declared its independence from France, no further French slave ship carrying slaves from Africa landed in newly independent Haiti. By 1794, three years after the beginning of the Saint-Domingue slave revolt, British slave ships started to dominate the slave trade in Cabinda and Malembo.[67] Yet French slave ships sailed to Africa to purchase enslaved people approximately fifty-three times between 1803 and 1817. Eventually, the French slave trade from Africa was prohibited in 1817, even though illegal trafficking continued until 1864, when the French slave vessel *Pondichery* transported enslaved people from the Congo River to Cuba.[68]

But with the banning of the British slave trade in 1807, Britain's further efforts to prohibit the slave trade north of the equator favored the Portuguese presence in the slave ports north of the Congo River, including those on the Loango coast, such as Cabinda and Malembo. Moreover, following Brazil's independence from Portugal in 1822, Brazilian slave merchants started to acquire slaves on the Loango coast "to avoid having their vessels confiscated if they sailed to the Portuguese ports."[69] At the same time, in the second half of the nineteenth century, French traders became important actors in the transition to the "legitimate" commerce of palm oil in Dahomey through companies such as the Maison Régis. This context favored not only the exchanges among agents from Europe, Africa, and the Americas, but also propelled growing interactions among ports of West Africa and West Central Africa. Therefore, the connections between Portuguese and Brazilian agents operating in the ports of Cabinda and Ouidah during the nineteenth century, including during the rise of the so-called legitimate trade in palm oil and after the end of the slave trade in the Bight of Benin and the Loango coast, does not allow the total exclusion of the possibility that the French silver *kimpaba* could also have been transferred to Dahomey during the nineteenth century. Yet it is more likely that the silver *kimpaba* made its way to Abomey in the context of the French slave trade and through the same circle of French slave traders who brought the sword to Cabinda in 1777. As we see in Chapter 6, regardless of what happened with the silver *kimpaba* after the death of Andris Pukuta, the sword of prestige left its imprint in Cabinda and on the Loango coast more broadly. Slave traders and colonizers increasingly commissioned European manufacturers to make silver *bimpaba* to be provided as gifts to *Mfukas*, whose swords of prestige became even stronger symbols of power. Far from the Loango coast, Abomey's royalty and artisans also embraced Pukuta's silver *kimpaba* as an exquisite and exotic object of power.

6

Ngoyo Meets Dahomey

The French silver *kimpaba* was taken from Cabinda and possibly brought back to La Rochelle, from where it was likely transported either directly to Ouidah, perhaps through Porto-Novo, and then carried to Abomey, the capital of the powerful Kingdom of Dahomey. As noted in Chapter 5, this long itinerary of displacement can be understood within the complex dynamic of the Atlantic slave trade on the Loango coast and the Bight of Benin. Ouidah was the main West African slave-trading port and the second busiest port after Luanda in West Central Africa. Ouidah was also where the French had been trading in enslaved people since the seventeenth century. In the Bight of Benin, local states and their commercial agents competed among themselves to sell enslaved people to European slave merchants. As on the Loango coast, European traders were also fighting each other to obtain the best African captives in the largest numbers, and within the shortest period.

The silver *kimpaba*'s false edge was engraved with a dedication to Andris Pukuta. Admittedly, none of the rulers of Dahomey between the eighteenth and the nineteenth centuries read European languages such as French, Portuguese, and English. But, there were interpreters in Abomey, some of whom were kept as captives in the capital. These men, often nationals of France, Portugal, Brazil, or England, could certainly read that the engraved message was addressed to the "just of Cabinda," and not to any of the kings who had ruled Dahomey from 1787, when the *kimpaba* likely reached Abomey. Assuming that either a French trader or officer gave the *kimpaba* to the king of Dahomey as a gift or that Dahomean soldiers stole the silver item from French traders stationed in Porto-Novo or Ouidah, then more probably it entered Dahomey royal

collections during King Kpengla's reign (1774–1789). Yet it is possible
that the *kimpaba* made its way to Abomey during the reign of Agonglo (1789–1797), and less likely, although not impossible, that the item
reached Abomey during the rule of either Adandozan (1797–1818), Gezo
(1818–1848), or Glèlè (1848–1889); the rule of Béhanzin (1889–1894)
is much less likely.

6.1 DESTINATION ABOMEY

The possible specific path by which the silver *kimpaba* traveled to
Dahomey depended on who appropriated the object. Dahomean soldiers who attacked Porto-Novo would probably have carried their hostages and stolen goods to the northwest through existing interior paths
on land and water until they reached Abomey, the Dahomey's capital.
But if French agents transported the *kimpaba*, it is more likely they first
reached Ouidah's shore, which is not a protected harbor but rather an
open roadstead. To avoid the strong surf, European slave ships had to
anchor between 1 and 2 miles off the beach, and crewmembers had to use
canoes to arrive at the seashore. After reaching the beach, European officials had to travel approximately 2 miles inland to reach the town, where
the French, English, and Portuguese forts were located. In Dahomey, porters traveled inland mostly on foot and occasionally employed canoes
when crossing the lagoons.[1] Hence, to reach Ouidah's town, affluent
European agents hired porters who transported them on devices similar
to palanquins, which consisted of hammocks suspended by huge bamboo
poles carried over their shoulders.[2] During the eighteenth and nineteenth
centuries, they traveled likewise to Abomey, situated 60 miles north of
Ouidah. These journeys could take more than twenty walking hours over
two days at best. European traders and travelers also hired porters to
transport them in these suspended hammocks and in sedan chairs.[3]

   In the late eighteenth century, the Kingdom of Dahomey was located
on a strip of land stretching from the coast to about 200 miles inland.
Archibald Dalzel, a Scottish slave trader who served as the director of
the English fort in Ouidah between 1767 and 1770, was one of the first
European contemporary observers to publish a written account describing Dahomey. According to him, the country had a "deep, rich clay, of a
reddish colour," with a rich fauna of buffaloes, deer, sheep, goats, hogs,
hens, and ducks, as well as rich markets where the meat of these animals
and a large variety of vegetables were sold.[4] Starting in the seventeenth
century, the Fon dynasty gradually conquered and occupied the region

surrounding the Abomey plateau, where they established the capital of the Kingdom of Dahomey.[5] In Abomey, as noted by Cameron Monroe, the kingdom's early founders built earthen buildings as residences "to commemorate their individual achievements."[6] With successive rulers over the eighteenth and the nineteenth centuries, the number of palaces also expanded. Enslaved Africans such as Mahommah Gardo Baquaqua and Cudjo Lewis (born Oluale Kossola), who passed through Abomey as they were transported to the coast in the nineteenth century, briefly described the capital's walls and palaces in their accounts. Likewise, European contemporary observers such as traders, officers, and travelers also left reports describing their journeys in words and visual images. Dalzel portrayed Abomey royal palace structures during the annual ceremonies. According to him, each building occupied an area of 1 square mile. During the nineteenth century, the palaces of Abomey had eight buildings, and in Cana, situated just a few miles southeast, there were secondary palaces.

The Abomey royal palaces consisted of one-story, thatched-roof earthen buildings constructed around internal courtyards, though in the nineteenth century King Gezo constructed Singbodji, a two-story building. In addition to being the residence of the king and his court, composed of dozens of wives and several hundred dependents, the palaces were also the government headquarters. The Fon of Dahomey honored multiple gods (*voduns*) that represented the elements (air, water, earth, and fire) as well as deceased ancestors who upon their demise also became deities. In the past, as today, ceremonies honoring *voduns* followed a specific annual calendar. Rituals included dance, music, as well as animal and human sacrifice. Annual public ceremonies honoring *voduns* were also performed before the walls of Abomey's palaces. Similar to royal palaces in other societies in Europe, Africa, and the Americas, the palaces of Abomey symbolized the king's political and symbolic authority. King Agaja may have started commissioning male artists and artisans to decorate the palace walls with painted bas-reliefs in the early eighteenth century.[7]

Although earthen wall decorations were also used in other smaller buildings and structures such as temples honoring various *voduns*, the colored bas-reliefs conveyed more elaborate and figurative depictions. They provided an official account of the kingdom's history, including representations of the emblems of the various kings as well as scenes of military campaigns led by Dahomey against neighboring polities. Dalzel noted that the king's palace was "surrounded with a very substantial clay wall, of a quadrangular form, and about twenty feet high," and that in

"the middle of each side of the wall is a guard-house ... with two senti-
nels at the gate" in addition to a "guard of armed women and eunuchs
within." Also, on "the thatched roofs of these guard-houses are ranged,
on small wooden stakes, many human skulls."[8] These displays certainly
surprised, and very probably scared, European visitors who started to
visit Abomey in the early eighteenth century to pay tributes and negotiate the terms of the Atlantic slave trade, as well as captives Africans
who were brought to the capital or who reached the region before being
transported to the coast.

6.2 DISTRIBUTING WEALTH DURING
THE ANNUAL CUSTOMS

At least once a year, European traders and the directors of the Portuguese, English, and French fortresses participated in the annual ceremonies during which they provided gifts, or in other words paid tributes,
to the king of Dahomey. Based mostly on British travelogues, scholars
slightly disagree about the names of each of these ceremonies and when
they were held. Relying on the 1851–1852 journals of British vice-consul
Louis Fraser and other European contemporary observers who sojourned
in Abomey during the second half of the nineteenth century, historian
Robin Law emphasizes that the cycle of the "annual customs" was
launched with the return of the Dahomean army from its annual campaign, and its dates varied over time, whereas another ceremony held
approximately in December was dedicated to honor the ruling king's
deceased father.[9]

Meanwhile, in his analysis of these ceremonies, anthropologist Luis
Nicolau Parés suggests that the term "custom" (*coutume* in French and
costume in Portuguese) has been used in the kingdoms of Hueda and
Jakin in the Bight of Benin since the early eighteenth century to designate
the payment of tributes or taxes by the European trader to local rulers
but with the rise of the Atlantic slave trade, the term came also to designate the ceremonies honoring the deceased kings.[10] According to him,
the "grand customs" (*Ahosutanu* in Fon language) were associated with
the death of the king. Yet during the rule of King Agaja, when Dahomey
conquered Hueda and took control of Ouidah and started actively participating in the Atlantic slave trade, these ceremonies started to be held
annually, therefore becoming "annual customs" (*Xwetanu* in Fon), cel-
ebrated just after Christmas in the Christian calendar, marking the end
of the rainy season and the beginning of the harvest.[11] From the early

nineteenth century, the calendar of the ceremonies expanded, with new ceremonies being held in the short dry season between July and August.[12]

Human sacrifice was part of these ceremonies that lasted approximately one month. Contemporary observers reported that between several hundred and a few thousand war prisoners and criminals were killed to honor various deities of Vodun religion and ancestral kings who became *voduns*. Referring to the annual customs as a "carnival," Dalzel noted that during the festival, palace women distributed food and drinks, such as *pitto* (a locally brewed alcoholic beverage). Dahomean subjects, local chiefs, and European traders and officials, including the directors of the forts, who attended the event offered gifts to the king. One of the most important moments of these festivities was the distribution of riches by the king. Although ceremonies of redistribution of wealth also existed in the Kingdom of Ngoyo on the Loango coast, and intensified with the rise of the Atlantic slave trade, in Dahomey they achieved great importance.[13] Dalzel's account explained that adjoining the palace was built a "large stage, of about 100 feet by 40 ... supported by a vast number of piles, 10 feet long, driven into the ground, upon which are laid joists and the branches of straws." Protecting the back of this stage was the palace wall, while rails stood at the sides and the front of the built structure. Flags, streamers, and huge colorful umbrellas, some of which were made in gold and silver materials, decorated the front and the sides of the stage, whereas carpets and local cloths covered the floor and the railing.

While Dalzel's account is illustrated by a detailed engraving portraying the luxurious stage displaying the kingdom's local and foreign goods (Figure 6.1), he also enumerated the panoply of goods distributed among the attendants, including piles of cowries, "pieces of brocade, and other silks, strings of corals, European and country cloths, Brazil tobacco, pipes, bottled liquors, and a variety of other articles."[14] His account includes *The Memoirs of the Reign of Bossa Ahadee, King of Dahomy*, by the English slave trader Robert Norris, who sojourned in Dahomey between 1740 and 1774.[15] Norris's narrative, covering the reign of King Tegbesu ("Bossa"), also described the annual customs he attended in 1772.[16] As in Dalzel's account, he mentioned the distribution of foreign textiles such as "silesias, checks, callicoes" as well as several other European and Indian goods and "many fine cotton clothes manufactured in Eyeo [Oyo] country."[17] As we see in Chapter 1 and Chapter 3, exactly as on the Loango coast, these textiles reached Dahomey and its inland capital as currencies to purchase enslaved people. However, the most luxurious textiles were reserved to be given as gifts to African agents. But

FIGURE 6.1 *Last Day of the Annual Customs for Watering the Graves of the King's Ancestors* in Archibald Dalzel, *The History of Dahomy: An Inland Kingdom of Africa* (London: T. Spilsbury and Son, 1793), 55.

unlike the kingdoms of the Loango coast, where the rulers (*Maloango, Manikakongo,* and *Maningoyo*) could not accept European items, in the kingdoms of the Bight of Benin, such as Allada and Hueda and then in Dahomey throughout the eighteenth and nineteenth centuries not only did the kings demand and receive specific lavish presents, but they also proudly preserved these objects and displayed them in public ceremonies. For example, Norris attended a procession of royal women during the annual customs in Dahomey. According to him, this parade was similar to the other displays he saw during the festival, except that "the dresses and ornaments of the women were much more showy" and included a "variety and abundance of rich silks, silver bracelets, and other ornaments, coral, and a profusion of other valuable beads." In addition, the pageant functioned as an itinerant exhibition of Dahomey's material culture, with the parade of another group of forty women wearing silver helmets and carrying the king's most precious objects, including "furniture and trinkets" and "fine swords" while another group held "silver-mounted guns ... gold or silver-headed canes ... candlesticks ... [and] lamps."[18] Although Norris did not provide detailed visual representations of these items, among the objects presented there were very likely locally manufactured as well as European and Asian articles.

In 1795, King Agonglo demanded that Portuguese rulers should provide him with luxury objects.[19] More than two decades later, in 1810, King Adandozan, Agonglo's son who succeeded his father on the throne, sent a letter to Prince Regent Dom João, in which he asked the Portuguese to send him several European articles of prestige. In his missive, Adandozan not only gave a detailed description of previous luxury items sent by previous Portuguese rulers to his great-grandfather (assumedly King Tegbesu), but also emphasized that several of those older items were still in his possession, including large and heavy "sunhats" (likely broad brimmed hats) in silk lined with crimson velvet, with gold fringes, a green-lined hat also with gold fringes, a light blue velvet with gallon ribbon stitching surrounded with gold lace and mirrors, a black-and-white velvet hat surrounded with gold lace, a damask hat lined with flower satin and adorned with golden fringes and mirrors, and a silk hat ornated with green fringes. All these hats were topped with decorative lions, as well as figures holding swords and pointing rifles.[20]

Through this enumeration, Adandozan confirmed that Dahomean rulers not only consumed these foreign objects, accessories, and clothing articles, but also stored and preserved them. Four decades later, British Navy officer Frederick Edwyn Forbes described King Gezo, Adandozan's half-brother, in his account illustrated by a detailed full-body portrait (Figure 6.2). In the image, Gezo is wearing a European broad brimmed hat, and is "plainly dressed, in a loose robe of yellow silk slashed with satins stars and half-moons, Mandingo sandals, and a Spanish hat trimmed with gold lace; the only ornament being a small gold chain of European manufacture."[21] Very possibly the "Spanish hat," whose description broadly corresponds to some of the hats described by Adandozan in his letter, was actually manufactured in Portugal; if this was the case, the accessory could have been either an older or a more recent gift from Portuguese or Brazilian traders. Certainly, when Forbes wrote his account, Brazil remained the main nation illegally trading in enslaved Africans in the Bight of Benin. Although independent from Portugal since 1822, Brazil still imported Portuguese hats, or at least their various parts to be locally assembled in Rio de

FIGURE 6.2 *Gezo, King of Dahomey* in Frederick Edwyn Forbes, *Dahomey and the Dahomans*. London: Longman, Brown, Green, and Longmans, 1851, facing title page.

Janeiro.[22] Therefore, when Adandozan requested the Portuguese ruler to send him luxurious items, he did not conceal the fact that the desired foreign items were markers of symbolic distinction, intended to impress the members of his court and his subjects, among whom his popularity was in decline: "I am asking you, because I want to have all these things to cause admiration in my people, for them to say to themselves: my King does not know how to read and write, but how does he own so many beautiful things of the white." These beautiful things from the land of the whites included "large porcelain or wooden figures depicting two lions and two dogs, a flag with a lion in the middle and another flag with the symbol of the House of Bragança, for when I will go out, I will bring them in front of me."[23] In the conclusion to his letter, Adandozan confirms that, as Dahomean rulers did during the annual customs' ceremonies, not only did they receive gifts, but they also sent locally manufactured presents to the Portuguese kings, which he carefully describes in the letter as "two bandoleers, for the gold of your pants. I send one more chair from my country, and a box to put your pipe in, which is mine, and three smaller ones for the servants who accompany your Majesty. Both of them, will conserve the pipes and prevent them from breaking ... I also send you a flag showing the wars I waged, the people I caught, and the heads I cut, for my Brother to see and to carry in front of him when going outside for a walk."[24]

6.3 DAHOMEY'S COSMOPOLITAN MATERIAL CULTURE

The cosmopolitan material culture embraced by Dahomey kings has been defined by art historian Suzanne Preston Blier as a "desire to refashion the Other" that "strategically employed image appropriation in a manner that paralleled local military engagements."[25] Contemporary observers who visited Abomey royal palaces, starting with that of King Agaja (who reigned approximately between 1716/1718 up to his death in 1740), until the end of the nineteenth century, when the French removed King Béhanzin from power, described an impressively large number of European and Asian articles given as gifts to the various rulers and displayed in Abomey royal palaces.[26]

One nineteenth-century French visitor reported the display of a panoply of items such as "pieces of silk, damask brocaded with gold, luxury furniture, tables, armchairs, glass and crystal, bottles of perfume and confections, and a great number of lithographs representing the diverse episodes of war with the Orient" as well as portraits of the French emperor and empress, in addition to flags, and even "fetiches of the whites, eight half life-size statues of saints, in papier mâché."[27] Other European traders and officers enumerated a large array of objects, including

carriages, sedan chairs ... bath chairs ... printed handkerchiefs ... mass books ... German prints, sculped figures of silver and bronze, decanters, chased work, silver and gilt waiters, crystal, Delft plates, Toby pots, chamber pots, basins, tubs, glass chandeliers, candelabrum, English and Dutch crowns, scepters, coats of mail, music boxes, bedsteads inlaid with gold, Louis XIV brass legged tables, Indian and Japanese cabinets, arm chairs, rocking chairs, folding screens, Turkish carpets, clocks, a spinning wheel, globe reflectors, arms, kites, umbrellas, bonnets, buckles, armlets, pipes.[28]

Although these travelers rarely provided detailed descriptions of specific imported items, their accounts reveal the existence of many European silver objects displayed in Abomey's royal palaces. Brazilian Catholic priest Vicente Ferreira Pires, who along with his half-brother Cipriano Pires Sardinha sojourned in Abomey between 1796 and 1798

to convert King Agonglo to Catholicism, reported in his travel account
that the king (referred to as Adarunzá) had embedded in a silver shield
the skull of the ruler of a neighboring enemy kingdom. Upon meeting
the chief eunuch and guardian of the king's harem, they were offered
two bottles of *aguardente* in a huge silver bowl.[29] Pires also described
other silver objects that surrounded the king during their audiences,
including a silver stove, a silver purse, a silver platter, and silver *manil-*
las.[30] Pires, who was in Abomey when King Agonglo was assassinated
following a palace plot, partly described Dahomean royal funerary
practices, which included human sacrifices and also the depositing of
the deceased king's precious articles such as silks, gold, and silver items
in the burial pit, which remained open for three days. Not surprisingly,
once the three-day period had passed, and at the moment of closing
the burial pit, the king's secretary and wives were allowed to take back
these valuable items.[31] Pires makes clear that as in other regions of
Atlantic Africa, such as the Loango coast, traders needed the king's
permission to trade tobacco, *aguardente*, and slaves. But only the king
could trade precious metals and goods such as gold, coral, gunpowder,
and rifles, as well as silver.[32]

Nearly fifty years after Pires, Forbes also mentioned numerous silver
items in King Gezo's royal palace, including silver caps, and ornaments,
as well as a silver spittoon. Probably manufactured in Europe, spittoons
were essential items for kings who loved smoking Brazilian tobacco in
large wooden or clay pipes.[33] For example, one of the gifts sent by Adandozan to Prince Dom João in 1810, was a huge pipe box ("a box to
put your pipe in"), witnessing the huge size of the pipes used by Dahomean kings (Figure 6.3). Likewise, in his travel account, British ento-
mologist J. Alfred Skertchly, who stayed for eight months in Dahomey
in 1871, described a large array of silver articles, including King Glèlè's
"silver-bowled pipe," a "silver-mounted pipe, [a] silver ring jingled round
one of his ankles," and "a silver spittoon," probably the same one owned
by his father Gezo and described by Forbes.[34] The king's wives wore silver jewelry as well. According to Skertchly, "[t]heir hair was frizzed out
in the turban style, and a row of silver coins, attached to chains of the
same metal, jingled in a circlet around their brows. A profusion of silver
necklaces, coral beads, and other finery, with several armlets, completed
their get-up."[35] As late as 1931, an inventory of the objects composing
the "Tresor of the royal palace of Abomey" listed dozens of locally manufactured objects, including items recovered from the kings' tombs. In
addition to royal insignia such as thrones, *récades, asen* portable altars,

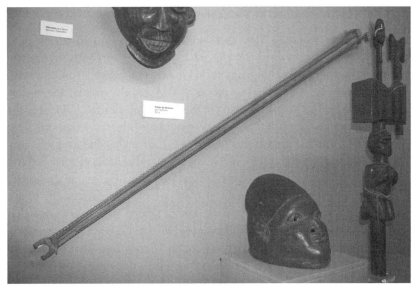

FIGURE 6.3 Fon artist, pipe box, wood, *c.* 1810. Gift from King Adandozan to Prince Regent Dom João. Museu Nacional, Rio de Janeiro, Brazil. Photograph: Ana Lucia Araujo, 2009.

and objects depicting animals evoking several Dahomean kings in a variety of materials such as iron, copper, silver, and wood, the inventory also included items such as thrones and porcelain spittoons manufactured in Europe, "dragon" iron helmets, porcelain vases, and as well as a ring in gold and diamonds, and other pieces of jewelry such as rings, necklaces, crosses, and chains in gold, silver, and copper.[36]

Among the dozens of silver articles described by Skertchly were a "silver candlestick of Brazilian workmanship ... [a] tall silver candelabrum in the form of a tree, about five feet high, with candles of silver; a six-foot silver stork ... an immense silver skull, and a smaller silver tree about four feet high."[37] Unlike several other objects, and except for the Brazilian-made candlestick, Dahomean royal silversmiths produced most of these articles. Dahomean rulers' interest in imported silver items as early as the eighteenth century suggests that regardless of how Pukuta's silver *kimpaba* reached Abomey, in the king of Dahomey's eyes the exquisite article certainly stood out as a unique and precious object. This interest can be assumed not only to have been because the *kimpaba* was made of silver but also because it carried formal elements present in other European articles known to Dahomean rulers.

6.4 SIMILARITIES BETWEEN WOYO AND FON INSIGNIAS

Pukuta's silver *kimpaba* also had similarities with Fon royal insignias such as scepters and swords fabricated by Abomey's artisans. In French, a scepter (*makpo* in Fon language) was known as a *récade*, from the word *recado* in Portuguese, meaning message.[38] A royal insignia, the *récade* was carried by the king and also by the king's messenger.[39] Hence, the *récade*'s function was similar to the Woyo *mbele* (knife in Kikongo). This ceremonial knife, as discussed in Chapter 4, preceded the *kimpaba* and was also carried by the ruler's messenger. Several *récades* feature a spiral shape symbolizing *dàn*, a serpent associated with the name Dahomey (*Danxomɛ*), meaning in the belly of Dan, which also evoked the king's transcendental power. As each king had a strong name or motto that was accompanied by emblems associated with his slogan, wooden scepters were adorned with a variety of metal shapes representing each of these symbols that also appeared on bas-reliefs decorating the walls of the royal palaces and on the colorful appliqué hangings. Like the West Central African *bimpaba*, Dahomean scepters were objects of prestige that embodied the ruler's presence even in his absence.

French invaders looted and dispersed many of these scepters after the conquest of Dahomey in 1894. But in 1910, French colonial administrator Auguste Le Hérissé commissioned Abomey's craftsmen of the Houndo and Hountondji workshops to create *récades* honoring the kings Kpengla, Béhanzin, and Agoli-Agbo, represented respectively by a cannon, a shark, and a leg (Figure 6.4). Although fabricated after the demise of these kings, these wooden scepters decorated with iron provide an accurate image of the various original royal Fon wooden scepters decorated with animal heads such as birds, lions, and sharks. Dahomean royal *récades* were not unique. They were closely connected to other scepters carried by African and European rulers to display their power. Although the first Fon *récades* may have been created as early as the seventeenth century, their formal elements are also in dialogue with French and English wooden royal canes, which were decorated with handles made of various materials, including metal. During the nineteenth century, these canes became fashionable items among European urban upper classes who wanted to publicly display their affluent status.[40] Like the Dahomean scepters, the handles of these European walking sticks also depicted animals such as birds, dogs, and lions. This international trend may have encouraged Abomey artists to produce a greater variety of *récades* during the nineteenth century.

FIGURE 6.4 Fon *récades*, iron and wood, *c.* 1910. Musée du Quai Branly, Paris, France. Photograph: Ana Lucia Araujo, 2019.

6.5 FON SILVER

Some Dahomean scepters, probably created in the late eighteenth century, during the same period when the silver *kimpaba* reached Abomey, were fully covered with silver. One of these wooden *récades* (Figure 6.5), measuring nearly 25 inches, consists of thin silver sheets hammered and nailed to the wood core. As explained by Blier, the "sheet metal technique enabled artists to produce works of precious metal without the vastly greater expense entailed in casting by the lost-wax method."[41] The *récade*'s curved shaft is thicker than the stick, forming an angle of almost 90 degrees. Made of a separate piece of wood attached to the stick, the scepter's extremity is an ornament representing a pineapple, the symbol of King Agonglo, whose motto was "[l]ightning strikes the palm tree but never the pineapple plant, which is close to the earth," a slogan evoking the ruler's ability to outlive his enemies, although ironically Agonglo was eventually assassinated by his opponents.[42] The silver sheets covering the scepter's pineapple-shape handle and stick are embossed and punched

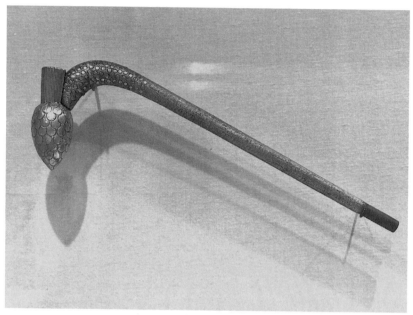

FIGURE 6.5 Fon royal scepter (*Makpo*), nineteenth century, silver (silver/ copper alloy), wood, h. 24⅞ × w. 8⅛ × d. 2⅛ inches. Metropolitan Museum of Art, New York City, United States. Photograph: Ana Lucia Araujo, 2019.

with dotted lines and circles, with the extremity engraved with semicircles and vertical lines to depict the fruit and its crown of leaves.

Many other Fon royal articles produced during the eighteenth and the nineteenth centuries were made of silver. During the reign of King Gezo (1818–1858), jewelry, coins, and raw metals such as silver and copper were stored in one section of the public area of his palace.[43] But despite the existence of silver mines in various African regions, there were no silver mines in Dahomey. During the height of the Atlantic slave trade, European and Hausa traders were the most important suppliers of silver to the kingdom.[44] Historian Edna G. Bay states that from the nineteenth century, silver was undoubtedly the "prestige metal" in Dahomey. She emphasizes that such prominence was not associated with Dahomean taste but rather related to the fact that silver was the most "easily available luxury metal."[45] It is likely these two dimensions were not opposed; that both taste and availability played a role in making silver a prestige metal in Dahomey.

In addition to all silver manufactured articles enumerated by European traders and officers in their accounts, Dahomean artisans used melted European silver coins to produce silver jewelry and other objects. The existence of Fon silver necklaces incorporating actual French and British

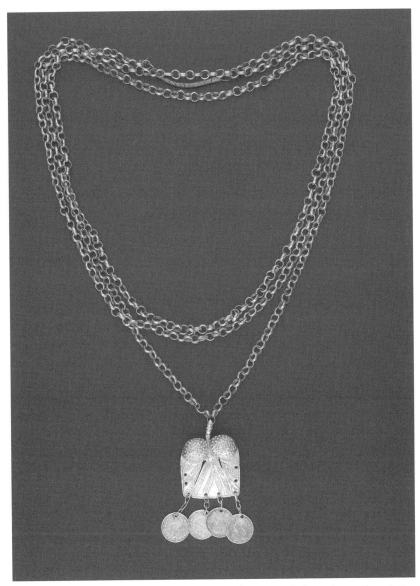

FIGURE 6.6 Fon artist, necklace, nineteenth or twentieth century, silver, EO 1978.21.1, Royal Museum for Central Africa, Tervuren, Belgium. Photograph: J. Van de Vyver, CC-BY 4.0.

coins (Figure 6.6) produced in the late nineteenth century and early twentieth century also confirms that European coins were the primary source of silver for Fon artisans. Among these objects were a variety of sculptures using the sheet metal technique that represented animals such as

FIGURE 6.7 Fon artist, elephant figure, nineteenth century, silver (silver/copper alloy), h. 8⅝ × w. 5½ × d. 23⅝ inches. Metropolitan Museum of Art, New York City, United States. Photograph: Ana Lucia Araujo, 2019.

elephants, lions, and buffalos. Symbolizing the Dahomean kings, these sculptures were also "power objects (*bocio*), able both to repel danger and attract well-being to the kingdom."[46]

Take the examples of two late nineteenth-century silver animal power objects symbolizing King Gezo housed in the collections of the Metropolitan Museum of Art in New York. Whereas one figure is a beautiful hollow silver elephant (Figure 6.7), the second is an astonishingly delicate wooden buffalo (Figure 6.8) covered with multiple silver sheets. An "x-ray radiography, metallography, and x-ray spectroscopy" analysis revealed that the silver composing these two objects "conformed in composition to traditional European standards," therefore containing 70 to 80 percent of silver and approximately 20 to 30 percent copper, comparable to available silver coins in the period preceding French colonization, hence confirming the silver's European origin.[47] An analogous composition was found in an equally striking silver powder horn ornament (Figure 6.9) on display at the Baltimore Museum of Art in Maryland, United States. The object's core is a domestic goat horn. Silver sheets wrap the horn's bottom third and the horn's upper third. Both the horn's extremities and

FIGURE 6.8 Fon artist, buffalo figure, Fon, nineteenth century, silver, iron, wood, h. 13³⁄₁₆ × w. 9 × d. 18¾ inches. Metropolitan Museum of Art, New York City, United States. Photograph: Ana Lucia Araujo, 2019.

the center are surrounded with lines formed by small silver rings. One side of the ornament's surface is adorned with the figures of a serpent and a bird. As in other pieces of Fon jewelry, a delicate silver chain holds the object's two extremities. As there is no open area to introduce gunpowder into the horn's interior, the object was likely worn as a necklace. Spectrometry has revealed that the silver covering the horn is mixed with copper and contains traces of iron, therefore also suggesting that like the silver buffalo and elephant, the silver used to create the object was probably derived from European coins.[48] Ultimately, the incorporation of imported items in West African artworks resulted from several centuries of global exchanges in which Europeans incorporated African currencies such as cloth and iron bars, whereas African articles increasingly embraced foreign materials as well.[49] Still, the analysis of Fon jewelry items produced a few years later during the twentieth century with the rise of French colonialism reveal that the alloy included mostly copper and only a smaller amount of silver and zinc.[50] This newer composition perhaps suggests that silver was no longer available as a prime material

FIGURE 6.9 Unidentified Fon artist, personal ornament, Fon, second half of the nineteenth century, silver alloy, horn, h. 9 × w. 3 × d. 2 inches. Courtesy: Baltimore Museum of Art, Baltimore, MD, United States.

for Dahomey artisans after the end of the Atlantic slave trade and the rise of French colonial rule.

Each king established one or more guild workshops in Abomey and its environs. These family guilds of artisans were the only ones authorized to produce royal artifacts in various materials. For example, the

FIGURE 6.10 Fon artist, throne, wood, *c.* 1810. Gift from King Adandozan to Prince Regent Dom João. Museu Nacional, Rio de Janeiro, Brazil. Photograph: Ana Lucia Araujo, 2009.

Aklosi and Drè families produced wooden items, especially thrones and drums. Thrones produced during the nineteenth century embraced African, European, and American elements. For instance, among the gifts sent by King Adandozan to Brazil in 1810 was a wooden throne that like other Dahomean stools incorporated the format of Akan wooden thrones (Figure 6.10). Years later, King Gezo's throne (Figure 6.11) also mixed Akan and Luso-Brazilian features. Although this influence may

FIGURE 6.11 Fon artist, throne, wood, and metal, early nineteenth century. Musée du Quai Branly, Paris, France. Photograph: Ana Lucia Araujo, 2019.

have been associated with the earlier wooden furniture given as gifts by Portuguese traders to Dahomean kings, it may also have been introduced by Afro-Brazilian carpenters who were members of a growing community composed of slave merchants and formerly enslaved men and women who returned from Brazil to the Bight of Benin especially during the first half of the nineteenth century.[51] The design of this impressively large throne features forms of scallop shells and palm trees, whose cultivation for production of palm oil increased during Gezo's rule. Male and female members of the Yémadjé family specialized in the appliqué technique. Whereas men created patterns, cut the fabric, and created the composition, the women sewed the pieces.[52] Appliqué technique was used to produce umbrellas and appliqué hangings decorated with colorful figures symbolizing *voduns*, Dahomey kings, and the kings' praise names, as well as a variety of warfare scenes.[53]

Members of the Hountondji royal guild in Abomey were descendants of smiths who likely migrated from Allada to Cana in the eighteenth century and then settled in Abomey during the reign of King Gezo.[54] The Hountondji fabricated items in noble metals such as silver, brass, and copper, including sculptures, jewelry, scepters, and a panoply of royal objects. They also created works in iron, such as the royal *asen*, portable altars or shrines in the form of memorial metal staffs that were often described by European travelers and traders who visited Abomey. In addition to honoring deceased Dahomey kings, some *asen* were created to illustrate a particular idea for the resolution of judicial matters and to convey specific royal messages in assemblies of commoners, like the Woyo pot lids discussed in Chapter 4.[55]

6.6 RECREATING AND REEMPOWERING

Whereas Dahomean kings incorporated a great number of European gifts in the royal collections and redistributed some of these articles during the annual ceremonies, royal artists and artisans also appropriated foreign artworks and artistic styles. The Dahomey army captured prisoners during the military campaigns against its neighbors. War captives with artistic and craft skills were kept in Abomey. In these incursions into surrounding territories, soldiers also looted artifacts that were incorporated into the royal collections. Through these human, material, and visual exchanges, royal artists and artisans borrowed, adapted, and transformed foreign shapes and themes to create new objects and artworks and invent new artistic styles.[56] The names of the individual artists and artisans who designed and manufactured the smaller royal silver items discussed in these pages remain unknown. But very likely they were conceived and produced by the members of the Hountondji royal guild, whose silversmiths had the reputation of being able to reproduce any object Europeans brought to Abomey.[57]

Most probably, Pukuta's French silver *kimpaba* was exhibited among other treasures in the Abomey palaces. Perhaps the ruling kings displayed the valuable silver item during their public appearances as well. But Hountondji silversmiths certainly took the *kimpaba* and added their marks to the precious silver item. As discussed in Chapter 4, the silver sword gifted by La Rochelle agents to Andris Pukuta embodied the *kimpaba*'s format, but its handle and the engraved garlands and dedication were foreign to existing West Central African swords of prestige. However, the openwork on the false blade differs from the openwork of other *bimpaba* (Figure 4.6), whose blades include raised and cutout forms or glyphs that evoke the clan and region of the *kimpaba*'s holder. Although the openwork on Pukuta's silver *kimpaba* also includes geometrical figures, these forms were clearly not part of the original artifact created and fabricated at Chaslon's workshop in La Rochelle.

It is not impossible that the openwork was added to the *kimpaba*'s false blade when the artifact was still in Cabinda. But this hypothesis is unlikely because in contrast with Dahomey, the Kingdom of Ngoyo had no silversmith tradition. However, because Woyo peoples smelted iron, local blacksmiths could easily cast any other metal, including silver.[58] Moreover, as discussed in Chapter 4, although the geometric forms of the ornament seem to be related to other signs decorating West Central African *bimpaba*, they subtly differ from those in the Loango coast. Even though only a technical analysis of the Pukuta's *kimpaba*'s silver could help to confirm this hypothesis, it is possible to infer that once the *kimpaba* reached Abomey, the king commissioned a Hountondji smith to design and add the openwork to it.[59] By doing so, this artisan was adhering to a long-standing Dahomean tradition of dialogue with alien arts and crafts. As already discussed, these cross-cultural interactions encompassed African and European sources, and consisted of engaging, appropriating, incorporating, and transforming foreign designs and artifacts to create new visual vocabularies.[60]

Today, the eighteenth-century silver *kimpaba*'s originality is still striking. However, amending silver items was not a Dahomean invention. European and Asian elites melted down silver articles, not only to fulfill specific economic needs, but also to refashion the silver and create new objects that followed new design trends. In France, the practice of melting down silver articles to craft new objects explains why so few silver items prior to the eighteenth century have survived.[61] This was no different in the African continent. The practice of amending objects to adorn them is also found in other West African societies where "[c]utlasses and machetes of varying quality were imported in large quantities from Europe and traded along the coast of West Africa, though again the hilts were embellished by local craftsmen."[62] The king of Dahomey and the royal silversmiths certainly regarded the astonishing silver *kimpaba* as an object of power, the same way they viewed other insignias representing the kings. To reactivate the power of an alien object taken from the distant Kingdom of Ngoyo, Abomey's silversmiths reappropriated the *kimpaba* by adding to its edge's false blade a set of shapes evoking *voduns* deities and symbols.

The *kimpaba*'s added openwork includes eleven symbols divided into three sets, as described in Chapter 4. Some of these geometric forms are comparable with the cutout figures found in Fon ceremonial swords, known as *gubasa* that gave birth to the *vodun* Gu, the Fon god of war and metal.[63] King Glèlè commissioned the artist Akati Zomabodo Glenegbe Ekplekendo to create an iron sculpture (Figure 6.12) of Gu to commemorate his father Gezo.[64] This sculpture may have been modeled after two silver sculptures representing two soldiers fighting given as gifts by Portuguese officials to King Gezo.[65] Today displayed at the Louvre Museum, this artwork is in dialogue with the silver *kimpaba*, because in addition to diamond shapes, the huge *gubasa* (Figure 6.13) held by the iron warrior bears circle shapes as well as two opposing triangles. This symbol evokes the double-bladed axe associated with the *vodun* Hevioso of thunder and an equivalent of the orisha Ṣàngó in the Yoruba pantheon. The jagged semicircle symbolizing the moon and the circle signifying the sun likely evoke the feminine-masculine deities Mawu-Lisa.[66]

Associated with the creation of the world, the couple Mawu-Lisa embody the division between the world of the living (sun) and the dead (moon), the day and the night, the sky and the earth, and their complementary nature is what devised Dahomey's political organization, which was divided into masculine and feminine realms.[67] If this interpretation is correct, the added openwork on the blade of the silver *kimpaba* became a unique object of power and prestige that engaged central dimensions of Dahomean cosmology by activating Hevioso, Gu, and Mawu-Lisa. The duality represented by these symbols was not exclusive to Dahomey; it was also part of the cosmology of Loango coast societies, where crosses, diamonds, ovals, and crescent shapes signifying the sun and the moon also appear on pot lids, *bimpaba*, and later on tombstones of the early twentieth century.[68] Hence, after the addition of the openwork, the silver *kimpaba* started embodying the symbolic duality that characterized the political structure of both Ngoyo and Dahomey.[69] By introducing in the silver *kimpaba* symbols found in the powerful Fon *gubasa*, the Hountondji

FIGURE 6.12 Sculpture representing Gu, Fon, iron, attributed to Akati
Zomabodo Glenegbe Ekplekendo, before 1858. Louvre Museum, Paris, France.
Photograph: Ana Lucia Araujo, 2019.

artist also created a metanarrative analogous to the one found in Woyo
pot lids incorporating representations of *bimpada* (Figure 4.7) and in Fon
appliqué hangings (Figure 6.14) that also depict the *gubasa*.

FIGURE 6.13 Detail. Sculpture representing Gu, Fon, iron, attributed to Ekplekendo Akati, before 1858. Louvre Museum, Paris, France. Photograph: Ana Lucia Araujo, 2019.

Finally, another element of the silver *kimpaba* deserves to be revisited. The Latin cross (Figure 6.15) at the tip of the blade is carved at the same location where the *dikenga* symbol was usually cut out in Woyo swords. In Chapter 4, the Latin cross was examined as being part of the original French design. However, the cross may have been added to the sword after it reached Abomey. It is unlikely that Garesché and his agents wanted to use the silver *kimpaba* to promote the Christian doctrine to the Cabinda's *Mfuka* because, like many other shipowners and slave merchants in La Rochelle, he was not a Catholic but rather a Protestant, as noted in Chapter 2. Likewise, Jean Chaslon, the silversmith who created the *kimpaba*, was a Freemason, and Catholics could not join Masonic lodges. Ultimately, although European slave merchants of various nations and religious affiliations offered gifts to African agents, only Catholics were known for using material culture as an instrument of conversion during the era of the Atlantic slave trade.[70] These three arguments alone can challenge the hypothesis that the Latin cross was part of the original

FIGURE 6.14 Fon artist, appliqué hanging, Fon, cotton, Musée Théodore
Monod d'Art africain, Dakar, Senegal. Photograph: Bess Sadler, License CC
Attribution 2.0.

design. Yet, as noted in Chapter 2, Lessenne, the ship captain, was Catholic. Hence, could the cross shape on the silver *kimpaba*'s round tip be a sign of his influence on the object's design? It is possible, but except for the French silver *kimpaba*, no other *kimpaba* fabricated in Europe to be offered to African agents and bearing a carved cross on its blade has been identified to this day.[71] However, Greek and Latin crosses are carved on the blades of at least two Fon *récades*. The first scepter consists of a wooden stick (Figure 6.16) attached to an axe-like iron blade. At the joint of the blade with the wooden stick is a raised metal spiral shape, similar to the ones found in other *récades* (Figure 6.4). One extremity of the blade

FIGURE 6.15 Detail. *Kimpaba*, silver, Musée du Nouveau Monde de La Rochelle, La Rochelle, France. Photograph: Max Roy. Courtesy: Musée du Nouveau Monde de La Rochelle.

is engraved with a figure representing a pineapple associated with King Agonglo, who, as already discussed, was assassinated after bringing two Catholic priests to Dahomey, having promised them he would convert to Catholicism. Carved in the middle of the blade, the cross shape is also reinforced by an engraved contour line. A similar scepter is a *récade* made of copper and iron (Figure 6.17). A copper lion head, analogous to the handle of a Woyo *bimpaba* (Figure 4.5), connects the iron blade to the iron stick whose lower extremity is surrounded by a copper ring engraved with fine lines. A horizontal line formed by three small circles and a cross is carved along the iron blade, then a vertical line composed of four small carved circles decorates the blade's edge. Taking all these factors into consideration, it is possible that along with the symbols associated to *voduns*, Abomey artisans also cut the Latin cross on the blade of the *Mfuka*'s *kimpaba*. After all this, and passing through the hands of La Rochelle's slave traders and silversmiths, Woyo agents, and Abomey silversmiths, the *kimpaba* was transformed into a complex cross-cultural power object.

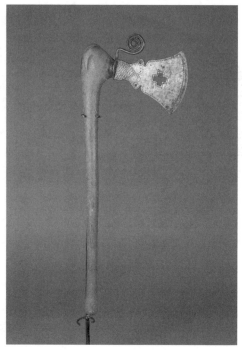

FIGURE 6.16 *Récade*, Fon, wood and iron, h. 21.2 × w. 8 × d. 1.5 inches. Muséum d'histoire naturelle de La Rochelle, La Rochelle, France. Courtesy: Muséum d'histoire naturelle de La Rochelle.

As a speaking object of power, the silver *kimpaba* is the bearer of several messages. The French words praising the *Mfuka*'s qualities as a righteous man engaged Cabinda's agents by reinforcing Pukuta's importance and political prestige. The added openwork with pictograms evoking *voduns* addressed the members of the Dahomey royal court and commoners who may have occasionally admired the king bearing the *kimpaba* during public appearances. Undoubtedly, the gift made by La Rochelle's ship captain to Pukuta marked an important moment in the Atlantic slave trade on the Loango coast. Whereas the *Mfuka* acquired increasing wealth and power, European merchants who sailed to the region to acquire enslaved Africans witnessed growing rivalries, especially during the second half of the eighteenth century. This new configuration gave more power to local men who acted on behalf of the king as middlemen in the inhuman commerce. The Cabinda's *Mfuka*, like the *Mfukas* of Malembo and Loango, were among these intermediaries. The *kimpaba* also came to embody the connections between the trade in people and the artistic traditions of the Loango coast and the Bight of Benin.

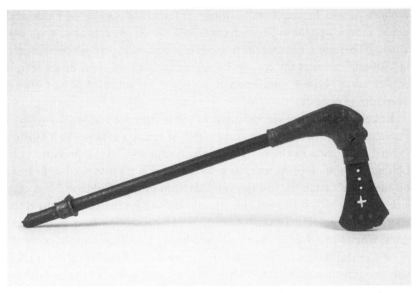

FIGURE 6.17 *Récade*, Fon, iron and copper alloy, h. 21.2 × w. 7.2 inches. Musée d'Aquitaine, Bordeaux, France. Photograph: Lysiane Gauthier, Mairie de Bordeaux. Courtesy: Musée d'Aquitaine.

6.7 *KIMPABA*'S LEGACY AND NGOYO'S FRAGMENTATION

After the British abolition of the Atlantic slave trade in 1807, Portuguese and Brazilian slave traders started dominating the trade in enslaved Africans on the Loango coast, as Portugal continued to make attempts to annex the region to its colony of Angola. Over the first five decades of the nineteenth century, Cabinda was controlled by three main families: Nkata Kolombo (whose one branch was referred to as Jack), Npuna or Puna, and Nsambo (also referred to as Sambo or Samba).[72] All three families were historically associated with the trade in enslaved Africans to the Americas. Moreover, whereas five of the seven known kings of Ngoyo were members of these families, all seven *Mambuku* came from these three families as well.[73] The family Nsambo is relevant to our story. As mentioned in Chapter 4, Andris Nsambo is said to have succeeded Andris Pukuta as the Cabinda's *Mfuka* after his death. According to Grandpré, by the time of his stay on the Loango coast, Nsambo was a powerful slave owner.[74] But in the next decades, certainly before 1840, the Franque family took over Nsambo's family village. The founder of the Franque family was a man named Kokelo (or Kokolo) Franque, who is said to have purchased the office of *Mfuka* at some point in the late eighteenth century. However, brokers named Frank, Franke, Jonge Franke, and Oude (or Oude and Oudt) Franck appear in Dutch records in Cabinda as early as in 1749 and 1767.[75] Therefore, because the number of men holding the office of *Mfuka* in Cabinda towards the end of the eighteenth century remains unclear, it is likely that Nsambo and Franque occupied the office of *Mfuka* during overlapping periods.

Kokelo may have taken the name Franque from his European owner, a Frenchman, whose last name was Franck or Franque, names that already existed in France in the early eighteenth century.[76] Like previous men holding the office of *Mfuka*, Kokelo owned his own *kimpaba*, bearing on the blade's back the inscription "Maffuca Franke Cokeloo."[77] A very rich man, Kokelo was even able to send his son Francisco Franque to be educated in Brazil in 1784.[78] As explained by historian Roquinaldo Ferreira, when the Atlantic slave trade had been made illegal on the coasts of West Central Africa in the 1830s, the presence of Brazilian slave traders was prominent in Cabinda.[79] Therefore, starting in the 1830s and during the 1850s, Francisco Franque "became an essential piece of Portuguese diplomacy with African chiefs in Cabinda."[80]

During the first decades of the nineteenth century, the Franque clan took over Nsambo's village.[81] Through this move they appropriated at least in part the fortune made by Andris Pukuta and his successor Andris Nsambo. Yet the name Sambo, associated with local princes of Ngoyo, continues to appear in British records side by side with the Franques until the end of the nineteenth century. A Prince "Sambo" and other dignitaries named Sambo (Nsambo) also signed the Simulambuco Treaty on February 1, 1885.[82] In response to the negotiations taking place at the Berlin Conference that led to the signature of the General Act of February 26, 1885, which brought about the partition of the African continent among various European nations, this treaty put Cabinda under Portugal's control. The signatures of individuals associated with the Nsambo family suggest that despite the rise of the Franque family, the Nsambo continued playing an important role in Cabinda's internal and external affairs during Portuguese colonial rule.[83] However, the competition among these lineages and conflicts with the Portuguese officials did not end. According to a Portuguese report, there were complaints that one of the Franques who had been appointed as an interpreter had stolen a silver *kimpaba* that bore the name of another local chief.[84]

The growing number of local agents acting as *Mfukas* confirms that the intensification of the slave trade created internal divisions between the rulers of the Loango coast and their increasingly rich agents. The trade also provoked conflicts among these wealthy intermediaries. As Carlos Serrano reminds us, the external trade contributed to displace the power of the old lineages, including those associated with the king who resided in the interior, in favor of new lineages that emerged on the coastal area, where exchanges with European traders took place.[85] As the Atlantic slave trade intensified and continued developing during the first five decades of the nineteenth century, especially with the involvement of Portuguese and Brazilian and then Spanish and Cuban slave traders in Havana, these divisions increased. These fractures ultimately led to the collapse of these centralized states in the nineteenth century, opening the door for the French and Portuguese conquest and colonization of the region.

During this period marking the final decades of the Atlantic slave trade and the rise of European colonial rule, the practice of using gifts of prestige persisted on the Loango coast. In 1850, the Brazilian slave trade was finally abolished after an initial unsuccessful attempt in 1831. Despite several repressive measures undertaken by the British Navy, which since the abolition of its own slave trade in 1807 had been patrolling the Atlantic coasts of Africa, the illegal slave trade continued until the 1860s. While envisioning occupation of parts of the African continent, British Navy officers attempted to convince African agents to stop selling enslaved people through the signature of treaties with local rulers, including the king of Ngoyo.[86] One of these British officers was Henry Need, who was part of the crew of the sloop *Linnet* commissioned to suppress the Atlantic slave trade between 1852 and 1856. In a letter dated January 30, 1855, addressed to Commodore John Adams, Need reported his meeting with the *Maningoyo* (referred to as "King of Cabinda"). According to Need, upon his arrival in Cabinda, he wrote to the king to inform him he had gifts on board and wanted to meet him to present them. These gifts were intended to seal a treaty that had previously been signed with the Ngoyo's ruler. At this time, both the English and the Portuguese were attempting to take control of the area.[87] But "after some delay," Need was told by Francisco Franque that "the King could not receive [the gifts], for if he did the Chiefs would dethrone him," and in a later interview the king informed him that "he could not receive the presents without a written declaration from the captain that they were 'for nothing,' although he was told that no new condition would be imposed on him through their acceptance."[88] By this time, British officers were describing Franque as the richest and "most influential man in Cabinda."[89] But unlike the Loango coast's *Mfukas* and the kings of Dahomey, the king of Ngoyo remained forbidden to accept foreign gifts, while his agents became increasingly wealthy by the middle of the nineteenth century.

Despite having left Cabinda at some point after Pukuta's death, the silver *kimpaba*'s legacy remained active on the Loango coast for many decades. The circumstances that led to the rise of wealthy *Mfukas* and other middlemen beneath them who, unlike the king, greatly benefited from accepting European presents also explain the proliferation of *bimpaba* during the nineteenth century. According to Pechuël-Loesche's report of his participation in the Loango expedition from 1873 to 1876, there were several silver imitations of *tschimpäpa* (*kimpaba*) circulating in the region.[90] The German naturalist even identified probably one of the last local creators of these artifacts, a man named Vinga, who was a *Maboma*, or dignitary in charge of judiciary measures in the Lubu region, in twenty-first century's central Democratic Republic of the Congo, whose uncle had taught him how to create *bimpaba*.[91] But, as already observed by Grandpré in the eighteenth century regarding European slave merchants, Pechuël-Loesche also noted that European companies that had emerged during the transition from the Atlantic slave trade to the "legitimate" commerce had started producing silver *bimpaba* to be given as gifts to local chiefs.

Several examples of locally made *bimpaba*, as well as silver models fabricated in Europe, are housed today in the Royal Museum for Central Africa in Tervuren. This institution was originally created by King Leopold II of Belgium in 1898 to house a huge variety of items, including looted artworks and artifacts from his privately owned Congo Free State, which was later annexed by Belgium as the Belgian Congo. One *kimpaba* (Figure 6.18) bears the engraved name Valle-Azevedo & Co., indicating that the item was commissioned by this Portuguese company to be given as a gift to a local agent in the Lower Congo region.[92] Like Pukuta's *kimpaba*, this sword is made of silver. However, in the Portuguese-made sword, the geometrical symbols conveying proverbs are cut out from the false blade, as in the traditional *bimpaba* fabricated in the region. Still, two different elements stand out. First, engraved along the entire extension of the *kimpaba*'s spine is the image of a snake, probably evoking Mbumba, the Woyo deity represented by the cosmic serpent that forms a rainbow, also to be found in similar forms in other West Central African and West African societies, including Dahomey.[93] Second, the sword's grip represents a lion, which by the end of the nineteenth century was a widespread cross-cultural symbol. An insignia of European powers such as England, the lion was also the symbol of King Glèlè in Dahomey. The lion handle of the Valle-Azevedo's *kimpaba* is also similar to the one

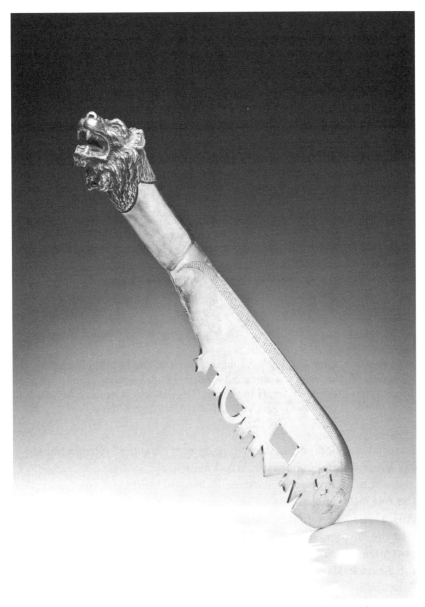

FIGURE 6.18 *Kimpaba*, silver, 21 inches, EO.1977.33.1. Photograph: J. Van de Vyver, CC-BY 4.0. Courtesy: Royal Museum for Central Africa, Tervuren, Belgium.

FIGURE 6.19 *Kimpaba*, silver, 21 inches, *Insignia*, late nineteenth century, The Christina N. and Swan J. Turnblad Memorial Fund, accession number 98.203, Minneapolis Institute of Art, Photograph: Dan Dennehy. Courtesy: Minneapolis Institute of Art, Minneapolis, MN, United States.

featured in a Dahomean *récade* (Figure 6.17) and the *kimpaba* housed in the Virginia Museum of Fine Arts (Figure 4.5).

Curiously, another Valle-Azevedo *kimpaba* (Figure 6.19), identical to the one belonging to the collections of the Royal Museum of Central Africa, is to be found in the Minneapolis Institute of Art, confirming that the Portuguese embraced the *bimpaba* as objects of prestige to support their control of the Loango coast in the period of transition from the Atlantic slave trade to colonialism during the nineteenth century. Admittedly, while several *bimpaba* were stolen from local rulers, these dignitaries may also have given or sold these items to European agents, who later offered them to European and North American museums. Still, many other *bimpaba* were kept in local families. In 1971, Portuguese anthropologist Benjamin Pereira photographed Mayor Idika, a Woyo dignitary, holding a silver *kimpaba* (Figure 6.20) given to his ancestor, a Ngoyo chief, as a gift by Portuguese King Carlos I in the late nineteenth

FIGURE 6.20 *O regedor Idika segurando a Tchimpada, símbolo de realeza* (the Mayor Idika holding a Tchimpada, symbol of royalty). Nova Estrela, Cabinda, Angola. Photographer: Benjamin Pereira, 1971. Photography Archive, Museu Nacional de Etnologia, Lisbon, Portugal. Courtesy: Museu Nacional de Etnologia.

century.[94] Unlike other existing photographs showing local leaders holding these swords, the dignitary is gripping the *kimpaba* upside down, probably to highlight the huge grip in the form of a man crossing his arms over his own chest. The handle's representation of the African male figure conveys an ambiguous message. On the one hand, the body position suggests the gesture of acceptance, which is also found in images of the Virgin Mary in several premodern paintings representing the Annunciation, therefore evoking the idea of accepting conversion to Catholicism. On the other hand, crossing arms can indicate defensiveness. More probably, the two interpretations convey the ways in which Woyo rulers perceived Portuguese colonization of the region – a promise of protection and also a hostile presence requiring physical and spiritual defense. As in the two Valle-Azevedo's *bimpaba*, a snake borders the entire blade. Eating its own tail, this time the snake's image evoking Mbumba is not engraved but it consists, instead, of a high-relief figure added to the blade.

6.8 THE FRENCH TAKE ABOMEY

After the official ban of the Atlantic slave trade to Brazil in 1850 and to Cuba in 1866, the slave trade from Ouidah and the other ports of the Bight of Benin to the Americas came to an end. From the 1850s, the Portuguese, the British, and the French had sought to use their long-lasting presence in the region from the era of the Atlantic slave trade to permanently settle in the Bight of Benin and on the Loango coast. These attempts were accompanied by the signature of several treaties. By 1861, the British had attacked the Kingdom of Porto-Novo. The invasion was justified to repress the continuous slave trade in the region. When the Kingdom of Porto-Novo, which had been a tributary to the Kingdom of Dahomey since the early nineteenth century, attempted to obtain protection from the French, Dahomey obviously rejected the deal. In 1874, King Toffa became the ruler of Porto-Novo. After an attack by Dahomey in 1882, Porto-Novo once again reestablished a French protectorate. The alliance between Porto-Novo and the French provoked new attacks by Dahomey, which eventually led to the first war between France and Dahomey. King Béhanzin was enthroned in January 1890, and the war started a month later in February 1890. Commanded by the then Colonel Alfred Amédée Dodds, the French forces faced the Dahomean army with its thousands of soldiers, including its famous all-female regiment of Amazons. But overall, France had more firepower and was also supported by ships. Eventually, in October 1890, Dahomey and France

signed a treaty in which Dahomey recognized Porto-Novo's French protectorate and also ceded Cotonou. But the peace did not last long, and
a second war started in June 1892, with France deploying nearly 3,000
soldiers to the region. After several battles, with the French forces gradually getting closer to Abomey, King Béhanzin along with his army and
royal court fled the capital and took refuge in the region, from where he
organized a resistance.[95] But before their departure, his troops set the
king's palace on fire. In late December 1893, after the French troops
entered the capital, and under the pressure of the invaders, the royal
family enthroned Béhanzin's brother Goutchili as King Agoli-Agbo, who
was formally accepted by the French as king of Dahomey on January 15,
1894. Ten days later, Béhanzin went to meet Dodds and was eventually
captured, then sent into exile to Senegal in early February 1894, thence
to Martinique, and finally to Algeria, where he died in 1906. In 1900,
France removed Agoli-Agbo from power as well and sent him into exile
in Gabon. French colonial rule in Dahomey continued until 1960.

The French hoped to take control of Dahomey's resources such as
gold and silver mines, but once in Abomey they were confronted by a
different reality.[96] Gaëlle Beaujean emphasizes that although existing
sources do not reveal any public instruction to loot Abomey's treasures,
on November 17, 1892, the French started digging around Abomey's
palaces searching for treasures.[97] But what was left seemed to be of little
commercial and artistic interest. On November 20, the diggers found
seventy-five boxes and thirty-one barrels containing cartridges, rifles,
umbrellas, textiles, and a great number of objects belonging to Béhanzin.[98] Locally manufactured precious wooden thrones, statues, *récades*,
and other silver objects were seized by Dodds's soldiers. Among these
objects were the two power objects in silver copper alloy representing
an elephant (Figure 6.7) and a buffalo (Figure 6.8). None of the written
reports included descriptions of any precious objects such as Pukuta's silver *kimpaba*. Whereas most artworks and artifacts taken from Dahomey
were incorporated into the collections of the Musée d'Ethnographie du
Trocadéro, and later entered the Musée de l'Homme and the Musée du
Quai Branly in Paris, members of Dodds's expeditionary force also kept
valuable articles as souvenirs of their participation in the campaign. One
of the officers took the silver *kimpaba* for a second time and carried it
back to France. Shaped by the conflictual exchanges during the era of
the Atlantic slave trade, the gift given by Garesché and his agents to the
Mfuka Andris Pukuta also came to embody the complex problem of tangible heritage that was looted during the scramble for Africa.

Conclusion

Objects That Shaped the Slave Trade and Colonialism

With the defeat of Dahomey during the French invasion and conquest that followed the Second Franco-Dahomean War between 1892 and 1894, the troops led by Alfred Amédée Dodds looted the treasures housed in the royal palaces of Abomey and Cana. Whereas no written document ordering the plunder of Dahomey's artifacts has yet been found, it is likely that the French never established a detailed inventory of the objects looted during these campaigns.[1] This apparent lack of coordination allowed various officers to take individual objects according to their preferences and according to the value of the artifacts. One officer took Andris Pukuta's silver *kimpaba* and brought it to France as a souvenir from the Dahomean campaign. Between the late nineteenth century and the first decade of the twenty-first century, this object has remained in the family of this officer, whose identity remains unknown. This was not a unique case. To this day, descendants of other high-ranking French officers have maintained in their homes collections of Abomey's royal objects, including silver items.[2] In the twentieth century, some valuable objects such as the silver elephant and buffalo figures (Figures 6.7 and 6.8) were sold in the private market and acquired by private institutions such as the Metropolitan Museum of Art in New York City in 2002, but the fate of other valuable objects remains unknown. In a letter dated June 9, 1894, France's Minister of the Public Instruction and Fine Arts informed the director of the national museums and the École du Louvre that "the Ministry of Navy expresses the desire of offering to the Louvre's Navy Museum [Musée de la Marine du Louvre] the crown of King Béhanzin, which [then] General Dodds brought from Dahomey," and that the crown was deposited at the Secretariat of the Navy Ministry.[3] Despite the

FIGURE C.1 *Un palabre chez Toffa,* wood engraving after a photograph. M.
Alexandre-L. d'Albéca, "Au Dahomey," *Le tour du monde: Nouveau journal
des voyages,* August 4, 1894, 89.

importance of this insignia, identified at the time as belonging to Béhanzin, the letter neither describes the crown nor provides any mention of
the material it was made of. Was this article really Béhanzin's crown?
Indeed, the object described could also have been the crown of Toffa,
who was the king of Porto-Novo at the time of the French conquest. An
existing wooden engraving executed after a photograph portrays Toffa
wearing a lavish crown surmounted by a lion (Figure c.1). This lion
suggests that Toffa's crown may have originally been given as a gift to
Glèlè, king of Dahomey, who was symbolized by a lion, by the German
company Goedelt. This venture was established in Ouidah in 1883, on
the eve of the Berlin Conference that partitioned the African continent
among European powers, including Germany. The depiction of Toffa's
crown reminds us of the seventeenth-century crown (Figure 1.1) that
English traders intended to give as a gift to the king of Allada. The crown
was seen for the last time when it was exhibited in the Dahomey pavilion
of the 1900 Paris Exposition. Regardless of who held the crown taken
by Dodds and brought to Paris, the fate of Behanzin's alleged crown and
Toffa's crown remain unknown.[4]

The French officer who took the silver *kimpada* passed it down to his children and grandchildren, therefore allowing it to remain in the family for more than a century. But in 2015, his granddaughter contacted the Rossini auction house in Paris to offer the silver *kimpaba* for sale. During an auction held in June 2015, the Musée du Nouveau Monde of La Rochelle purchased it for €20,500 and brought it back to the former slave port where it had originally been manufactured. Exhibited today in La Rochelle, the silver ceremonial sword became an important piece of the multisited and multilayered archive of the Atlantic slave trade and colonialism, offering historians an opportunity to explore connections between La Rochelle, Cabinda, Ouidah, Porto-Novo, and Abomey.

Despite the many gaps in our knowledge about the specific trajectory of the silver *kimpaba* from La Rochelle, through Cabinda, possibly Porto-Novo, then Ouidah, and finally Abomey, the path of this gift shows us that the study of material culture is central to understanding the history of the slave trade and colonialism. The silver *kimpaba* also problematizes the notions of origin and ownership that are today at the heart of demands for restitutions of African heritage that are being addressed to Western museums. The *kimpaba* was certainly manufactured in France, but as a gift it was supposed to be an inalienable movable property. Yet it was taken from Cabinda and incorporated into the royal collections of another African kingdom. Therefore, when French officers looted it from Dahomey, they appropriated the object as they did with other artifacts made in Dahomey by Fon artisans. However, since the silver *kimpaba* reemerged in the private market in 2015, seemingly there has been no contestation about the object being French, even though it was originally a gift to a Ngoyo's agent.

Although the demands of restitution of African heritage looted by European powers date back to the period of decolonization of the African continent, in the past fifteen years these demands have once again reemerged in the public sphere. International media began paying growing attention to restitutions in 2006, when the Musée du Quai Branly was unveiled in France, and a decade later in 2017, after French president Emmanuel Macron gave a speech at Ouagadougou (Burkina Faso), in which he lamented that a "large share of several African countries' cultural heritage be kept in France."[5] Following the Ouagadougou speech, Macron commissioned French art historian Bénédicte Savoy and Senegalese writer and economist Felwine Sarr to produce a report on restitution of African cultural heritage.

Released in November 2018, this long and provocative document urged France to return artworks and artifacts from its museum collections to

West African countries.[6] More precisely, the report emphasized the need to repatriate to the Republic of Benin eight of the twenty-seven items of the royal treasure that had been stolen from the palaces of Abomey, the inland capital of the Kingdom of Dahomey, by the French troops led by Dodds during the conquest of Dahomey between 1892 and 1894.[7] These objects, first offered by Dodds to the Musée d'ethnographie du Trocadéro that later became the Musée de l'Homme, have been housed in the Musée du Louvre and the Musée du Quai Branly.

But the French army also looted hundreds of other artifacts from the palaces of Abomey and Cana. Over the years, these articles were spread around several public and private museums in France and elsewhere. Many other items are kept in private collections, whereas others remain circulating in the private market. In addition to locally produced items such as gold and silver jewelry, wooden carved artifacts, and textiles, the Dahomean royal court's collections also incorporated objects plundered from other African neighboring states during military campaigns. These African royal collections also included a variety of foreign gifts offered to the kings by European officials. Despite the focus on 1894, during several decades of colonial rule in West Africa, administrators, officers, and scholars carried many thousands of African items of all kinds to French museums. Whereas some of these items may have been purchased from local communities, others could have been given as gifts. However, many objects were stolen from African colonized subjects or acquired through deceptive means. Throughout the twentieth century, objects made in Africa, Europe, Asia, and the Americas continued to circulate in the African continent. Hence, the silver *kimpaba* was not the only object taken from the Kingdom of Ngoyo that ended up in Dahomey. For example, the Museum of Natural History of Le Havre holds a Ngoyo's Ndunga ceremonial mask that was purchased in Dahomey in 1902 and sold to the French museum a year later. Woyo masks such as this one can also be found in other European museums such as the Sociedade de Geografia de Lisboa. These masks were associated with a secret society in charge of overseeing the respect of social order, the cult of the ancestors, and were usually seen during funerals and when a new ruler took power. Ultimately, this book emphasizes that the continuous circulation of gifts of prestige impacted the rise of the Atlantic slave trade and colonialism. Recognizing the complexity of these movements can certainly help us to better understand the current calls for restitution and repatriation of African heritage that was plundered during the colonial era.

Notes

INTRODUCTION

1 See Annick Notter, "Un témoignage de la traite rochelaise sur la 'côte d'Angole'," *La Revue des Musées de France, Revue du Louvre*, no. 4 (2016): 57–62.

2 Annick Notter, *Guide de visite* (La Rochelle: Musée du Nouveau Monde, 2016), 15.

3 Arjun Appadurai, "Introduction: Commodities and the Politics of Value," in *The Social Life of Things: Commodities in Cultural Perspective*, ed. Arjun Appadurai (New York: Cambridge University Press, 1986), 3, 6.

4 Francesca Trivellato, *The Familiarity of Strangers: The Sephardic Diaspora, Livorno, and Cross-Cultural Trade in the Early Modern Period* (New Haven, CT: Yale University Press, 2009), 7–8.

5 Although not specifically focusing on the era of the Atlantic slave trade, Jane I. Guyer theorizes about the conversions of gifts of prestige and other goods in Atlantic Africa. See Jane I. Guyer, *Marginal Gains: Monetary Transactions in Atlantic Africa* (Chicago: University of Chicago Press, 2004), 27–40.

6 On Atlantic gift exchanges at the Niger Delta at the end of the nineteenth century, see Julia T. S. Binter, "Becoming Imperial: The Politicisation of the Gift in Atlantic Africa," in *Exploring Materiality and Connectivity in Anthropology and Beyond*, ed. Phillip Schorch, Martin Saxer, and Marlen Elders (London: University College London Press, 2020), 53–71.

7 See, for example, Toby Green, *A Fistful of Shells: West Africa from the Rise of the Slave Trade to the Age of Revolution* (University of Chicago Press, 2019) and Colleen Kriger, *Making Money: Life, Death, and Early Modern Trade on Africa's Guinea Coast* (Athens: Ohio University Press, 2017).

8 For a general study, see Stanley B. Alpern, "What Africans Got for Their Slaves: A Master List of European Trade Goods," *History in Africa* 22 (1995): 5–43. David Richardson also explores this topic in a section of a book chapter, even though the chapter is mostly based on secondary sources. See David Richardson, "Consuming Goods, Consuming People: Reflections

on the Transatlantic Slave Trade," in *The Rise and Demise of Slavery and the Slave Trade in the Atlantic World*, ed. Kristin Mann and Philip Misevich (Rochester, NY: Rochester University Press, 2016), 31–63. On the French slave trade on the Loango coast examining the trade of the La Rochelle's slave ship *La Bonne Société*, see Amanda Gregg and Anne Ruderman, "Cross-Cultural Trade and The Slave Ship the Bonne Société: Baskets of Goods, Diverse Sellers, and Time Pressure on the African Coast," *Economic History Working Papers*, no. 333 (London: Department of Economic History, London School of Economics and Political Science, 2021), 1–60. On the Luso-Brazilian slave trade in West Central Africa, see Daniel Domingues da Silva, *The Atlantic Slave Trade from West Central Africa, 1780–1867* (New York: Cambridge University Press, 2017), 122–141 and Mariana P. Candido, "Women's Material World in Nineteenth-Century Benguela," in *African Women in the Atlantic World: Property, Vulnerability and Mobility, 1660– 1880*, ed. Mariana P. Candido and Adam Jones (Woodbridge: Boydell and Brewer, 2019), 70–85, as well as Mariana P. Candido, *An African Slaving Port and the Atlantic World: Benguela and Its Hinterland* (New York: Cambridge University Press, 2013), 173–175. On the Bight of Benin, see Carlos da Silva Jr., "Enslaving Commodities: Tobacco, Gold, Cowry Trade and Trans-Imperial Networks in the Bight of Benin (c. 1690s–c.1790s)," *African Economic History* 49, no 2 (2021): 1–30 and Ana Lucia Araujo, "Did Rodney Get It Wrong? Europe Underdeveloped Africa, But Enslaved People Were Not Always Purchased with Rubbish," *African Economic History Review* 50, no. 2 (2022): 22–32.

9 Among the recent monographs published in English covering ports in the region of Senegambia, see Walter Hawthorne, *From Africa to Brazil: Culture, Identity, and an Atlantic Slave Trade, 1600–1830* (New York: Cambridge University Press, 2010) and Toby Green, *The Rise of the Transatlantic Slave Trade in Western Africa, 1300–1589* (New York: Cambridge University Press, 2011); on the Gold Coast, see Rebecca Shumway, *The Fante and the Transatlantic Slave Trade* (Rochester, NY: Rochester University Press, 2011) and Randy J. Sparks, *Where the Negroes Are Masters: An African Port in the Era of the Slave Trade* (Cambridge, MA: Harvard University Press, 2014); on the Bight of Benin, see Robin Law, *Ouidah: The Social History of a West African Slaving Port 1727–1892* (Athens: Ohio University Press, 2004) and Kristin Mann, *Slavery and the Birth of an African City: Lagos, 1760–1900* (Bloomington: Indiana University Press, 2007); on the Bight of Biafra, see G. Ugo Nwokeji, *The Slave Trade and Culture in the Bight of Biafra: An African Society in the Atlantic World* (New York: Cambridge University Press, 2014); on Luanda and Benguela, see Linda Heywood and John K. Thornton, *Central Africans, Atlantic Creoles and the Foundation of the Americas* (New York: Cambridge University Press, 2007); Roquinaldo Ferreira, *Cross-Cultural Exchange in the Atlantic World* (New York: Cambridge University Press, 2014) and Candido, *An African Slaving Port and the Atlantic World.*

10 Phyllis M. Martin, *The External Trade of the Loango Coast, 1576–1870: The Effects of Changing Commercial Relations on the Vili Kingdom of Loango* (Oxford: Clarendon Press, 1972) remains the only monograph about the

slave trade on the Loango coast published in English. Since its publication, two monographs focusing on the trade in the region have been published in French. See Annie Merlet, *Autour du Loango (XIVe–XIXe siècle): Histoire des peuples du sud-ouest du Gabon au temps du royaume de Loango et du «Congo français»* (Libreville: Centre Culturel Français de Libreville, 1991) and Arsène Francoeur Nganga, *La traite négrière sur la baie de Loango pour la colonie du Suriname* (Saint-Denis: Edilivre, 2018). Four other important doctoral dissertations that cover the history of the Atlantic slave trade on the Loango coast remain unpublished: Susan Herlin Broadhead, "Trade and Politics on the Congo Coast: 1770–1870" (PhD dissertation, Boston University, 1971); Norm Schrag, "Mboma and the Lower Zaire: A Socioeconomic Study of a Kongo Trading Community, C. 1785–1885" (PhD dissertation, University of Indiana, 1985); Stacey Jean Muriel Sommerdyk, "Trade and Merchant Community of the Loango Coast in the Eighteenth Century" (PhD dissertation, University of Hull, 2012) and Christina Frances Mobley, "The Kongolese Atlantic: Central Africa Slavery and Culture from Mayombe to Haiti" (PhD dissertation, Duke University, 2015). However, two recent books covering West Central Africa give some attention to the trade on the Loango coast. See Silva, *The Atlantic Slave Trade from West Central Africa, 1780–1867* and John K. Thornton, *A History of West Central Africa to 1850* (New York: Cambridge University Press, 2020).

11 David Eltis and David Richardson, *Atlas of the Transatlantic Slave Trade* (New Haven, CT: Yale University Press, 2015), 90.

12 Appadurai, "Introduction: Commodities and the Politics of Value," 5.

13 Homer, *The Odyssey*, trans. Emily Wilson, Book 4 (New York: W. W. Norton, 2018), 170.

14 Homer, *The Odyssey*, 171.

15 Homer, *The Odyssey*, 233.

16 Marcel Mauss, *Essai sur le don: Forme et raison de l'échange dans les sociétés archaïques* (Paris: Presses universitaires de France, 2002), 62. The translation is from the English edition; see Marcel Mauss, *The Gift: The Form and Reason for Exchange in Archaic Societies* (London and New York: Routledge, 2002), 2.

17 See Verena Krebs, *Medieval Ethiopian Kingship, Craft, and Diplomacy with Latin Europe* (Cham: Palgrave Macmillan, 2021). On gift exchanges internal to early modern France, see Natalie Zemon Davis, *The Gift in Sixteenth-Century France* (Madison: University of Wisconsin Press, 2000). On the Mediterranean, see Maria G. Parani, "Intercultural Exchange in the Field of Material Culture in the Eastern Mediterranean: The Evidence of Byzantine Legal Documents (11th to 15th Centuries)," in *Diplomatics in the Eastern Mediterranean 1000–1500: Aspects of Cross-Cultural Communication*, ed. Alexander D. Beinammer, Maria G. Parani, and Christopher D. Schabel (Leiden: Brill, 2008), 349–372.

18 For example Dutch, English, French, and Indian merchants offered thousands of gifts, including Asian textiles, firearms, and spices, to traders in Yemen in the seventeenth and eighteenth centuries, Nancy Um, *Shipped But Not Sold: Material Culture and The Social Protocols of Trade during Yemen's Age of Coffee* (Honolulu: University of Hawai'i Press, 2017).

19 On these early exchanges between the Kingdom of Kongo and the Kingdom of Portugal, see Cécile Fromont, *The Art of Conversion: Christian Visual Culture in the Kingdom of Kongo* (Chapel Hill: University of North Carolina Press, 2014). See also Edward S. Cook, Jr., *Global Objects: Toward a Connected Art History* (Princeton, NJ: Princeton University Press, 2022), 178–180.

20 Christina Brauner, "Connecting Things: Trading Companies and Diplomatic-Giving on the Gold and Slave Coasts in the Seventeenth and Eighteenth Centuries," *Journal of Early Modern History* 20 (2016): 412. See also Christina Brauner, *Kompanien, Könige und caboceers: Interkulturelle Diplomatie an Gold- und Slavenküste im 17. Und 18. Jahrhundert* (Cologne, Weimar, Vienna: Böhlau Verlag, 2015).

21 Beinecke Library, Yale University (hereafter BLY), José Freire de Montarroyos Mascarenhas, *Relacam da Embayxada, que o poderoso Rey de Angome Kiayy Chiri Broncom, Senhor dos dila- tadissimos Sertõs de Guiné mandou ao Illustrissimo e Excellentissimo Senhor D. Luiz Peregrino de Ataide, Conde de Atouguia, Senhor das Villas de Atouguia, Peniche, Cernache, Monforte, Vilhaens, Lomba, e Pa͟co da Ilha Dezerta, Cõmendador das Cõmendas de Santa Maria de Adaufe, e Villa velha de Rodam, na Ordem de Christo, do Conselho de Sua Magestade, Governador, e Capitão General, que foy do Reyno de Algarve & actualmente Vice-Rey do Estado do Brasil: pedindo a amizade, e aliança do muito alto; e poderoso Senhor Rey de Portugal Nosso Senhor* (Lisbon: Na Officina de Francisco da Silva, 1751), 11 and Pierre Verger, *Fluxo e refluxo do tráfico de escravos entre o Golfo do Benin e a Bahia de Todos os Santos dos séculos XVII a XIX* (São Paulo: Editora Corrupio, 1987), 285. On this embassy see Ana Lucia Araujo, "Dahomey, Portugal, and Bahia: King Adandozan and the Atlantic Slave Trade," *Slavery and Abolition* 3, no. 1 (2012): 1–19. Earlier in the seventeenth century, the Kingdom of Allada also sent an embassy carrying gifts to France. See Christina Brauner, "To Be the Key for Two Coffers: A West African Embassy to France (1670/1)," *Institut français de recherche en Afrique Nigeria, E-papers series*, no. 30 (October 10, 2013): 1–26.

22 On Forbes's voyage in Dahomey, see Frederick E. Forbes, *Dahomey and the Dahomans: Being the Journey of Two Missions to the King of Dahomey, and his Residence at the Capital, in the Years 1849 and 1850* (London: Longman, Brown, Green, and Longmans, 1851), vols. 1 and 2. On Bonetta as a diplomatic gift, see Paul Brummell, *Diplomatic Gifts: A History in Fifty Presents* (London: Hurst, 2022), 203–214.

23 Here I agree with Appadurai, "Introduction: Commodities and the Politics of Value," 11. See also Nicholas Thomas, *Entangled Objects: Exchange, Material Culture, and Colonialism in the Pacific* (Cambridge, MA: Harvard University Press, 1991), 28–29 and David Graeber, *Toward an Anthropological Theory of Value: The False Coin of Our Dreams* (New York: Palgrave, 2001), 36.

24 Mauss, *Essai sur le don*, 64. Translation from Mauss, *The Gift*, 3.

25 Alain Caillé, *Anthropologie du don* (Paris: La Découverte, 2007), 49.

26 For an accessible introduction to Mauss and the problem of gifts and exchanges, see Hirozaku Miyazaki, "Gifts and Exchange," in *The Oxford*

Handbook of Material Culture Studies, ed. Dan Hicks and Mary C. Beaudry (Oxford: Oxford University Press, 2010), 246–264.
27 Mauss, *The Gift*, 50.
28 Mauss, *The Gift*, 18–19.
29 Thomas, *Entangled Objects*, 19.

1 THE LOANGO COAST AND THE RISE
OF THE ATLANTIC SLAVE TRADE

1 Linda M. Heywood and John K. Thornton, *Central Africans, Atlantic Creoles, and the Foundation of the Americas, 1585–1660* (New York: Cambridge University Press, 2007), 57.
2 "Descoberta do Reino do Congo (1482)," in *Monumenta Missionaria Africana: África Ocidental (1471–1531)*, ed. António Brásio (Lisbon: Agência Geral do Ultramar, 1952), vol. 1, 40. All English translations are my own, except otherwise indicated.
3 For a comprehensive and concise overview of the history of West Central Africa and the Atlantic world, see Roquinaldo Ferreira, "Central Africa and the Atlantic World," *Oxford Research Encyclopedia of African History*, October 30, 2019, https://oxfordre.com/africanhistory/view/10.1093/acrefore/9780190277734 .001.0001/acrefore-9780190277734-e-53C1kX3QTaPoG28MhKT3Ue/ Exmvoyhh22d.
4 After Luanda, Ouidah was the second largest slave port during the era of the Atlantic slave trade, having exported 1,004,000 enslaved Africans to the Americas between 1501 and 1867. See David Eltis and David Richardson, *Atlas of the Transatlantic Slave Trade* (New Haven, CT: Yale University Press, 2015), 90.
5 Arquivo Histórico Ultramarino (hereafter AHU), Conselho Ultramarino, Angola, Cx. 3, D. 334, Carta do governador e capitão-general de Angola, Pedro César de Meneses, ao Rei [D. João IV], March 9, 1643, fl. 1v.
6 I borrow the mid-eighteenth-century notion of the term "merchant," from Windham Beawes, through Francesca Trivellato's work, who defines it as "him who buys and fells any Commodities in Gross, or deals in Exchange; that traffcks in the way of Commerce, either by Importation, or Exportation; or that carries on Bufiness by way of Emption, Vendition, Barter, Permutation, or Exchange; and that makes a continued Assiduity or frequent Negociation in the Mystery of Merchandizing his sole Bufiness." See Wyndham Beawes, *Lex Mercatoria Rediviva: Or, The Merchant's Directory* (Dublin: Printed for Peter Wilson, 1754), 25. Even if Trivellato is not examining the trade in enslaved Africans, Beawes mentions "slaves" numerous times in his guide. See Trivellato, *The Familiarity of Strangers*, ix.
7 Jan Vansina, *Paths in the Rainforests: Toward a History of Political Tradition in Equatorial Africa* (Madison: The University of Wisconsin Press, 1990), 202.
8 Phyllis Martin, *The External Trade of the Loango Coast 1576–1870: The Effects of Changing Commercial Relations on the Vili Kingdom of Loango*

(Oxford: Clarendon Press, 1972), 3; The Vili (Civili) is a Zone H10 Bantu language, part of the Kongo clade. See Malcolm Guthrie, *The Classification of the Bantu Languages* (Oxford: Oxford University Press, 1948), 50.

9 "Al de zwarten, die ae den zeekant wonen, hebben hunne rechten, wetten van die van Pombo bekomen" ("All blacks who live on the coast obtained their laws and customs from those of Pombo"). See Olfert Dapper, *Naukeurige beschrijvinge der Afrikaensche gewesten van Egypten, Barbaryen, Lybien, Biledulgerid, Negroslant, Guinea, Ethiopiën, Abyssinie* (Amsterdam: J. van Meurs, 1676), vol. 2, 219; See also Jean Vansina, "Notes sur l'origine du Royaume du Kongo," *The Journal of African History* 4, no. 1 (1963): 37 and Martin, *The External Trade of the Loango Coast*, 4.

10 Martin, *The External Trade of the Loango Coast*, 9 and John K. Thornton, "The Origins of Kongo: A Revised Vision," in *The Kongo Kingdom: The Origins, Dynamics and Cosmopolitan Culture of an African Polity*, ed. Koen Bostoen and Inge Brinkman (Cambridge: Cambridge University Press, 2018), 39.

11 Vansina, *Paths in the Rainforests*, 156.

12 The capital was located about 4 miles from the coast, according to Olfert Dapper, *Description de l'Afrique, contenant les noms, la situation et les confins de toutes les parties, leur rivières, leurs villes et leurs habitations, leurs plantes et leurs animaux; les mœurs, les coûtumes, la langue, les richesses, la religion et le gouvernement de ses peuples* (Amsterdam: Chez Wolfang, Waesberge, Bom & van Someren, 1686), 321 and Thornton and Heywood, *Central Africans*, 106.

13 Martin suggests that Kakongo and Ngoyo may have been already independent from Loango by the middle of the seventeenth century. See Martin, *The External Trade of the Loango Coast*, 31. Both Sommerdyk and Mobley suggest that full independence may have occurred in the eighteenth century. See Stacey Sommerdyk, "Trade and Merchant Community of the Loango Coast in the Eighteenth Century" (PhD dissertation, University of Hull, 2012), 141–142 and Christina Mobley, "The Kongolese Atlantic: Central Africa Slavery and Culture from Mayombe to Haiti" (PhD dissertation, Duke University, 2015), 71. Grandpré suggested that Kakongo and Ngoyo paid tributes to Loango until the end of the eighteenth century when he visited the region. Louis-Marie-Joseph Ohier de Grandpré, *Voyage à la côte occidentale d'Afrique: fait dans les années 1786 et 1787, contenant la description des mœurs, usages, lois, gouvernement et commerce des états du Congo; suivi d'un voyage au cap de Bonne-Espérance: contenant la description militaire de cette colonie* (Paris: Dentu, 1801), vol. 1, 167.

14 Habi Buganza Mulinda, "Aux origines du royaume de Ngoyo," *Civilisations: Revue internationale d'anthropologie et des sciences humaines*, no. 41 (1993): 167.

15 Pieter van den Broecke and James D. La Fleur, *Pieter Van Den Broecke's Journal of Voyages to Cape Verde, Guinea and Angola: (1605–1612)* (London: Hakluyt Society, 2000), 89. But according to Grandpré it was ten *lieues* or a two-day walking distance from Cabinda. See Grandpré, *Voyage à*

la côte occidentale d'Afrique, vol. 1, 165; Martin, *The External Trade of the Loango Coast*, 30 and Phyllis M. Martin, "Family Strategies in Nineteenth-Century Cabinda," *The Journal of African History* 28, no. 1 (1987): 69.

16 See Martin, *The External Trade of the Loango Coast*, 30. See also Gilles-Maurice de Schryver, Rebecca Grollemund, Simon Branford, and Koen Bostoen, "Introducing A State-of-The-Art Phylogenetic Classification of the Kikongo Language Cluster," *Africana Linguistica* 21 (2015): 98; Mobley, "The Kongolese Atlantic," 190, and Koen Bostoen and Gilles-Maurice de Schryver, "Seventeenth-Century Kikongo Is Not the Ancestor of Present-Day Kikongo," in *The Kongo Kingdom: The Origins, Dynamics and Cosmopolitan Culture of an African Polity*, ed. Koen Bostoen and Inge Brinkman (New York: Cambridge University Press, 2018), 72.

17 I have explored this problem in a previous study focusing on illustrated travel accounts. See Ana Lucia Araujo, *Brazil through French Eyes: A Nineteenth-Century Artist in the Tropics* (Albuquerque: New Mexico University Press, 2015). For a recent assessment of how Europeans represented Africa and Africans in early modern travelogues, see Herman L. Bennett, *African Kings and Black Slaves: Sovereignty and Dispossession in the Early Modern Atlantic* (Philadelphia: University of Pennsylvania Press, 2019).

18 Samuel Purchas, *Hakluytus Posthumus or Purchas His Pilgrimes in Twenty Volumes, Contayning a History of the World in Sea Voyages and Lande Travells by Englishmen and Others* (Glasgow: James MacLehose and Sons, 1905), vol. 6, 393.

19 Broecke and La Fleur, *Pieter van den Broecke's Journal*, 95. For an early discussion on the various editions of Battell's accounts see Jan Vansina, "On Ravestein's Edition of Battell's Adventures in Angola and Loango," *History in Africa* 34 (2007): 321–347. See also, Jared Staller, *Converging on Cannibals: Terrors of Slaving in Atlantic Africa, 1509–1670* (Athens: Ohio University Press, 2019), 92–95.

20 Broecke and La Fleur, *Pieter Van Den Broecke's Journal*, 96.

21 Broadhead, "Trade and Politics on the Congo Coast," 58; Buganza, "Aux origines du Royaume de Ngoyo," 178 and Mobley, "The Kongolese Atlantic," 43–44.

22 Abbé Liévin-Bonaventure Proyart, *Histoire de Loango, Kakongo et autres royaumes d'Afrique* (Paris: C. P. Berton, 1776), 145–146 and Grandpré, *Voyage à la côte occidentale d'Afrique*, vol. 1, 192–193.

23 Proyart, *Histoire de Loango*, 145.

24 Proyart, *Histoire de Loango*, 146.

25 Purchas, *Hakluytus Posthumus*, vol. 6, 395–396. See also Martin, *The External Trade of the Loango Coast*, 25.

26 Proyart, *Histoire de Loango*, 127–128. On the Kondi, see Martin, *The External Trade of the Loango Coast,* 8; 25.

27 See Proyart, *Histoire de Loango*, 130 and "Chronica das missões," *Portugal em Africa*, vol. 3 (Lisbon: Typographia e Lithographia de A. E. Barata, 1896), 179.

28 Proyart, *Histoire de Loango*, 133–135.

29 Proyart, *Histoire de Loango*, 131.
30 Purchas, *Hakluytus Posthumus*, vol. 6, 396; Martin, *The External Trade of the Loango Coast*, 25 and John K. Thornton, *A History of West Central Africa to 1850* (New York: Cambridge University Press, 2020), 136–137. Martin refers to these princes as holding the titles of Manicaye, Manibock, Manisalag, and Manicabango. Thornton refers to the very same fiefs using Kikongo spelling: Kaye, Boke, Selage, and Kabongo.
31 Proyart, *Histoire de Loango*, 132.
32 See Karl Edward Laman, *Dictionnaire Kikongo-Français avec une étude phonétique décrivant les dialectes les plus importants de la langue dite Kikongo* (Brussels: Georges van Campenhout, 1936), 224. Therefore, one can infer that the term *kaïa* is related to the word *Makaya*.
33 *Mission de Loango. Mémoire sur l'établissement d'une mission dans les royaumes de Loango, Kakongo en Afrique* (Paris: Knapen, 1772), 11.
34 Grandpré, *Voyage à la côte occidentale d'Afrique*, vol. 1, 196–197.
35 See Martin, *The External Trade of the Loango Coast*, 25 and Mobley, "The Kongolese Atlantic," 88; 165.
36 See Buganza, "Aux origines du Royaume de Ngoyo," 177–178.
37 Martin, *The External Trade of the Loango Coast*, 43 and Thornton, *A History of West Central Africa to 1850*, 97; 136.
38 Filipa Ribeiro da Silva, *Dutch and Portuguese in Western Africa: Empires, Merchants and the Atlantic System, 1580–1674* (Leiden: Brill, 2011), 175–179.
39 On the Portuguese presence on the Loango coast during the seventeenth century see Ferreira, "Central Africa and the Atlantic World."
40 Broecke and La Fleur, *Pieter van den Broecke's Journal*, 54–55. On these Dutch vessels, although without comments about this specific incident, see Sommerdyk, "Trade and Merchant Community," 84 and Silva, *Dutch and Portuguese in Western Africa*, 175.
41 *Pterocarpus soyauxii*, and *Ptincotirus Welw*. See Broecke and La Fleur, *Pieter van den Broecke's Journal*, 73, n.2.
42 Broecke and La Fleur, *Pieter van den Broecke's Journal*, 89.
43 Broecke and La Fleur, *Pieter van den Broecke's Journal*, 90 and Martin, *The External Trade of the Loango Coast*, 30.
44 Dapper, *Description de l'Afrique*, 340.
45 Thornton, *A History of West Central Africa to 1850*, 139.
46 Broecke and La Fleur, *Pieter van den Broecke's Journal*, 55, n.6.
47 Broecke and La Fleur, *Pieter van den Broecke's Journal*, 56. Martin, *The External Trade of the Loango Coast*, 106, refers to the palm cloth currency unit as *macoute*, but the Kikongo word for piece of folded corner of cloth is *kutu*, whose plural is *makutu*. Laman, *Dictionnaire Kikongo-Français*, 344; Thornton spells "*makuta*," see Thornton, *A History of West Central Africa to 1850*, 196.
48 "Memoriais de Pedro Sardinha ao Conselho de Estado (1612?)," in *Monumenta Missionaria Africana: Africa Ocidental*, ed. António Brásio (Lisbon: Agência Geral do Ultramar, 1955), vol. 6, 104. See Phyllis M. Martin, "Power, Cloth and Currency on the Loango Coast," *African Economic History*, no. 15 (1986): 1–12.

49 As already mentioned, the Portuguese controlled Luanda and Benguela. But from 1641 to 1648, the Dutch took control of these colonies and seaports. Martin, *The External Trade of the Loango Coast*, 60; Mariana P. Candido, *An African Slaving Port and the Atlantic World: Benguela and Its Hinterland*. (New York: Cambridge University Press, 2013), 68 and Thornton, *A History of West Central Africa to 1850*, 165; 196.

50 Proyart, *Histoire de Loango*, 108.

51 Purchas, *Hakluytus Posthumus*, vol. 6, 371 and Martin, *The External Trade of the Loango Coast*, 35–36.

52 Frederik W. Rademarkers, Nicolas Nikis, Thierry de Putter and Patrick Degryse, "Copper Production and Trade in the Niari Basin (Republic of Congo) During the Thirteenth to Nineteenth Centuries CE: Chemical and Lead Isotope Characterization," *Archaeometry* (2018), 1251–1270.

53 Martin, *The External Trade of the Loango Coast*, 40–41. See also Eugenia W. Herbert, *Red Gold of Africa: Copper in Precolonial History and Culture* (Madison: University of Wisconsin Press, 1984), 142–143.

54 Martin, *The External Trade of the Loango Coast*, 27. Yet the idea of wealth in people is not specific to African societies and slave ownership was not the only form of wealth. On this discussion, see Mariana P. Candido, *Wealth, Land and Property in Angola: A History of Dispossession, Slavery, and Inequality* (New York: Cambridge University Press, 2022), 4–16.

55 Dapper, *Description de l'Afrique*, 327.

56 Proyart, *Histoire de Loango*, 254.

57 On *takula* acquired on the Loango coast, see "Alvitre de Pedro Sardinha (1611?)," in *Monumenta Missionaria Africana*, ed. António Brásio (Lisbon: Agência Geral do Ultramar, 1955), vol. 6, 54. On *takula*, ivory, and copper see Martin, *The External Trade of the Loango Coast*, 29.

58 Phyllis M. Martin, "The Kingdom of Loango," in *Kongo: Power of Majesty*, ed. Alisa Lagamma (New York: The Metropolitan Museum of Art, 2015), 34; 57.

59 See Mobley, "The Kongolese Atlantic," 54–55; 59–60. On the English slave trade in the region, see Arsène Francoeur Nganga, "La Compagnie royale d'Afrique et les commerçants négriers anglais sur la baie de Loango (entre 1650 et 1838)," *Études caribéennes* 42 (2019), https://journals.openedition.org/etudescaribeennes/15466

60 Dapper, *Description de l'Afrique*, 328.

61 Proyart, *Histoire de Loango, Kakongo et autres royaumes d'Afrique*, 2; 63.

62 The interdiction of enslaving a kingdom's own subjects was not specific to the kingdoms of the Loango coast. On enslaved persons as outsiders, see Paul E. Lovejoy, *Transformations in Slavery: A History of Slavery in Africa*. New York: Cambridge University Press, 2011), 1. On a similar custom from the sixteenth until the middle of the seventeenth century in the Kingdom of Kongo, see Linda M. Heywood, "Slavery and its Transformation in the Kingdom of Kongo: 1491–1800," *Journal of African History* 50 (2009):

6, 8. Likewise, in West Central African states such as Viye in the hinterland of Benguela there were similar principles, even though there were always exceptions allowing to enslave the kingdom's own subjects and the line separating outsiders from insiders was often blurred, see Candido, *An African Slaving Port*, 228–230. In Dahomey, the principle preventing the enslavement of kingdom's subjects dated back to the seventeenth century, during the rule of King Wegbaja, see Auguste Le Herissé, *Royaume du Dahomey: Moeurs, Religion, Histoire* (Paris: Emile Larose, 1911), 56, and Robin Law, *Ouidah: The Social History of a West African Slaving Port (1727–1892)*, 149. Yet this rule was broken as the slave trade intensified in the Bight of Benin, during the eighteenth and nineteenth centuries, see Ana Lucia Araujo, "Dahomey, Portugal, and Bahia: King Adandozan and the Atlantic Slave Trade," *Slavery & Abolition* 3, no. 1 (2012): 1–19. On the slave trade initially targeting outsiders and later virtually making anyone eligible to be enslaved in Upper Guinea, see Hawthorne, *From Africa to Brazil*, 64.

63 Proyart, *Histoire de Loango, Kakongo et autres royaumes d'Afrique*, 63, 150; 158.

64 Martin, *The External Trade of the Loango Coast*, 117–118.

65 Mobley, "The Kongolese Atlantic," 151–153.

66 Mobley, "The Kongolese Atlantic," 135–229.

67 See Thornton, *A History of West Central Africa to 1850*, 304–307.

68 See Kathryn M de. Luna, "Sounding the African Atlantic," *The William and Mary Quarterly* 78, no. 4 (2021): 581–616.

69 For the case of the brothers Adandozan and Gezo in Dahomey, see Ana Lucia Araujo, "History, Memory and Imagination: Na Agontimé, a Dahomean Queen in Brazil," in *Beyond Tradition: African Women and their Cultural Spaces*, ed. Toyin Falola and Sati U. Fwatshak (Trenton, NJ: Africa World Press, 2011), 45–68.

70 Grandpré, *Voyage à la côte occidentale d'Afrique*, vol. 1, 107–108.

71 Broecke and La Fleur, *Pieter van den Broecke's Journal*, 88.

72 Martin, *The External Trade of the Loango Coast*, 66 and Arsène Francoeur Nganga, "La Compagnie royale d'Afrique et les commerçants négriers anglais sur la baie de Loango (entre 1650 et 1838)," *Études caribéennes* 42 (2019), https://journals.openedition.org/etudescaribeennes/15466.

73 Joseph C. Miller, *Way of Death: Merchant Capitalism and the Angolan Slave Trade 1730–1830* (Madison: University of Wisconsin Madison, 1988), 50–51.

74 Candido, *An African Slaving Port*, 45.

75 Dapper, *Description de l'Afrique*, 340. On Dutch's gifts provided to the Maloango and his agents, see also Mark Meuwese, *Brothers in Arms, Partners in Trade: Dutch-Indigenous Alliances in the Atlantic World, 1595–1674* (Leiden: Brill, 2012), 87.

76 "Lettre de M. Descourvières Missionnaire apostolique à Loango écrite à M. Féris, supérieur du séminaire de Nantes," in *Documents sur une mission française au Kakongo, 1766–1776*, ed. Jean Cuvelier (Brussels: Institut Royal Colonial Belge, 1953), 38.

77 On the Guinea Coast, see Kriger, *Making Money*, 66. On the Bight of Benin, see Araujo, "Dahomey, Portugal, and Bahia," 1–19 and Mariza de Carvalho Soares, "Trocando galanterias: a diplomacia do comércio de escravos, Brasil-Daomé, 1810–1812," *Afro-Ásia*, no. 49 (2014): 229–271. On the Gold Coast, see Shumway, *The Fante and the Transatlantic Slave Trade*, 110; 113; Sparks, *Where the Negroes Are Masters*, 64, 133 and Christina Brauner, "Connecting Things," 408–428.

78 Mulinda Habi Buganza, "Aux origines du Royaume de Ngoyo," *Civilisations* 41, no. 1/2 (1993): 179.

79 J. Van Wing and C. Penders, *Le plus ancien dictionnaire bantu: Vocabularium P. Georgii Gelensis* (Louvain: Imprimerie J. Kuyl-Otto, 1928), 191.

80 Laman, *Dictionnaire Kikongo-Français*, 113.

81 Laman, *Dictionnaire Kikongo-Français*, 115.

82 Laman, *Dictionnaire Kikongo-Français*, 327.

83 Sommerdyk, "Trade and Merchant Community," 187.

84 "Chronica das missões," 180.

85 Susan Herlin Broadhead, "Trade and Politics on the Congo Coast: 1770–1870" (PhD dissertation, Boston University, 1971), 157.

86 Martin, *The External Trade of the Loango Coast*, 98–99.

87 Martin, *The External Trade of the Loango Coast*, 99. See also Buganza, "Aux origines du Royaume de Ngoyo," 179, who describes the *Mangovo* as a nobleman.

88 Grandpré, *Voyage à la côte occidentale d'Afrique*, vol. 1, 202.

89 Proyart, *Histoire de Loango, Kakongo et autres royaumes d'Afrique*, 125.

90 Martin, *The External Trade of the Loango Coast*, 99.

91 Martin, *The External Trade of the Loango Coast*, 99 and Buganza, "Aux origines du Royaume de Ngoyo," 179.

92 Buganza, "Aux origines du Royaume de Ngoyo," 179.

93 Martin, *The External Trade of the Loango Coast*, 100.

94 Martin, "Family Strategies in Nineteenth-Century Cabinda," 69; Carlos Serrano, "Tráfico e mudança no Reino Ngoyo (Cabinda no século XIX)," *Estudos Afro-Asiáticos*, 32 (1997): 97–108 and Miller, *Way of Death*, 184–185. See also David Graeber and Marshal Sahlins, *On Kings* (Chicago: HAU Books, 2017), 413.

95 Grandpré, *Voyage à la côte occidentale d'Afrique*, vol. 1, xxiii.

96 Grandpré, *Voyage à la côte occidentale d'Afrique*, vol. 1, 191; Martin, *The External Trade of the Loango Coast*, 79; Mobley, "The Kongolese Atlantic," 88 and Sommerdyk, "Trade and Merchant Community," 102; 168.

97 Martin, *The External Trade of the Loango Coast*, 97.

98 John K. Thornton, *A Cultural History of the Atlantic World, 1250–1820* (New York: Cambridge University Press, 2012), 472.

99 Sommerdyk, "Trade and Merchant Community," 102.

100 Silva, *Dutch and Portuguese in Western Africa*, 178.

101 Martin, "The Kingdom of Loango," 75; Sommerdyk, "Trade and Merchant Community," 179 and Mobley, "The Kongolese Atlantic," 83; 85–86.

102 In the port of Benguela, south to the Congo River, attacks led by local rulers were not uncommon. See Candido, *An African Slaving Port*, 46.

2 LA ROCHELLE AND ATLANTIC AFRICA

1 Jean-Michel Deveau, *La traite rochelaise* (Paris: Karthala, 2009), 15. An ivory turner is a craftsman who worked producing delicate objects made in ivory, such as handles, pieces of musical instruments, and chess sets.

2 Manuel Covo, *Entrepôt of Revolutions: Saint-Domingue, Commercial Sovereignty, and the French American Alliance* (New York: Oxford University Press, 2022), 5.

3 See Brice Marinetti, *Les négociants de La Rochelle au XVIIIe siècle* (Paris: Presses universitaires de Rennes, 2013), 27.

4 Robert Louis Stein, *The French Slave Trade in the Eighteenth Century: An Old Regime Business* (Madison: University of Wisconsin Press, 1979), 14.

5 Éric Saugera, *Bordeaux port négrier: XVIIe-XIXe siècles* (Paris: Karthala, 2002), 249.

6 The numbers vary. Whereas 420 documented slave voyages are featured in David Eltis and David Richardson, *Atlas of the Transatlantic Slave Trade*, (New Haven, CT: Yale University Press, 2015), 39, as well as in *SlaveVoyages*, www.slavevoyages.org, this number is likely higher. Brice Martinetti refers to a total of 476 slave voyages, including the seventeenth century and the period of the illegal slave trade. See Brice Martinetti, "La traite rochelaise et la côte des esclaves: des coopérations locales aux prises d'otages, des décalages sociétaux aux intérêts divergents," *Dix-huitième siècle* 1, no. 44 (2012): 79.

7 See Jean Meyer, *L'armement nantais dans la deuxième moitié du XVIIIe siècle* (Paris: Éditions de l'École des Hautes Études en Sciences Sociales, 1999), 73–94.

8 Martinetti, *Les négociants de La Rochelle au XVIIIe siècle*, 35.

9 Martinetti, *Les négociants de La Rochelle au XVIIIe siècle*, 36.

10 John C. Clark, *La Rochelle and the Atlantic Economy during the Eighteenth Century* (Baltimore, MD: Johns Hopkins University Press, 1981), 5.

11 On trading diasporas, see Philip D. Curtin, *Cross-Cultural Trade in World History* (Cambridge: Cambridge University Press, 1984). For a discussion of trading diasporas, and especially the Sephardim trading diaspora, see Trivellato, *The Familiarity of Strangers*. On the Huguenot diaspora, see Deveau, *La traite rochelaise*, 34, and Jennifer L. Palmer, *Intimate Bonds: Family and Slavery in the French Atlantic* (Philadelphia: University of Pennsylvania Press, 2016), 10.

12 Martinetti, *Les négociants de La Rochelle au XVIIIe siècle*, 75.

13 Clark, *La Rochelle and the Atlantic Economy*, 42.

14 Archives départementales de la Charente Maritime (hereafter ADCM) 17, 4J 45 2318, "Mémoires de Jacques Proa dit Proa des îles," publiés par Jean Arcand, typed manuscript, n/d, 4.

15 Martinetti, *Les négociants de La Rochelle au XVIIIe siècle*, 68–75.

16 Martinetti, *Les négociants de La Rochelle au XVIIIe siècle*, 302–303.

17 Martinetti, *Les négociants de La Rochelle au XVIIIe siècle*, 54–55.

18 ADCM 4J 4030/5, May 8, 1773, doc. 108, fl 1.

19 Clark, *La Rochelle and the Atlantic Economy*, 159–160.

20 Madeleine Dobie, "Patrimoine mobilier: entre colonialisme et orientalisme," *In Situ: Revue des patrimoines* 20 (2013): 2.

21 On the great variety of prohibited textiles that were reserved to be exported, see Colette Establet, *Répertoire des tissus indiens importés en France entre 1687 et 1769* (Aix-en-Provence: Institut de recherches et d'études sur les mondes arabes et musulmans, 2017), 27–29.

22 On prohibitions in Europe, see Sarah Fee, ed. *Cloth That Changed the World: The Art and Fashion of Indian Chintz* (Toronto and New Haven, CT: Royal Ontario Museum and Yale University Press, 2019), 16.

23 See Aziza Gril-Mariotte, "Indiennes, toiles peintes et toiles de Jouy, de nouvelles étoffes d'ameublement au XVIIIe siècle," *Histoire de l'art*, no. 65 (2009): 141–152 and Aziza Gril-Mariotte, "La consommation des indiennes à Marseille (fin XVIIIe-début XIXe siècle)," *Rives méditerranéennes*, no. 29 (2008):141–152. On popular consumption of chintz, see also Virginia Postrel, *The Fabric of Civilization: How Textiles Made the World* (New York: Basic Books, 2020), 194–199.

24 Dieudonné Rinchon, *Les armements négriers au XVIIIe siècle d'après la correspondance et la comptabilité des armateurs et des capitaines nantais* (Brussels: Académie royale des sciences coloniales, 1955), 17.

25 Guyer, *Marginal Gains*, 37.

26 The *livre* or *livre tournois* was the currency of the Kingdom of France from 781 CE. The *livre* was also referred to as *franc* or *franc d'argent*.

27 See Stanley B. Alpern, "What Africans Got for Their Slaves: A Master List of European Trade Goods," *History in Africa* 22 (1995), 7, 10.

28 Deveau, *La traite rochelaise*, 13.

29 On the term as it was used by the Portuguese, see Beatrix Heintze, "Traite de 'pièces' en Angola: Ce qui n'est pas dit dans nos sources," in *De la traite à l'esclavage: Actes du colloque international sur la traite des Noirs, Nantes 1985, tome 1: Ve-XVIIIe siècle*, ed. Serge Daget (Nantes and Paris: Centre de recherche sur l'histoire du monde atlantique and Société française d'histoire d'outre-mer, 1985), 147–172, at 151.

30 See Deveau, *La traite rochelaise*, 74–75.

31 The numbers vary. One watercolor states that the ship transported 307 captives. But the *SlaveVoyages*, voyage ID 30910 refers to 312 enslaved people who embarked in Africa and 302 who disembarked alive in Cap-Français in Saint-Domingue in 1770.

32 See Krystel Gualdé, *L'abîme: Nantes dans la traite atlantique et l'esclavage colonial, 1707–1830* (Nantes: Musée d'histoire de Nantes and Fondation pour la mémoire de l'esclavage, 2021), 170; Bertrand Guilet, *La Marie-Séraphique: Navire négrier* (Nantes: Musée d'histoire de Nantes, 2009), 64–65.

33 Stein, *The French Slave Trade in the Eighteenth Century*, 71.

34 Alpern, "What Africans Got for Their Slaves," 6.

35 Descriptions of these textiles slightly vary. See Alain Yacou, *Journaux de bord et de traite de Joseph Crassous de Médeuil: De La Rochelle à la côte de Guinée et aux Antilles (1772–1776)* (Paris: Karthala, 2001), 53, and Guilet, *La Marie-Séraphique*, 50.

36 The watercolor, not reproduced here, is currently held in a private collection, and is reproduced in Gualdé, *L'abîme*, 149.

37   The French spelling of these textile names greatly varied. For a description of these fabrics, see Guilet, *La Marie-Séraphique*, 87. For a description of these fabrics in English, see Alpern, "What Africans Got for Their Slaves."

38   He uses *franc*, another term to designate the currency *livre*.

39   ADCM 17, 4J 45 2318, "Mémoires de Jacques Proa dit Proa des îles," 113.

40   Usually only high-rank officers were authorized to carry pacotilles. See Deveau, *La traite rochelaise*, 123.

41   ADCM 17, 4J 45 2318, "Mémoires de Jacques Proa dit Proa des îles," 89.

42   Louis-Marie-Joseph Ohier de Grandpré, *Voyage à la côte occidentale d'Afrique: fait dans les années 1786 et 1787, contenant la description des mœurs, usages, lois, gouvernement et commerce des états du Congo; suivi d'un voyage au cap de Bonne-Espérance: contenant la description militaire de cette colonie* (Paris: Dentu, 1801), vol. 1, 75.

43   *Le commerce de l'Amérique par Marseille ou Explications des Lettres-Patentes du Roi, portant règlement pour le Commerce qu'il se fait de Marseille aux Isles Françoises de l'Amérique, données au mois de Février 1719 et des Lettres-Patentes du Roi, pour la liberté du Commerce à la Côte de Guinée. Données à Paris au mois de Janvier 1716* (Leiden and Aix: Pierre Chambon, 1782), vol. II, 381 and Alain Yacou, *Journaux de bord et de traite de Joseph Crassous de Médeuil: De La Rochelle à la côte de Guinée et aux Antilles (1772–1776)* (Paris: Karthala, 2001), 144–155. On coral trade from Marseille, see Olivier Raveux, "The Coral Trade in Smyrna at the End of the 17th Century as Seen through Several of François Garnier's Business Deals," *Rives méditerranéenes*, no. 59 (2019): 135–151.

44   See Jean Mettas, Serge Daget and Michèle Daget, ed. *Répertoire des expéditions négrières françaises au XVIIIe siècle*, tome II: Ports autres que Nantes (Paris: Société française d'outre-mer 1984), 338.

45   ADCM 17, 4J 45 2318, "Mémoires de Jacques Proa dit Proa des îles," 84.

46   See Deveau, *La traite rochelaise*, 83–84 and Rinchon, *Les armements négriers au XVIIIe siècle*, 16. On the central role of Brazilian tobacco in the slave trade between Brazil and the Bight of Benin and the attempts by the French and the English to imitate the flavor of Brazilian third-rate tobacco, see Pierre Verger, *Fluxo e refluxo, do tráfico de escravos entre o Golfo do Benin e a Bahia de Todos os Santos dos séculos XVII a XIX* (São Paulo: Editora Corrupio, 1987), 44–49. On the tobacco trade and local use in the Bight of Benin, see also Carlos da Silva Jr., "Enslaving Commodities: Tobacco, Gold, Cowry Trade and Trans-Imperial Networks in the Bight of Benin (c. 1690s–c.1790s)," *African Economic History* 49, no. 2 (2021): 1–30, at 5–12.

47   ADCM 17, 4J 45 2318, "Mémoires de Jacques Proa dit Proa des îles," 94–95.

48   Louis Esnoul de Sénéchal, "Un manuel du parfait traitant au XVIIIe siècle," *Mémoires de la société d'Histoire et d'archéologie de Bretagne* 13 (1932), 199–200.

49   ADCM 4J 4030/5, "Mémoire à consulter," doc. 136, fl. 1.

50   See ADCM 4J 4030/5, doc. 139, fl. 1. Dorothy Garesché Holland, *The Garesché, De Baudy, and Des Chapelles Families: History and Genealogy* (Saint Louis, MO: Schneider Printing Company, 1963), 9.

51 Their business and presence in Saint-Domingue are attested in several family notarized documents, see ADCM 4J 4030/5, April 12, 1770, fl. 60.

52 In 1768, he became lieutenant of the *compagnie des dragons blancs ou dragons mulâtres libres* (company of white dragons or free mulatto dragons) in Port-au-Prince, and in 1775 he was appointed captain of the *compagnie des dragons mulâtres libres* (company of free mulatto dragons) of Port-au-Prince. See Société des archives historiques de la Saintonge et de l'Aunis, *Bulletin de la Société des archives historiques de la Saintonge et de l'Aunis* (Paris and Saintes: A. Picard and Mme Z. Mortreuil, 1896), 293.

53 His postmortem inventory lists a slave-trading journal of 1771. ADCM 4J 4030/5, April 23, 1775, doc. 105, iv. See also ADCM 4J 4030/5, May 8, 1773, doc. 108, fl. 1.

54 *Affiches américaines*, July 8, 1767, 216. On the term griffe, see Jean-Pierre Le Glaunec, *Esclaves mais résistants: Dans le monde des annonces pour esclaves en fuite, Louisiane, Jamaïque, Caroline du Sud (1801–1815)* (Paris: Karthala, 2021), 136, and Jason Daniels, "Recovering the Fugitive History of Marronage in Saint-Domingue, 1770–1791," *The Journal of Caribbean History* 46, no. 2 (2012): 138.

55 *Affiches américaines*, January 4, 1769, 2.

56 *Affiches américaines*, May 11, 1768, 160; October 4, 1769, 372; February 14, 1770, 80; May 20, 1772, 248; July 22, 1772, 356; May 19, 1773, 236; October 27, 1773, 512; March 16, 1774, 162–163; April 6, 1774, 163; November 30, 1774, 572; December 20, 1775, 608; February 19, 1777, 92; March 10, 1778, 76–77; October 5, 1779, 2; April 11, 1780, 4 and February 15, 1783, 4.

57 *Affiches américaines*, August 16, 1775, 391.

58 ADCM 4J 1610 1, doc. 283, fl. 1.

59 *Affiches américaines*, November 30, 1774, 570.

60 *Affiches américaines*, December 7, 1774, 1.

61 See Mettas, Daget, and Daget, ed. *Répertoire des expéditions négrières françaises au XVIIIe siècle*, tome II: Ports autres que Nantes, 451. See also *SlaveVoyages*, www.slavevoyages.org, voyage ID 32593.

62 Édouard Delobette, "Ces Messieurs du Havre. Négociants, commissionnaires et armateurs de 1680 à 1830" (PhD dissertation, Université de Caen, 2008), note 6891, 2248.

63 ADCM 4. J 1610 4, "Acte de société entre nous soussignés," 1777, fl. 2. On Tiamba and Arada see Philip D. Curtin, *The Atlantic Slave Trade: A Census* (Madison: University of Wisconsin Press, 1969), 192.

64 Holland, *The Gareschê, De Baudy, and Des Chapelles Families*, 240 and Clark, *La Rochelle and the Atlantic Economy*, 135.

65 *Revue de Saintonge et d'Aunis: Bulletin de la Société des archives historiques* (Saintes: Mortreuil, 1896), 291.

66 See for example, Correspondance commerciale de Gareschê et Billoteau à Port-au-Prince (1777–1786), ADCM 4J art 1610 (folder 1–100), June 28, 1777 doc. 7, fls.1–1v; July 24, 1778, doc.14, fl.1–1v; August 17, 1779, doc. 17, 1v and July 31, 1780, doc. 88, 1v.

67 *Revue de Saintonge et d'Aunis*, 292.

68 ADCM 4. J 1610 4, "Second expedition...Par devant leur notaire...," May 3, 1784.

69 Archives nationales d'outre-mer, Aix-en-Provence, France (hereafter FR ANOM) COL E 14, fls. 1–2, We know Babet was owned by Jean Garesché du Rocher because in 1794 she is mentioned in a letter sent by his daughter from La Rochelle to Philadelphia, where he went into exile during the Saint-Domingue Revolution. See Holland, *The Garesché, De Baudy, and Des Chapelles Families*, 27–28.

70 He was elected director of the Chamber of Commerce on July 9, 1766 and remained in the office until June 20, 1768. See B. Martinetti, *Les négociants de La Rochelle au XVIIIe siècle* (Paris: Presses universitaires de Rennes, 2013), 398.

71 Clark, *La Rochelle and the Atlantic Economy*, 80.

72 See Mettas, Daget, and Daget, ed. *Répertoire des expéditions négrières françaises au XVIIIe siècle*, tome II: Ports autres que Nantes, 312 and *SlaveVoyages*, www.slavevoyages.org, voyage ID 32257.

73 See Mettas, Daget, and Daget, ed. *Répertoire des expéditions négrières françaises au XVIIIe siècle*, tome II: Ports autres que Nantes, 316, 322, 328, 340, 351, 363, 384, 392 and *SlaveVoyages*, www.slavevoyages.org, voyages ID 32267, 32279, 32296, 32324, 32380, 32423 and 32445.

74 *Affiches américaines*, January 21, 1775, 33.

75 ADCM 4J 1610 1 (folder 100–199), doc 105, letter of July 15, 1780, fl. 1v.

76 According to the *SlaveVoyages*, www.slavevoyages.org.

77 See *SlaveVoyages*, www.slavevoyages.org, voyages ID 32420 and 32374.

78 See *SlaveVoyages*, www.slavevoyages.org, voyages ID 32260, 32277, 32293, 32313, 32436 and 32449. See also Mettas, Daget, and Daget, ed. *Répertoire des expéditions négrières françaises au XVIIIe siècle*, tome II: Ports autres que Nantes, 313.

79 ADCM 3 E 1680, liasse 2, November 2, 1769, fl. 518–521.

80 See Jean-Pierre Queguiner, "Jean-Amable Lessenne, Louisbourg 1739-La Rochelle 1818. Capitaine de navire négrier, président trésorier au bureau des finances de la généralité de La Rochelle, propriétaire du château de La Tourtillère (Puilboreau) et de l'hôtel particulier du Petit-Val (La Rochelle)," *Écrits d'Ouest* 12 (2004): 109.

81 Queguiner, "Jean-Amable Lessenne,"112.

82 Mettas, Daget, and Daget, ed. *Répertoire des expéditions négrières françaises au XVIIIe siècle*, tome II: Ports autres que Nantes, 313 and *Affiches américaines*, December 12, 1770, 1. See also *SlaveVoyages*, www.slavevoyages.org, voyage ID 32260.

83 Mettas, Daget, and Daget, ed. *Répertoire des expéditions négrières françaises au XVIIIe siècle*, tome II: Ports autres que Nantes, 321; *SlaveVoyages*, www.slavevoyages.org, voyage ID 32277 and *Affiches américaines*, June 5, 1773, 261.

84 Martinetti, *Les négociants de La Rochelle au XVIIIe siècle*, 236.

85 Martinetti, *Les négociants de La Rochelle au XVIIIe siècle*, 335.

86 Queguiner, "Jean-Amable Lessenne," 119–123.

87 Daniel Domingues da Silva, *The Atlantic Slave Trade from West Central Africa, 1780–1867* (New York: Cambridge University Press, 2017), 29.

3 SLAVE TRADERS TURNED PIRATES

1 In a study about the La Rochelle slave ship *La Bonne Société* that traded in Loango in the late eighteenth century, Gregg and Ruderman showed that prices of captives increased proportionally to the time the slave ship captain spent on the coast. See Amanda Gregg and Anne Ruderman, "Cross-Cultural Trade and the Slave Ship the Bonne Société: Baskets of Goods, Diverse Sellers, and Time Pressure on the African Coast," *Economic History Working Papers*, no. 333 (London: Department of Economic History, London School of Economics and Political Science, 2021), 1–60, at 3. See also Robert Louis Stein, *The French Slave Trade in the Eighteenth Century: An Old Regime Business.* Madison: University of Wisconsin Press, 1979, 75.

2 Daniel Domingues da Silva, "The Supply from Luanda, 1768–1806: Records of Anselmo da Fonseca Coutinho," *African Economic History* 38 (2010): 56.

3 The National Archives, Kew, hereafter TNA, T 70 1216, fl. 12–12v. See also *Slave Voyages*, www.slavevoyages.org, voyage ID 9897.

4 Louis-Marie-Joseph Ohier de Grandpré, *Voyage à la côte occidentale d'Afrique: fait dans les années 1786 et 1787, contenant la description des mœurs, usages, lois, gouvernement et commerce des états du Congo; suivi d'un voyage au cap de Bonne-Espérance: contenant la description militaire de cette colonie* (Paris: Dentu, 1801), vol. 1, 16.

5 Léon Vignols, "El asiento francés (1701–1713) e inglés (1713–1750) y el Comercio franco-español desde 1700 hasta 1730," *Anuario de historia del derecho español*, no. 5 (1928): 266–300.

6 *Journal d'un voyage sur les costes d'Afrique et aux Indes d'Espagne avec une description particulière de la Rivière de La Plata; de Buenosayres, & autres lieux; commencé en 1701 & fini en 1706* (Amsterdam: 1723), 2–3.

7 *Journal d'un voyage sur les costes d'Afrique*, 61.

8 *Journal d'un voyage sur les costes d'Afrique*, 88–97.

9 *Journal d'un voyage sur les costes d'Afrique*, 96–97

10 FR ANOM, COL C8 A 15, fl. 109. On *L'Opiniâtre* and *L'Aigle*, see also *Slave Voyages*, www.slavevoyages.org, voyages ID 33504 and 33501.

11 *Journal d'un voyage sur les costes d'Afrique*, 134.

12 *Journal d'un voyage sur les costes d'Afrique*, 104.

13 In addition, they rented the trading post for 10 *pièces*. The *Maningoyo* (king) assigned one of his slaves to work at the trading post for 15 *pièces* and another ten slaves, each of whom was paid 10 *pièces* as well. See *Journal d'un voyage sur les costes d'Afrique*, 136.

14 FR ANOM COL C8 A 15, fl. 109v.

15 FR ANOM COL C8 A 15, fl. 109v. The French distance measure *lieue* changed over time, and during the eighteenth century there were several types of *lieues*. Moreover, the measure of a *lieue* also depended on whether

the distance was measured on land (1 *lieue* measuring approximately 276 miles) or water (1 *lieue* measuring approximately 3.4 miles).

16 Mariana P. Candido, *An African Slaving Port and the Atlantic World: Benguela and Its Hinterland* (New York: Cambridge University Press, 2013), 75, 93.

17 TNA T70 1225, fls. 9, 16, 17, 21.

18 Phyllis Martin, *The External Trade of the Loango Coast 1576–1870: The Effects of Changing Commercial Relations on the Vili Kingdom of Loango* (Oxford: Clarendon Press, 1972), 81–83.

19 K. H. Ledward, ed. *Journals of the Board of Trade and Plantations*, vol. 5: January 1723–December 1728 (London: H.M. Stationery Office, 1928), 234. See also TNA T70 1225, fl. 9,

20 Archives nationales, Paris, France (hereafter ANF) MAR B 4 77, fl. 20.

21 The accounts vary slightly. See *Journal encyclopédique par une société de gens de lettres*, tome V: troisième partie (Liège: Everard Kints, 1757), 163–164; M. Chabaud-Arnault, "Études historiques sur la marine militaire de France, La marine française avant et pendant la guerre de sept ans (suites)," in *Revue maritime et coloniale* (Paris: Librairie Militaire de L. Baudoin, 1892), 485; *Mercure de France* 26 (1758): 180–181 and Alfred Graincourt, *Histoire des hommes illustres de la marine française, suivie de l'expédition française au Mexique en 1863* (Niort: Robin et L. Favre, 1863), 178.

22 ANF MAR B 4 77, Campagne aux côtes d'Afrique, 1757, fl. 17v.

23 ANF MAR B4 77, "Copie du traité fait avec le prince Classe Maffouk et les habitants du pays de Cabinde ...," 8–8v. On the treaty see also Martin, *The External Trade of the Loango Coast 1576–1870*, 85 and Christina Frances Mobley, "The Kongolese Atlantic: Central Africa Slavery and Culture from Mayombe to Haiti" (PhD dissertation, Duke University, 2015), 93. Both Martin and Mobley refer to Mfuka "Klaus" but the exact transcription is "Classe."

24 ANF MAR B4 77, "Copie du traité fait avec le prince Classe Maffouk et les habitants du pays de Cabinde ...," 8–8v.

25 Jean Mettas, Serge Daget, and Michèle Daget, ed. *Répertoire des expéditions négrières françaises au XVIIIe siècle,* tome II: Ports autres que Nantes (Paris: Société française d'histoire d'outre-mer, 1984), 36 and Eric Saugera, *Bordeaux port négrier: XVIIe–XIXe siècles* (Paris: Karthala, 2002), 353.

26 ANF MAR C 7 74, doc. 7, fl.1–fl4v.

27 See Jean Mettas, Serge Daget, and Michèle Daget, eds., *Répertoire des expéditions négrières françaises au XVIIIe siècle,* tome I: Nantes (Paris: Société française d'histoire d'outre-mer, 1978), 480–481 and Mettas, Daget, and Daget, eds., *Répertoire des expéditions négrières françaises au XVIIIe siècle,* tome II, 41, 28.

28 ANF MAR C 7 74, fl. 3v.

29 *Affiches américaines*, January 14, 1767, 9.

30 *Affiches américaines*, February 25, 1767, 57 and *Affiches américaines*, March 18, 1767, 81.

31 *Affiches américaines*, April 22, 1767, 121 and *Affiches américaines*, April 29, 1767, 129.

32 Mettas, Daget, and Daget, ed. *Répertoire des expéditions négrières françaises au XVIIIe siècle*, tome II, 36 and Saugera, *Bordeaux port négrier: XVIIe–XIXe siècles*, 43; 45.

33 See "Lettre de M. Descouvrières, actuellement à Malimbe dans le Royaume de Loango en Afrique, en date du 30 8bre 1768," and "Relation du voyage et de l'établissement des Missionnaires françois dans le royaume de Kakongo proche de celui de Loango en Afrique," in *Documents sur une mission francaise au Kakongo, 1766–1776*, ed. Jean Cuvelier (Brussels: Institut Royal Colonial Belge, 1953), 35, 103. See also Mobley, "The Kongolese Atlantic," 75–76.

34 The spelling of *Le Montyon* varies depending on the voyage to the African coast. *Le Montyon* appears in *SlaveVoyages*, www.slavevoyages.org voyage ID 32315 and ADCM 41 ETP 210/6533, fl. 1. *Le Monthion* according to Mettas, Daget, and Daget, ed. *Répertoire des expéditions négrières françaises au XVIIIe siècle*, tome II, 330.

35 Archives de la Marine à Rochefort (hereafter AMR) 6P6 7, fl. 22, no. 87, AMR, 6P6 30, 1776, no. 25.

36 ADCM, January 17, 1761, 3 E 1672 liasse 1, fl. 35.

37 AMR, 6P6 30, 1775, fl. 28, no. 87.

38 Médiathèque Michel-Crépeau (hereafter MMC), Ms 2286, Traite des noirs, fl. 49.

39 For more details on the sea currents and winds, see David Eltis and David Richardson, *Atlas of the Transatlantic Slave Trade* (New Haven, CT: Yale University Press, 2015), 8.

40 Existing ship logs show that numerous slave ships stopped especially at São Tomé and Príncipe. See Alain Yacou, *Journaux de bord et de traite de Joseph Crassous de Médeuil: De La Rochelle à la côte de Guinée et aux Antilles (1772–1776)* (Paris: Karthala, 2001), 173. See also Bertrand Guilet, *La Marie-Séraphique: Navire négrier* (Nantes: Musée d'histoire de Nantes, 2009), 73.

41 Daniel Domingues da Silva, *The Atlantic Slave Trade from West Central Africa, 1780–1867* (New York: Cambridge University Press, 2017), 22.

42 Abbé Liévin-Bonaventure Proyart, *Histoire de Loango, Kakongo et autres royaumes d'Afrique* (Paris: C. P. Berton, 1776), 151–152.

43 The *pièce* as a standard set of goods was also used on the Loango coast and other West Central African ports such as Luanda. The *pièce* consisted of a bundle that included cloth and other trading items. Obviously, contents of a piece or bundle varied over time and space. See Miller, *Way of Death*, 67; 299. On bundles on the Loango coast, see also Gregg and Ruderman, "Cross-Cultural Trade and the Slave Ship the Bonne Société," 4–5.

44 Phyllis M. Martin, "Power, Cloth and Currency on the Loango Coast," *African Economic History*, no. 15 (1986): 3–4.

45 On textiles in Kongo and Angola and the symbolic importance of white, blue, and other colors see Cécile Fromont, "Common Threads: Cloth, Colour, and the Slave Trade in Early Modern Kongo and Angola," *Art History* 41, no. 5 (2018): 853–867.

46 Grandpré, *Voyage à la côte occidentale d'Afrique*, vol. 1, 80–81.

47 Guilet, *La Marie-Séraphique*, 86 and MMC, Ms 2286, Traite des noirs, fl. 49.
48 Proyart, *Histoire de Loango, Kakongo et autres royaumes d'Afrique*, 155.
49 ADCM, 41 ETP 217 6660, July 18, 1776, fl. 1.
50 ADCM, 41 ETP 217 6660, July 18, 1776, fl. 1.
51 *L'Hirondelle* owned by Daniel Garesché does not appear in armament and disarmament records for the period 1776–1777. It is also absent from *Slave Voyages* and Mettas, Daget, and Daget, ed. *Répertoire des expéditions négrières françaises au XVIIIe siècle*, tome II: Ports autres que Nantes.
52 AMR, 6P6 36, *Désarmements année 1782*, no. 18.
53 For *L'Hirondelle*'s voyage in 1783, see *Slave Voyages*, voyage ID 32334 and AMR 6P6 16, Armément au mois de mars 1783, no. 8.
54 ADCM, 41 ETP 217 6660, July 18, 1776, fl. 1.
55 The name Pukuta has been associated in the oral tradition with Mibimbi Pukuta, the father of Mwe (or Mõe) Panzo and Mwe Pukuta, who successively became the kings of Ngoyo (*Maningoyo*), see José Domingos Franque and Manuel de Resende, *Nós, Os Cabindas, pelo príncipe negro* (Lisbon: Editora Argo, 1940), 20; Carlos Serrano, *Os senhores da terra e os homens do mar: Antropologia política de um reino africano* (São Paulo: Faculdade de Filosofia, Letras e Ciências Humans, Universidade de São Paulo, 1983), 62 and Alberto Oliveira Pinto, *Nós, os Cabindas: Domingos José Franque e a história oral das linhagens de Cabinda* (Lisbon: Novo Imbondeiro, 2003), 23–24.
56 See Jean-Michel Deveau, *La traite rochelaise* (Paris: Karthala, 2009), 74–75.
57 ADCM, 41 ETP 217/6660, July 18, 1776, fl. 1v. Martin Dubouscoua was an officer from Bayonne and appears in the list of officers of *Le Montyon*, see AMR 6P6 30, 1775, fl. 22, no. 28.
58 ADCM, 41 ETP 217/6660, July 18, 1776, fl. 1v.
59 ADCM, 41 ETP 217/6660, July 18, 1776, fl. 1v.
60 Bloyet's *Le Saint Charles* arrived on Loango on December 8, 1774, where it purchased 167 enslaved Africans, then moved to Malembo, where it acquired 184 enslaved Africans, and left the port to Port-au-Prince on November 26, 1775, see Mettas, Daget, and Daget, *Répertoire des expéditions négrières françaises au XVIIIe siècle*, tome I, 584.
61 ADCM, 41 ETP 217/6660, July 18, 1776, fl. 2.
62 ADCM, 41 ETP 217/6660, fl. 2v.
63 My thanks to David Eltis, Daniel Domingues da Silva, and Alex Borucki for helping me to figure out the role of *L'Hirondelle*.
64 ADCM 41 ETP 17, July 23, 1776, fl. 42.
65 ADCM, 41 ETP 217 6662, August 27, 1776, fl 1–1v.
66 ADCM 41 ETP 17, October 27. 1776, fl. 45.
67 *Slave Voyages*, www.slavevoyages.org, voyage ID 32300; Mettas, Daget, and Daget, ed. *Répertoire des expéditions négrières françaises au XVIIIe siècle*, tome II, 330 and *Supplément aux Affiches américaines*, January 20, 1776, 33.
68 *Supplément aux Affiches américaines*, January 27, 1776, 45.
69 *Slave Voyages*, www.slavevoyages.org, voyage ID 32605; Mettas, Daget, and Daget, ed. *Répertoire des expéditions négrières françaises au XVIIIe siècle*, tome II, 456 and *Supplément aux Affiches américaines*, December 23, 1775, 609.

70   *Slave Voyages*, www.slavevoyages.org, voyage ID 32603; Mettas, Daget, and Daget, ed. *Répertoire des expéditions négrières françaises au XVIIIe siècle*, tome II, 455 and *Supplément aux Affiches américaines*, January 20, 1776, 33.
71   *Slave Voyages*, www.slavevoyages.org, voyage ID 31613; Mettas, Daget, and Daget, ed. *Répertoire des expéditions négrières françaises au XVIIIe siècle*, tome II, 64; Saugera, *Bordeaux port négrier: XVIIe–XIXe siècles*, 355 and *Supplément aux Affiches américaines*, April 6, 1776, 165.
72   See FR ANOM COL E 136, October 20, 1783, fl. 2.
73   See Candido, *An African Slaving Port and the Atlantic World*, 74–76; 169–170.
74   Letter from José Onorio de Valladares e Aboim, July 11, 1783 in "Angola: O Forte de Cabinda," Ministério das colônias, *Arquivos das colônias*, III July-December (1918): 194.
75   "Letter from Luiz Candido Cordeiro Pinheiro Furtado, Forte de Cabinda, November 5, 1783" in "Angola: O Forte de Cabinda," Ministério das colônias, *Arquivos das colônias*, III, no. 17 (1918): 172.
76   Letter from José Onorio de Valladares e Aboim, July 11, 1783, 195.
77   José Curto, *Enslaving Spirits: The Portuguese-Brazilian Alcohol Trade at Luanda and its Hinterland, c. 1550–1830* (Leiden: Brill, 2004), 153.
78   Letter from José Onorio de Valladares e Aboim, July 11, 1783, 196.
79   Letter from José Onorio de Valladares e Aboim, July 11, 1783, 196.
80   Martin, *The External Trade of the Loango Coast 1576–1870*, 87–88 and Daniel B. Domingues da Silva, "The Transatlantic Slave Trade from Angola: A Port-by-Port Estimate of Slaves Embarked, 1701–1867," *International Journal of African Historical Studies* 46, no. 1 (2013): 117.
81   The Portuguese often portrayed West Central Africans as the perpetrators while depicting themselves as victims. In 1618, before the conflicts in Cabinda, they developed a similar narrative to justify their attacks against the state of Peringue at the Bay of Benguela, when its rulers resisted against treaties of vassalage. See Candido, *An African Slaving Port and the Atlantic World*, 54–55.
82   For more on land clashes between the Portuguese and West Central African rulers see Mariana P. Candido, *Wealth, Land and Property in Angola: A History of Dispossession, Slavery, and Inequality* (New York: Cambridge University Press, 2022), 46–62.
83   FR ANOM 16 DFC MEM 137, XIII, carton 75, fl. 1–1v.
84   FR ANOM 16 DFC MEM 137, XIII, carton 75, fl. 2
85   FR ANOM 16 DFC MEM 124, XIII, carton 75, "Relation de l'expédition de Cabende," fl. 2–2v.
86   FR ANOM 16 DFC MEM 124, XIII, carton 75, "Relation de l'expédition de Cabende," fl. 1v.
87   FR ANOM 16 DFC MEM 132, XIII, carton 75, "Journal et détail de tout ce qui s'est passé depuis le 17 juin..." fl. 5v.
88   Musée d'histoire de Nantes (hereafter MHN), Correspondance de Mr de Marigny dans son expédition de Cabinde sur la Côte d'Affrique en 1784, June 17, 1784, 2001.9.1, fl. 2.
89   FR ANOM 16 DFC MEM 124, XIII, carton 75, "Relation de l'expédition de Cabende." fl. 3.

90   FR ANOM 16 DFC 132, "Journal et détail de tout ce qui s'est passé depuis le 17 juin," fl. 8v–fl 9. See also Silva, "The Transatlantic Slave Trade from Angola," 117. The report and journal first refer to the Portuguese agreeing to raze (*"raser"*) the fort to the ground but as the Portuguese surrendered, they referred to the French demolishing the fort.

91   FR ANOM 16 DFC 132, "Journal et détail de tout ce qui s'est passé depuis le 17 juin," fl. 9–9v.

92   AHU, Governo Geral de Angola, Correspondência confidencial, códice 1642, "Carta do governo interino escrita para Cabinda ao Capitão de Mare-Guerra António Januário do Vale," October 10, 1783, fl. 2.

93   See Mettas, Daget, and Daget, ed. *Répertoire des expéditions négrières françaises au XVIIIe siècle*, tome I, 626. The vessel arrived on November 4, 1783, see *Affiches américaines*, November 12, 1783, 649.

94   MHN, Correspondance de Mr de Marigny dans son expédition de Cabinde sur la Côte d'Affrique en 1784, June 17, 1784, 2001.9.1, fl. 2v.

95   Grandpré, *Voyage à la côte occidentale d'Afrique*, vol. 1, 82.

96   Mobley, "The Kongolese Atlantic," 105.

97   *Affiches américaines*, February 11, 1784, 103 and *Supplément aux Affiches américaines*, February 28, 1784, 148.

98   Mettas, Daget, and Daget, ed. *Répertoire des expéditions négrières françaises au XVIIIe siècle*, tome II, 477.

99   Mettas, Daget, and Daget, ed. *Répertoire des expéditions négrières françaises au XVIIIe siècle*, tome II, 488.

100 Mettas, Daget, and Daget, ed. *Répertoire des expéditions négrières françaises au XVIIIe siècle*, tome II, 89, 103.

101 Mettas, Daget, and Daget, ed. *Répertoire des expéditions négrières françaises au XVIIIe siècle*, tome II, 496.

102 Mettas, Daget, and Daget, ed. *Répertoire des expéditions négrières françaises au XVIIIe siècle*, tome II, 513.

103 Mettas, Daget, and Daget, ed. *Répertoire des expéditions négrières françaises au XVIIIe siècle*, tome II, 492.

4   DECIPHERING THE GIFT

1   ADCM, Amirauté La Rochelle, Soumissions 1720–1792, B259, fl. 139.

2   AMLR, 6P6 30, 1776, no. 25.

3   Despite the lack of broad studies, the examination of particular cases shows that shipowners and slave traders made profits in the eighteenth century. See, for example, Cheryl Susan McWatters, "Investment Returns and la traite négrière: Evidence from Eighteenth-Century France, Accounting," *Business & Financial History* 18, no. 2 (2008): 161–185.

4   AMLR, 6P6 11, 1777, ADCM B243 fl. 1v.

5   The silver sword emerged when Maison Rossini auctioned it in 2015. See Maison Rossini, *Dessins, tableaux anciens, art d'Asie, arts décoratifs du XXe, céramiques, montres, horlogerie, instruments scientifiques et de marine, objets d'art et d'ameublement* (Paris: Hôtel Drouot, salle Rossini le 5 juin

2015). That same year, Gaëlle Beaujean reproduced an image of the object in her PhD dissertation. See Gaëlle Beaujean, "L'art de la cour d'Abomey: le sens des objets" (PhD dissertation, École des Hautes Études en Sciences Sociales, 2015). In 2016, the then director of the Musée du Nouveau Monde in La Rochelle, wrote the first article about the *kimpaba*. See Annick Notter, "Un témoignage de la traite rochelaise sur la 'côte d'Angole'," *La Revue des Musées de France, Revue du Louvre*, no. 4 (2016): 57–62. Beaujean also reproduced the *kimpaba* in Gaelle Beaujean, *L'art de la cour d'Abomey: Le sens des objets* (Paris: Presses du Réel, 2019), 479–80, at 417. In 2021, two art historians respectively published a book chapter and an article briefly examining the *kimpaba*, see Cécile Fromont, "The Taste of Others: Finery, The Slave Trade, and Africa's Place in the Traffick of Early Modern Things," in *Early Modern Things: Objects and their Histories, 1500–1800*, ed. Paula Findlen (New York: Routledge: 2021), 273–294, and Julien Volper, "Trois cimpaaba d'argent: Échanges afro-européens sur les côtes kongo (XVIIe–XIXe siècles)," *Tribal Art magazine* XXV-4, no. 101 (2021): 83–95.

6 See Cécile Fromont, "From Image to Grave and Back: Multidisciplinary Inquiries into Kongo Christian Visual Culture," in *The Kongo Kingdom: The Origins, Dynamics and Cosmopolitan Culture of an African Polity*, ed. Koen Bostoen and Inge Brinkman (Cambridge: Cambridge University Press, 2018), 159–160.

7 Tristan Arbousse Bastide, *Du couteau au sabre: Armes traditionnelles d'Afrique. From Knife to Sabre: Traditional Arms of Africa 2* (Oxford: Archaeopress, 2008), 79–80.

8 "D. Manuel envia ao Congo letrados e religiosos (1504)," in *Monumenta Missionaria Africana: Africa Ocidental (1471–1531)*, ed. António Brásio (Lisbon: Agência Geral do Ultramar, 1952), vol. 1, 194–195.

9 Dieudonné Rinchon, *Pierre-Ignace-Liévin van Alstein: Capitaine négrier, Gand 1733-Nantes 1793* (Dakar: Institut de l'Afrique noire, 1964), 262.

10 Louis-Marie-Joseph Ohier de Grandpré, *Voyage à la côte occidentale d'Afrique: fait dans les années 1786 et 1787, contenant la description des mœurs, usages, lois, gouvernement et commerce des états du Congo; suivi d'un voyage au cap de Bonne-Espérance: contenant la description militaire de cette colonie* (Paris: Dentu, 1801), vol. 2, 24.

11 Stacey Sommerdyk, "Trade and Merchant Community of the Loango Coast in the Eighteenth Century" (PhD dissertation, University of Hull, 2012), 229.

12 Abbé Liévin-Bonaventure Proyart, *Histoire de Loango, Kakongo et autres royaumes d'Afrique* (Paris: C. P. Berton, 1776), 103.

13 Grandpré, *Voyage à la côte occidentale d'Afrique*, vol. 1, 199.

14 BLY, Lieutenant Durand, "Journal de bord d'un négrier, 1731–1732," Gen Mss, vol. 7. See also Robert W. Harms, *The Diligent: A Voyage through the Words of the Slave Trade* (New York: Basic Books, 2002).

15 See, for example visual depictions of African artifacts in Thomas Astley, ed. *A New General Collection of Voyages and Travels Consisting of the Most Esteemed Relations, Which Have Been Hitherto Published in Any Language: Comprehending Every Thing Remarkable in Its Kind, in Europe, Asia, Africa, and America* (London: Thomas Astley, 1745), vol. 2.

16   On two *bimpaba* from the nineteenth and twentieth centuries, see Suzanne Preston Blier, *Royal Arts of Africa: The Majesty of Form* (London: Laurence King Publishing, 2012), 200.

17   On eighteenth-century silversmiths in France and La Rochelle, see Solange Brault and Yves Bottineau, *L'orfèvrerie française du XVIIIe siècle* (Paris: Presses Universitaires de France, 1959), 18.

18   Notter, "Un témoignage de la traite rochelaise sur la 'côte d'Angole'," 4–5.

19   Thomas T. Hoopes, "French Silver of the Eighteenth Century," *Bulletin of the City Art Museum of St. Louis* 39, no. 1 (1954): 7.

20   On details about these hallmarks see Notter, "Un témoignage de la traite rochelaise sur la 'côte d'Angole'," 54.

21   See Notter, "Un témoignage de la traite rochelaise sur la 'côte d'Angole'," 57. On the silver oiler, see Christie's, Live Auction 3515, 500 ans: arts décoratifs européens, "Huilier en argent" probablement par Jean-Baptiste Chaslon, La Rochelle, 1775, 11 inches, Christie's auction, closed November 6, 2012, in *500 Ans: Arts décoratifs européens, Mercredi 7 novembre 2012* (Paris: Christie's, 2012).

22   According to Francis Masgnaud, *Franc-maçonnerie et francs-maçons en Aunis et Saintonge sous l'Ancien Régime et la Révolution* (La Rochelle: Rumeur des Ages, 1989), 41.

23   The apprenticeship contract indicates fourteen years old, which would make the year of his birth 1733; therefore, it is very possible that Jean's father increased his age. ADCM B 302 Registre, June 7, 1747, fl. 36v–37.

24   Lessenne purchased the Hôtel du Petit Val, Maîtresses Street in 1787. See Jean-Pierre Queguiner, "Jean-Amable Lessenne, Louisbourg 1739-La Rochelle 1818. Capitaine de navire négrier, président trésorier au bureau des finances de la généralité de La Rochelle, propriétaire du château de La Tourtillère (Puilboreau) et de l'hôtel particulier du Petit-Val (La Rochelle)," *Écrits d'Ouest* 12 (2004): 122.

25   MMC, Ms 641, fl. 97. His wife was possibly Marie Vrignaud, see B2106 (liasse), in M. Meschinet de Richemond, *Inventaire sommaire des Archives départementales antérieures à 1790: Charente-inférieure serie B (art 1829 à 2661), Jurisdictions secondaires relevant des présidiaux de La Rochelle et de Saintes* (La Rochelle: Eugène Martin, 1906), 131–132. On the discussion about the denominations merchant and master, see Jean Thuile, *L'orfèvrerie en Languedoc du XIIe au XVIIIe siècle. Géneralité de Montpellier* (Montpellier: Causse & Castlenau, 1966), 31.

26   AMR 6P6-7, 1775, no. 28, fl. 1v, AMR, 6P6 30, 1776, no. 25, fl.1.

27   Masgnaud, *Franc-maçonnerie et francs-maçons en Aunis et Saintonge* 41. Like Jean, Louis Chaslon was born in Marans, on August 20, 1738.

28   AMR, 6P 30, 1777, ADCM B243 fl. 1v and AMR 6P6 32, no. 16, fl. 1, 1778.

29   For example, the Islamic silver coin, *dirham*, François-Xavier Fauvelle, *The Golden Rhinoceros: Histories of the African Middle Ages* (Princeton, NJ: Princeton University Press, 2018), 9, 145. See also Joseph E. Inikori, *Africans and the Industrial Revolution in England: A Study in International Trade and Development* (Cambridge: Cambridge University Press, 2002), 203–206 and Toby Green, *A Fistful of Shells: West Africa from the Rise*

of the Slave Trade to the Age of Revolution (Chicago: Chicago University Press, 2019), 52.

30   See Kara Danielle Schultz, "'The Kingdom of Angola Is Not Very Far from Here': The Río de La Pata, Brazil, and Angola, 1580–1680" (PhD diss., Vanderbilt University, 2016), 20–29. See also, Green, *A Fistful of Shells*, 253–254.

31   Eugenia W. Herbert, *Red Gold of Africa: Copper in Precolonial History and Culture* (Madison: University of Wisconsin Press), xx, 3.

32   Green, *A Fistful of Shells*, 14–15.

33   Cécile Fromont, *The Art of Conversion: Christian Visual Culture in the Kingdom of Kongo* (Chapel Hill: University of North Carolina Press, 2014), 165.

34   See Kris Lane, *Potosí: The Silver City that Changed the World* (Oakland: California, 2019), and Peter John Bakewell, *Silver Mining and Society in Colonial Mexico, Zacatecas 1546–1700* (Cambridge: Cambridge University Press, 1972). On the Dutch trade of silver between the Río de La Plata and Europe, see David Freeman, *A Silver River in a Silver World: Dutch Trade in the Río de la Plata, 1648–1678* (New York: Cambridge University Press, 2020).

35   See Jorge Bohorquez, "Linking the Atlantic and Indian Oceans: Asian Textiles, Spanish Silver, Global Capital, and the Financing of the Portuguese-Brazilian Slave Trade (c. 1760–1808)," *Journal of Global History* 15, no. 1 (2020): 19–38, and Alex Borucki, "The US Slave Ship Ascension in the Río de La Plata: Slave Routes and Circuits of Silver in the Late Eighteenth-Century Atlantic and Beyond," *Colonial Latin American Review* 29, no. 4 (2020): 630–657.

36   Louis Dermigny, "Circuits de l'argent et milieux d'affaires au XVIIIe siècle," *Revue Historique* 212, no. 2 (1952): 239–278.

37   Grandpré, *Voyage à la côte occidentale d'Afrique*, vol. 1, 71.

38   Jérôme Jambu, "La circulation de la monnaie métallique et des métaux monétisables en Europe au XVIIIe siècle," in *Les circulations internationales en Europe, années 1680-années 1780*, ed. Pierre-Yves Beaurepaire and Pierrick Pourchasse (Rennes: Presses universitaires de Rennes, 2010), 153–155. See also Carlos Mancal, "The Spanish-American Silver Peso: Export Commodity and Global Money of the Ancien Regime, 1550–1800," in *From Silver to Cocaine: Latin American Commodity Chains and the Building of the World Economy, 1500–2000*, ed. Steven Topik, Carlos Marichal, and Zephyr Frank (Durham, NC: Duke University Press, 2006), 25–52.

39   Solange Brault and Yves Bottineau, *L'orfèvrerie française du XVIIIe siècle* (Paris: Presses universitaires de France, 1959), 4.

40   Denis Diderot and Jean le Rond d'Alembert, ed. *Encyclopédie ou Dictionnaire raisonné des sciences, des arts et des métiers par une société de gens de lettres*, vol. XI (Neuchâtel: Samuel Faulche, 1765), plate I.

41   For more on this process see Hoopes, "French Silver of the Eighteenth Century," 8–9.

42   Christopher C. Fennell, "Kongo and the Archaeology of Early African America" in *Kongo across the Waters*, ed. Susan Cooksey, Robin Poynor, and Hein Vanhee (Gainesville: University of Florida Press, 2013), 230–231.

43 Karl Edvard Laman, *Dictionnaire Kikongo-Français: une étude phonétique décrivant les dialecteds les plus importants de la langue dite Kikongo* (Brussels: Librairie Falk Fils, 1936), 255.

44 Carlos Serrano, "Símbolos do poder nos provérbios e nas representações gráficas Mabaya Manzangu dos Bawoyo de Cabinda, Angola," *Revista do Museu de Arqueologia e Etnologia* (1993): 142

45 Carlos Serrano, *Os senhores da terra e os homens do mar: Antropologia política de um reino africano* (São Paulo: Faculdade de Filosofia, Letras e Ciências Humans, Universidade de São Paulo, 1983), 94.

46 Mulinda Habi Buganza, "Aux origines du Royaume de Ngoyo," *Civilisations* 41, no. 1/2 (1993): 172 and Serrano, "Símbolos do poder nos provérbios," 142.

47 Padre Joaquim Martins, *Sabedoria Cabinda: Símbolos e provérbios* (Lisbon: Junta de investigações ultramar, 1968), 200–201.

48 Grandpré, *Voyage à la côte occidentale d'Afrique*, vol. 1, 204–205.

49 Grandpré, *Voyage à la côte occidentale d'Afrique*, vol. 2, 26.

50 Buganza, "Aux origines du royaume de Ngoyo," 179.

51 Zdenka Volavka and Wendy Anne Thomas, *Crown and Ritual: The Royal Insignia of Ngoyo* (Toronto: Toronto University Press, 1998), 35.

52 Martins, *Sabedoria Cabinda*, 65.

53 Volper, "Trois cimpaaba d'argent,": 83–95.

54 See Blier, *Royal Arts of Africa*, 210, and Serrano, "Símbolos do poder nos provérbios," 142.

55 Joseph Cornet, *Pictographies Woyo* (Milan: PORO, Associazione degli Amici dell'Arte Extraeuropea, 1980), 21–22.

56 On the proverbs on the pot lids, see Serrano, "Símbolos do poder nos provérbios," 137–146. See also Wyatt Macgaffey, "Os Kongo," in *Na Presença dos espíritos: Arte Africana do Museu Nacional de Etnologia, Lisboa*, ed. Frank Herreman (New York: Museum for African Art and Gent: Snoek-Ducaju, 2000), 51–53.

57 Cornet, *Pictographies Woyo*, 59.

58 Fromont, *The Art of Conversion*, 75.

59 Fromont, *The Art of Conversion*, 67.

60 Susan Cooksey, Robin Poynor, Hein Vanhee, and Carlee S. Forbes, ed. *Kongo across the Waters* (Gainesville: University Press of Florida, 2014), 113.

61 Martins, *Sabedoria Cabinda*, 479.

62 Martins, *Sabedoria Cabinda*, 64–65.

63 Cornet, *Pictographies Woyo*, 80.

64 Serrano, "Símbolos do poder nos provérbios," 142.

65 Cornet, *Pictographies Woyo*, 79–80, figures 34 and 35.

66 Joaquim Martins, *Cabindas: história, crença, usos e costumes* (Cabinda: Comissão de Turismo da Câmara Municipal de Cabinda, 1972), 105. See also João Baptista Luís, "O comércio do marfim e o poder nos territórios do Kongo, Ngoyo e Loango: 1796–1825" (MA thesis, Universidade de Lisboa, 2016), 56.

67 On speaking objects, see Jennifer Trimble, "The Zoninus Collar and the Archaelogy of Romany Slavery," *American Journal of Archaeology* 120, no. 3 (2016): 444–472.

68 Gérard van Krieken, *Corsaires et marchands: Les relations entre Alger et les Pays-Bas, 1604–1830* (Saint-Denis: Éditions Bouchène, 2002), 103–104.

69 For example, see Grandpré, *Voyage à la côte occidentale d'Afrique*, vol. 1, 188; 133.

70 See Sommerdyk, *Trade and the Merchant Community of the Loango Coast in the Eighteenth Century*, 225.

71 Alain Anselin, "Résistances africaines sur la Côte d'Angole au XVIIIe siècle," *Présence africaine*, no. 173 (2006): 195.

72 See *Slave Voyages*, www.slavevoyages.org, voyage ID 31504.

73 See *Slave Voyages*, www.slavevoyages.org, voyages ID 30989, 31559, and 31139.

74 *Madam Pookata* made nine voyages to the coasts of Africa, see *Slave Voyages*, see voyages ID 82415, 82417, 82418, 82419, 82420, 82421, 82422 and 82424, www.slavevoyages.org.

75 Anselin, "Résistances africaines sur la Côte d'Angole au XVIIIe siècle," 196.

76 Archives Départementales de la Loire Atlantique (hereafter ADLA), Rôles de bord, C 1396 (181 à 192), Armément et désarmement, *La Sainte Anne*, no. 174, 164 au désarmement, fl. 3.

77 Alain Roman, *Mes ennemis savent que je suis Breton: La vie d'Ohier de Grandpré, marin de Saint-Malo (1761–1846)* (Saint-Malo: Éditions Cristel, 2004), 61.

78 Grandpré, *Voyage à la côte occidentale d'Afrique*, vol. 1, 143.

79 Grandpré, *Voyage à la côte occidentale d'Afrique*, vol. 1, 146–147.

80 Grandpré, *Voyage à la côte occidentale d'Afrique*, vol. 1, 152.

81 Proyart, *Histoire de Loango, Kakongo et autres royaumes d'Afrique*, 199.

82 Proyart, *Histoire de Loango, Kakongo et autres royaumes d'Afrique*, 201.

83 See Volavka and Thomas, *Crown and Ritual*, 83; Josef Chavanne, *Reisen und Forschunen im alten und neuen Kongostaate in den Jahren 1884 und 1885* (Jena: Hermann Costenoble, 1887), 218 and Pechuel-Loesche, *Volkskunde*, 155–156.

84 "bis der Stoffklumpen die Gestalt einer ungeheuren Schmetterlingspuppe hatte, grosser als ein Elefant." See Eduard Pechuël-Loesche, *Volkskunde von Loango* (Stuttgart: Stecker and Schroder, 1907), 157.

85 Grandpré, *Voyage à la côte occidentale d'Afrique*, vol. 1, 153.

86 Grandpré, *Voyage à la côte occidentale d'Afrique*, vol. 1, 154. Several historians have commented on Grandpré's description of the funeral and the process of packing the body within a bundle of cloth. See Phyllis M. Martin, "Power, Cloth and Currency on the Loango Coast," *African Economic History* 15 (1986): 6–7, and Martin, "The Kingdom of Loango," 77. This treatment was also observed in Ngoyo and Loango by other travelers and scholars. See Joseph Chavanne, *Reisen und Forschungen im alten und neuen Kongstaate in den Jahren 1884 und 1885* (Jenna: Hermann Constenoble, 1887), 218, Pechuel-Loesche, *Volkskunde von Loango* (Stuggart: Stecker and Schröeder, 1907), 155–156, and in northern Kongo, see E. Manker, "Niombo. Die Totenbestattung der Babwende," *Zeitschrift für Ethnologie* 64, no. 4–6 (1932), 159–172 and Fromont, *The Art of Conversion: Christian Visual Culture in the Kingdom of Kongo* (Durham: University of North Carolina Press, 2014), 96. See also Volavka and Thomas, *Crown and Ritual*, 336, note 126.

87 Grandpré, *Voyage à la côte occidentale d'Afrique*, vol. 1, 155.
88 Arquivo Nacional da Torre do Tombo, MNEJ, 2a. inc. Mç 14, no. 145, cx. 42, Extrait des minutes déposées au Greffe de l'Amirauté du Cap, No. 4, November 25, 1783,

5 A DISPLACED GIFT

1 Zdenka Volavka and Wendy Anne Thomas, *Crown and Ritual: The Royal Insignia of Ngoyo* (Toronto: Toronto University Press, 1998), 83.

2 Louis-Marie-Joseph Ohier de Grandpré, *Voyage à la côte occidentale d'Afrique: fait dans les années 1786 et 1787, contenant la description des mœurs, usages, lois, gouvernement et commerce des états du Congo; suivi d'un voyage au cap de Bonne-Espérance: contenant la description militaire de cette colonie* (Paris: Dentu, 1801), vol. 1, 148.

3 Grandpré, *Voyage à la côte occidentale d'Afrique*, vol. 1, 147–148.

4 On this discussion see Volavka and Thomas, *Crown and Ritual*, 83–85.

5 John K. Thornton, "The Regalia of the Kingdom of Kongo, 1491–1895," in *Kings of Africa: Art and Authority in Central Africa*, ed. Erna Beumers and Hans-Joachim Koloss (Maastricht: Foundation Kings of Africa, 1992), 57.

6 Pieter van den Broecke and James D. La Fleur, *Pieter Van Den Broecke's Journal of Voyages to Cape Verde, Guinea and Angola: (1605–1612)* (London: Hakluyt Society, 2000), 58. As the Portuguese were present in the region since the late fifteenth century and because Van den Broecke visited the region during the period of the Iberian Union (1580–1640), when the kingdoms of Castile and Aragon and the Kingdom of Portugal were ruled by the Castilian Crown, it remains unclear whether the throne was Spanish-made or Portuguese-made or if it was modeled after Iberian thrones.

7 Thornton, "The Regalia of the Kingdom of Kongo," 58.

8 Thornton, "The Regalia of the Kingdom of Kongo," 59.

9 On this silver basin, see Elena Phipps, Johanna Hecht, and Cristina Esteras Martín, ed. *The Colonial Andes: Tapestries and Silverwork, 1530–1830* (New York and London: The Metropolitan Museum of Art and Yale University Press, 2004), 210–211, and Cécile Fromont, *The Art of Conversion: Christian Visual Culture in the Kingdom of Kongo* (Chapel Hill: University of North Carolina Press, 2014), 122.

10 Granpré, *Voyage à la côte occidentale d'Afrique*, vol. 1, 149–150.

11 Volavka, *Crown and Ritual*, 93.

12 Grandpré, *Voyage à la côte occidentale d'Afrique*, vol. 1, 187.

13 Joseph Cornet, *Pictographies Woyo* (Milan: PORO, Associazione degli Amici dell'Arte Extraeuropea, 1980), 82.

14 See Crystal Eddins, *Rituals, Runaways, and the Haitian Revolution: Collective Action in the African Diaspora* (New York: Cambridge University Press, 2022).

15 See Patrick Manning, *Slavery, Colonialism and Economic Growth in Dahomey, 1640–1960* (Cambridge: Cambridge University Press, 1982), 50–54. On this period of transition, see, Élisee A. Soumonni, "Dahomean

Economic Policy Under Ghezo 1818–1858: A Reconsideration," *Journal of the Historical Society of Nigeria* X, no. 2 (1980): 1–11, and Élisée Akpo Soumonni, "Trade and Politics in Dahomey, 1841–1892, With Particular Reference to the House of Regis" (PhD dissertation, University of Ife, 1983). See also Elisée Soumonni, "The Compatibility of the Slave and Palm Oil Trades in Dahomey, 1818–1858," in *From Slave Trade to 'Legitimate' Commerce: The Commercial Transition in Nineteenth Century West Africa,* ed. Robin Law (Cambridge: Cambridge University Press, 1995), 78–92.

16 Robin Law, *Ouidah: The Social History of a West African Slaving 'Port' 1727–1892* (Athens: Ohio University Press, 2004), 12, 31.

17 These voyages are recorded in *SlaveVoyages,* www.slavevoyages.org, voyages ID 33156, 33168, 33182, 33219, 33234, 33265, 33288 and 33306; and they also appear in Jean Mettas, Serge Daget, and Michèle Daget, ed. *Répertoire des expéditions négrières françaises au XVIIIe siècle,* tome II: Ports autres que Nantes (Paris: Société française d'histoire d'outre-mer, 1984), 704, 708, 714, 731, 738, 745, 752, 762, 768. On Louis-Athanase Ohier, see Alain Roman, *Saint-Malo au temps des négriers* (Paris: Karthala, 2001), 185–186; and on his first voyage to the Loango Coast, see also Alain Roman, *Mes ennemis savent que je suis Breton: La vie d'Ohier de Grandpré, marin de Saint-Malo (1761–1846)* (Saint-Malo: Éditions Cristel, 2004), 29–30, 61.

18 Grandpré, *Voyage à la côte occidentale d'Afrique,* vol. 1, 94.

19 Mettas, Daget, and Daget, ed. *Répertoire des expéditions négrières françaises au XVIIIe siècle,* tome II, 767. See also Roman, *Saint-Malo au temps des négriers,* 154.

20 Grandpré, *Voyage à la côte occidentale d'Afrique,* vol. 1, 21.

21 Roman, *Mes ennemis savent que je suis Breton,* 89. On the voyages of these three vessels, see Mettas, Daget, and Daget, ed. *Répertoire des expéditions négrières françaises au XVIIIe siècle,* tome II, 368, 369 and 371.

22 Grandpré, *Voyage à la côte occidentale d'Afrique,* vol. 1, 33.

23 See Mettas, Daget, and Daget, ed. *Répertoire des expéditions négrières françaises au XVIIIe siècle,* tome II, 362–363.

24 Grégoy is a reference to Glehue, the indigenous name of Ouidah in Fon language. On the fort, see Simone Berbain, *Le comptoir français: Le comptoir français de Juda (Ouidah) au XVIIIe siècle* (Paris: Librairie Larose, 1942).

25 Law, *Ouidah: The Social History,* 31–33.

26 Robin Law, "A Lagoonside Port on the Eighteenth-Century Slave Coast: The Early History of Badagri," *Canadian Journal of African Studies* 28, no. 1 (1994): 33.

27 Mettas, Daget, and Daget, ed. *Répertoire des expéditions négrières françaises au XVIIIe siècle,* tome II, 728.

28 Mettas, Daget, and Daget, ed. *Répertoire des expéditions négrières françaises au XVIIIe siècle,* tome II, 329.

29 Mettas, Daget, and Daget, ed. *Répertoire des expéditions négrières françaises au XVIIIe siècle,* tome II, 468.

30 Mettas, Daget, and Daget, ed. *Répertoire des expéditions négrières françaises au XVIIIe siècle,* tome II, 336.

31   Mettas, Daget, and Daget, ed. *Répertoire des expéditions négrières françaises au XVIIIe siècle*, tome II, 355.

32   Mettas, Daget, and Daget, ed. *Répertoire des expéditions négrières françaises au XVIIIe siècle*, tome II, 373–374, 719.

33   ADCM 41 ETP 219 6683, January 15, 1774. fl. 1–4v.

34   ADCM 41 ETP 209 6520, March 29, 1784 fl. 242.

35   ADCM 41 ETP 219 6684, July 13, 1786, fl. 1. See also ADCM 41 ETP 219 6685, July 16, 1786, fl. 1–2v.

36   ADCM 41 ETP 219 6684, July 13, 1786, fl. 2.

37   ADCM 41 ETP 219 6689, July 24, 1786, fl. 1–2. Slave trader and ship captain John Adams, who traded in West Africa between 1786 and 1800, mentions a Hausa man named Tammata, whose European name was Pierre, and was considered Porto-Novo's richest man. See John Adams, *Remarks on the Country Extending from Cape Palmas to the River Congo, including observations on the manners and customs of the inhabitants* (London: G. and W. B. Whittaker, 1823), 75. See also Pierre Verger, *Fluxo e refluxo, do tráfico de escravos entre o Golfo do Benin e a Bahia de Todos os Santos dos séculos XVII a XIX* (São Paulo: Editora Corrupio, 1987), 241.

38   ADCM 41 ETP 219 6691 bis, August 27, 1786, fl. 1–1v. For more on Hardy's efforts to build the new French fortresses on the Bight of Benin, see Brice Martinetti, *Les négociants de La Rochelle* (Paris: Presses universitaires de Rennes, 2013), 227–232. See also Brice Martinetti, "La traite rochelaise et la côte des esclaves: des coopérations locales aux prises d'otages, des décalages sociétaux aux intérêts divergents," *Dix-huitième siècle* 1, no. 44 (2012): 79–95.

39   ADCM 41 ETP 219 6695, October 29, 1787, fl. 1–2v.

40   The vessel is listed in Mettas, Daget, and Daget, ed. *Répertoire des expéditions négrières françaises au XVIIIe siècle*, tome II, 375. Yet the date of the attack by Dahomey is not July 6, but the night of June 5 to June 6, as in ADCM 41 ETP 219 6710, fl. 1.

41   ADCM 41 ETP 219 6695, October 29, 1787, fl. 1–1v.

42   ADCM 41 ETP 219 6710, fl. 1.

43   ADCM 41 ETP 219 6708, fl. 1.

44   ADCM 41 ETP 219 6710, fl. 1.

45   ADCM 41 ETP 219 6695, October 29, 1787, fl. 1–2v. On *La Jeune Thérèse*, see Mettas, Daget, and Daget, *Répertoire des expéditions négrières françaises au XVIIIe siècle*, tome I, 685.

46   Mettas, Daget, and Daget, ed. *Répertoire des expéditions négrières françaises au XVIIIe siècle*, tome II, 377–378. Note that there is an error in this entry – the date of departure from La Rochelle is February 19 and not December 19.

47   ADCM 41 ETP 219 6709, fl. 1–1v.

48   ADCM 41 ETP 219 6709, fl. 1.

49   ADCM 41 ETP 219 6709, fl. 1.

50   ADCM B 259 0380, February 13, 1788, fl. 30.

51   Mettas, Daget, and Daget, ed. *Répertoire des expéditions négrières françaises au XVIIIe siècle*, tome II, 371; 375–376.

52   AHU CU São Tomé e Príncipe, Cx. 7, D. 798. See also Verger, *Fluxo e refluxo*, 170.

53 When Gourg went to Abomey in 1787, he reported seeing some of the Portuguese hostages. See Verger, *Fluxo e refluxo*, 310, note 35.

54 FR ANOM COL E 209TER 1774/1793, Pierre Simon Gourg, écrivain principal des colonies, faisant fonction de commissaire ordonnateur au comptoir de Juda, "Mémoire du Sieur Gourg écrivain principal des colonies, faisant fonctions de commissaire directeur et donateur au comptoir de Juda, concernant son enlèvement et les violences exercées contre lui le 20 juillet 1789," 14 and FR ANOM 06 COL E 241 2374 A, "Notes sur les rachats des officiers, marchandises, matelots et nègres piroguiers enlevés à Portonove par les Dahomets le 6 juin 1787," 702–707, fl.1–3.

55 FR ANOM COL C6 27, no. 3, "Mémoire pour servir d'instruction au Directeur qui me succédera au Comptoir de Juda par M. Gourg, 1791," fl. 11v.

56 FR ANOM COL E 209TER 1774/1793, Pierre Simon Gourg, écrivain principal des colonies, faisant fonction de commissaire ordonnateur au comptoir de Juda, "Mémoire du Sieur Gourg écrivain principal des colonies, faisant fonctions de commissaire directeur et donateur au comptoir de Juda, concernant son enlèvement et les violences exercées contre lui le 20 juillet 1789," fl. 23.

57 ADCM B 1620, Enregistrement du procès-verbal de visite du navire Le Comte de Pontchartrain, fl. 78.

58 ADCM G 525 La Rochelle, Collection Communale, Paroissial, Baptêmes Mariage, Paroisse Saint-Nicolas 1782, fl. 16–16v.

59 Martinetti, *Les négociants de La Rochelle*, 35.

60 ADCM 41 ETP 215/6639, 1786, 1.

61 ADCM B 259, Registre des soumissions, commence le 24 juillet 1784 et fini le 1er mai 11787792, vol. 3, fl. 11 and *Feuille maritime de Nantes*, October 20, 1785, 2.

62 *Affiches américaines*, December 9, 1786, 1; Mettas, Daget, and Daget, ed. *Répertoire des expéditions négrières françaises au XVIIIe siècle*, tome II, 360 and *Feuille maritime de Nantes*, February 20, 1787, 3.

63 ADCM B 259, Registre des soumissions, commence le 24 juillet 1784 et fini le 1er mai 1792, vol. 3, fl. 34.

64 Mettas, Daget, and Daget, ed. *Répertoire des expéditions négrières françaises au XVIIIe siècle*, tome II, 383; *Feuille maritime de Nantes*, May 12, 1789, 3 and *Feuille maritime de Nantes*, November 20, 1789.

65 Mettas, Daget, and Daget, ed. *Répertoire des expéditions négrières françaises au XVIIIe siècle*, tome II, 394. See also *Slave Voyages*, www.slavevoyages .org, voyage ID 32449.

66 For more information on São Tomé and Príncipe as an Atlantic station to fetch supplies during the era of the Atlantic slave trade, see Arlindo Caldeira, "Learning the Ropes in the Tropics: Slavery and the Plantation System on the Island of São Tomé," *African Economic History* 39 (2011): 35–71.

67 See the *Slave Voyages*, www.slavevoyages.org.

68 On the slave trade during this period, see *Slave Voyages*, www.slavevoyages.org.

69 Daniel Domingues da Silva, "The Transatlantic Slave Trade from Angola: A Port-by-Port Estimate of Slaves Embarked, 1701–1867," *International Journal of African Historical Studies* 46, no. 1 (2013): 118.

6 NGOYO MEETS DAHOMEY

1 Robin Law, *Ouidah: The Social History of a West African Slaving 'Port' 1727–1892* (Athens: Ohio University Press, 2004), 136.

2 See, for example, ADCM 17, 4J 45 2318, "Mémoires de Jacques Proa dit Proa des îles," 96 and Vicente Ferreira Pires, *Viagem de África em o Reino de Dahomé escrita pelo Padre Vicente Ferreira Pires no anno de 1800 e até presente inédita* (São Paulo: Companhia Editora Nacional, 1957), 27.

3 Robert Norris, "A Journey to the Court of Bossa Ahadee, King of Dahomy, in the Year 1772," in *The History of Dahomy: An Inland Kingdom of Africa*, ed. Archibald Dalzel (London: T. Spilbury and Son, 1793), 106–107, 127–28.

4 Archibald Dalzel, *The History of Dahomy: An Inland Kingdom of Africa* (London: T. Spilbury and Son, 1793), ii–iii.

5 Isaac Adeagbo Akinjogbin, *Dahomey and Its Neighbours, 1708–1818* (Cambridge: Cambridge University Press, 1967), 25.

6 J. Cameron Monroe, *The Precolonial State in West Africa: Building Power in Dahomey* (New York: Cambridge University Press, 2014) 154.

7 Francesca Piqué and Leslie Rainer, *Palace Sculptures of Abomey: History Told on Walls* (London: The J. Paul Getty Trust, Thames and Hudson, 1999), 53. Gaëlle Beaujean explains that in the Fon language, there is a difference between the artist who creates and the artisan who executes, which is why I refer to artists and artisans, see Gaëlle Beaujean, *L'art de la cour d'Abomey: Le sens des objets* (Paris: Presses du Réel, 2019), 126.

8 Dalzel, *The History of Dahomy*, xiii.

9 Relying on Forbes, vol. 2, 171, Robin Law initially uses the term *hwenùwà* to designate "annual customs," but he also develops a detailed explanation of the various customs and their occurrence in the annual calendar, see Robin Law, ed. *Dahomey and the Ending of the Trans-Atlantic Slave Trade: The Journals and Correspondence of Vice-Consul Louis Fraser, 1851–1852* (Oxford: Oxford University Press, 2012), 263–270.

10 Luis Nicolau Parés, *O rei, o pai e a morte: A religião vodum na antiga Costa dos escravos na África Ocidental* (São Paulo: Companhia das Letras, 2016), 181–182. Parés explains that the term *hwenùwà* but cautions that this was a generic term.

11 Dalzel, *The History of Dahomy*, xx.

12 Parés, *O rei, o pai e a morte*, 182.

13 Serrano mentions these ceremonies. See Carlos Serrano, *Os senhores da terra e os homens do mar: Antropologia política de um reino africano* (São Paulo: Faculdade de Filosofia, Letras e Ciências Humans, Universidade de São Paulo, 1983), 118.

14 Dalzel, *The History of Dahomy*, xxiii. See also Monroe, *The Precolonial State in West Africa*, 81–82.

15 On Norris, see Robin Law "The Slave-Trader as Historian: Robert Norris and the History of Dahomey," *History in Africa* 16 (1989): 219–235.

16 According to Parés, *O rei, o pai e a morte*, 188.

17 Norris, "A Journey to the court of Bossa Ahadee," 146.

18 Norris, "A Journey to the court of Bossa Ahadee," 138.

19 Biblioteca Nacional, Rio de Janeiro, "Ofício do Rei de Dahomey a D. Fernando José de Portugal enviando um branco chamado Luís Caetano e dois embaixadores para serem enviados a El-Rei e falando sô bre a ida de navios a seu pôrto, Abome, 20 de março de 1795," II–34, 2, 10, Doc. 551, f. 1, March 20, 1795.

20 Instituto Histórico e Geográfico Brasileiro (hereafter IHGB), Lata 137, Pasta 62, Doc. 3, 6v, October 9, 1810.

21 Frederick E. Forbes, *Dahomey and the Dahomans: Being the Journey of Two Missions to the King of Dahomey, and his Residence at the Capital, in the Years 1849 and 1850* (London: Longman, Brown, Green, and Longmans, 1851), vol. 1, 77.

22 Lyndon de Araújo dos Santos, "Os Brácaros Chapeleiros Mundos e representações dos chapéus no Rio de Janeiro (1825–1898)," *Varia História* 31, no. 57 (2015): 787–818.

23 IHGB, Lata 137, Pasta 62, Doc. 3, fl.7, October 9, 1810.

24 IHGB, Lata 137, Pasta 62, Doc. 3, fl.7, October 9, 1810. For more on these gifts, see Ana Lucia Araujo, "Dahomey, Portugal, and Bahia: King Adandozan and the Atlantic Slave Trade," *Slavery & Abolition* 3, no. 1 (2012): 1–19. These items were received by Prince regent Dom João and remained housed in Brazil's National Museum until 2018, when a fire destroyed the museum and most of its collections. See Ana Lucia Araujo, "The Death of Brazil's National Museum," *The American Historical Review* 124, no. 2 (2019): 569–580. On Adandozan's gifts to Dom João, see Mariza de Carvalho Soares, *A coleção Adandozan do Museu Nacional: Brasil-Daomé, 1818–2018* (Rio de Janeiro: Mauad, 2022).

25 Suzanne Preston Blier, "Europa Mania: Contextualizing the European Other in Eighteenth and Nineteenth-Century Dahomey Art," in *Europe Observed: Multiple Gazes in Early Modern Encounters*, ed. Kumkum Chaterjee and Clement Hawes (Lewisburg, PA: Bucknell University Press, 2008), 239.

26 See Gaëlle Beaujean, "Le Cadeau dans les relations diplomatiques du Royaume du Danhomè au XXe siècle," *Politique africaine* 1, no. 165 (2022): 73–94.

27 Blier, "Europa Mania," 246–247.

28 Blier, "Europa Mania," 248.

29 Pires, *Viagem de África em o Reino de Dahomé*, 50–52. On this mission, see Júnia Ferreira Furtado, "The Eighteenth-Century Luso-Brazilian Journey to Dahomey: West Africa Through a Scientific Lens," *Atlantic Studies: Global Currents* 11, no. 2 (2014): 256–276.

30 Pires, *Viagem de África em o Reino de Dahomé*, 59–60.

31 Pires, *Viagem de África em o Reino de Dahomé*, 75.

32 Pires, *Viagem de África em o Reino de Dahomé*, 112. See also Akinjogbin, *Dahomey and Its Neighbours*, 103.

33 Forbes, *Dahomey and the Dahomans*, vol. 1, 78. European ship surgeon Johann Peter Oettinger, who visited the king of Hueda prior to the Dahomean conquest in 1693, also noticed that the king spit in a Chinese porcelain spittoon, see Roberto Zaugg, "Le crachoir chinois du roi: Marchandises

globales, culture de cour et vodun dans les royaumes de Hueda et du Dahomey (XVIIIᵉ- XIXᵉ siècle)," *Annales: Histoire, Sciences Sociales* 73, no. 1 (2018): 119–159. See also Johann Oettinger, Peter Craig Koslofsky, and Roberto Zaugg, *A German Barber-Surgeon in the Atlantic Slave Trade: The Seventeenth-Century Journal of Johann Peter Oettinger* (Charlottesville: University of Virginia Press, 2020), 40. In later years, Gaëlle Beaujean also mentions spittoons made in copper and calabash. See Beaujean, *L'art de la cour d'Abomey*, 79.

34 J. A. Sertchly, *Dahomey as It Is; Being a Narrative of Eight Months' Residence in That Country with a Full Account of the Notorious Annual Customs and the Social and Religious Institutions of the Ffons; Also an Appendix on Ashantee and Glossary of Dahoman Lords and Titles* (London: Chapman and Hall, 1871), 142, 165, 168.

35 Skertchly, *Dahomey as It Is*, 204.

36 Archives du Musée d'Ethnographie du Trocadéro et du Musée de l'Homme, 2 AM1 K78a, folder Porto Novo, inventaire des objets composant le Trésor du Palais Royal d'Abomey, 1931, 18 fls.

37 Skertchly, *Dahomey as It Is*, 255–256.

38 Elvira Stefania Tiberini, "La Recade Del Dahomey: Messagio-Simbolo D Potere," *Africa: Rivista trimestrale di studi e documentazione dell'Instituto italiano per l'Africa e l'Oriente* 37, no. 1–2(1982): 55.

39 For more on Dahomey's *récades* see Alexandre Adandè, *Les récades des rois du Dahomey* (Dakar: Institut de l'Afrique Noire, 1962). See also, Sandro Capo Chichi, "On the Origins of the Récades of the Kings of Dahomey," *African Arts* 56, no. 2 (2023): 10–19.

40 Mary Ellen Snodgrass, *An Encyclopedia of History, Culture, and Social Influence* (Abingdon: Routledge, 2014), vol. 1, 104–105.

41 Suzanne Preston Blier, *Royal Arts of Africa: The Majesty of Form* (London: Laurence King Publishing, 2012), 113.

42 Piqué and Rainer, *Palace Sculptures of Abomey*, 29.

43 Beaujean, *L'art de la cour d'Abomey*, 116.

44 Beaujean, *L'art de la cour d'Abomey*, 53.

45 Edna G. Bay, *Asen, Ancestors, and Vodun: Tracing Change in African Art* (Urbana and Chicago: University of Illinois Press, 2008), 70.

46 Blier, *Royal Arts of Africa*, 113.

47 To know more about this analysis, see Ellen Howe, "Fon Silver Jewelry of the 20th Century," *Met Objectives: Treatment and Research Notes* 1, no. 2 (2000): 4–5; 8.

48 Baltimore Museum of Arts, technical report 2002, 112.

49 Enid Schildkrout and Curtis A. Keim, "Objects and Agendas: Re-Collecting Congo," in *The Scramble for African Art*, ed. Enid Schildkrout and Curtis A. Keim (New York: Cambridge University Press, 1998), 26.

50 Howe, "Fon Silver Jewelry of the 20th Century," 5.

51 Beaujean, *L'art de la cour d'Abomey*, 174. On the professions of these Afro-Brazilians, Ana Lucia Araujo, *Public Memory of Slavery: Victims and Perpetrators in the South Atlantic* (Amherst, NY: Cambria Press, 2010), 108.

52 Beaujean, *L'art de la cour d'Abomey*, 135–136.

53 Blier, "Europa Mania," 242.

54 Bay, *Asen, Ancestors, and Vodun*, 61–63.

55 The *asen* appear among the Akan of the Gold Coast as well as among the Aja, Ewe, Fon, Hueda, Yoruba, and Edo peoples of the Bight of Benin. On the asen, see Suzanne Preston Blier, *Asen: Mémoires de fer forgé. Art vodun du Danhomè* (Geneva: Musée Barbier-Mueller, 2018), 11, 16.

56 On these different forms of appropriation and recreation see Suzanne Preston Blier, "The Art of Assemblage: Aesthetic Expression and Social Experience in Danhomè," *RES: Anthropology and Aesthetics*, no. 45 (2004): 186–210 and Beaujean, *L'art de la cour d'Abomey*, 126.

57 Bay, *Asen, Ancestors, and Vodun*, 64.

58 I am grateful to Allen F. Roberts who reminded me that although silver-smithing was not developed in Ngoyo, Woyo blacksmiths would have the skills to cast other metals, including silver. On metals and metalworking in West Central African region surrounding the kingdoms of the Loango coast, see Raoul Lehuard, *Art Bakongo: Insigne de pouvoir, le sceptre* (Arnouville: Arts d'Afrique Noire, 1998), vol. 4, 900–905. On ironwork-ing in Africa, see Allen F. Roberts, Tom Joyce, Marla Berns, William Joseph Dewey, Henry John Drewal, and Candice Lee Goucher, ed. *Striking Iron: The Art of African Blacksmiths* (Los Angeles California: Fowler Museum at UCLA, 2019). On iron craftsmen in West Central Africa see also Colleen Kriger, *Pride in Man: Ironworking in Nineteenth-Century West Central Africa* Africa (Westport, CT: Greenwood Press, 1999), and Crislayne Gloss Marão Alfagali, *Blacksmiths of Ilamba: A Social History of Labor at the Nova Oeiras Iron Foundry (Angola, Eighteenth Century)* (Berlin: De Gruyter, 2023).

59 As I revised this manuscript before final submission in April 2023, the Musée du Nouveau Monde de La Rochelle did not intend to conduct an X-ray spec-troscopic analysis of the Pukuta's *kimpaba*.

60 Blier, "The Art of Assemblage," 187–188.

61 Daniëlle Kisluk-Grosheide and Jeffrey Munger, *The Wrightsman Galleries for French Decorative Arts: The Metropolitan Museum of Art* (New York and New Haven, CT: The Metropolitan Museum and Yale University Press, 2010), 206.

62 Christopher Spring, *African Arms and Armor* (Washington, DC: Smithsonian Institution, 1993), 48.

63 Suzanne Preston Blier, *African Vodun: Art, Psychology, and Power* (Chicago: University of Chicago Press, 1995), 340.

64 Suzanne Preston Blier, "Words about Words about Icons: Iconologology and the Study of African Art," *Art Journal* 47, no. 2 (1988): 81.

65 Blier, "Europa Mania," 256.

66 Beaujean, *L'art de la cour d'Abomey*, 62.

67 See Melville J. Herskovits, "Some Aspects of Dahomean Ethnology," *Africa: Journal of the International African Institute* 5, no. 3 (1932): 286, Bernard Maupoil, *La géomancie à l'ancienne Côte des Esclaves* (Paris: Institut d'Eth-nologie, 1988), 71 and Parés, *O rei, o pai e a morte*, 210.

68 James Denbow, "Heart and Soul: Glimpses of Ideology and Cosmology in the Iconography of Tombstones from the Loango Coast of Central Africa," *The Journal of American Folklore* 112, no. 445 (1999): 410.

69 Carlos Serrano briefly explores the similarities of Ngoyo's and Dahomey's culture. See Serrano, *Os senhores da terra e os homens do mar*, 68–70.

70 See Cécile Fromont, *The Art of Conversion: Christian Visual Culture in the Kingdom of Kongo* (Chapel Hill: University of North Carolina Press, 2014).

71 The Latin cross does not appear in any *bimpaba* in various collections, including the Royal Museum of Central Africa in Belgium, the Virginia Museum of Fine Arts in the United States, and the Humboldt Forum in Germany, as well as the ones reproduced in Mário António Fernandes de Oliveira, "Insígnias do poder entre os Cabindas," in *Angola: Os Símbolos do Poder na Sociedade Tradicional*, ed. Manuel Laranjeira Rodrigues de Areia (Coimbra: Coimbra University Press, 1983), 19–24 and Joaquim Martins, *Cabindas: história, crença, usos e costumes* (Cabinda: Comissão de Turismo da Câmara Municipal de Cabinda, 1972), figures P 6, C 8, P 9, P 14, P 15, C 42. I am grateful to Carlos Serrano who also shared with me several photographs of *bimpaba*, but none of them bearing a Latin cross.

72 Serrano, *Os senhores da terra e os homens do mar*, 62; Phyllis Martin, "Family Strategies in Nineteenth-Century Cabinda," *The Journal of African History* 28, no. 1 (1987): 67 and Pinto, *Nós, os Cabindas*, 50. Pinto initially argues that the Nsambo family was not involved in the Atlantic slave trade, but later recognizes that the family's involvement declined or ended with the end of the French slave trade, see Alberto Oliveira Pinto, *Nós, os Cabindas: Domingos José Franque e a história oral das linhagens de Cabinda* (Lisbon: Novo Imbondeiro, 2003), 66.

73 Martin, "Family Strategies in Nineteenth-Century Cabinda," 67–68.

74 Louis-Marie-Joseph Ohier de Grandpré, *Voyage à la côte occidentale d'Afrique: fait dans les années 1786 et 1787, contenant la description des mœurs, usages, lois, gouvernement et commerce des états du Congo; suivi d'un voyage au cap de Bonne-Espérance: contenant la description militaire de cette colonie* (Paris: Dentu, 1801), vol. 1, 187.

75 See Stacey Sommerdyk, "Trade and Merchant Community of the Loango Coast in the Eighteenth Century" (PhD dissertation, University of Hull, 2012), 232, 235, 241.

76 In eighteenth-century France, the name Franque is associated with a family of architects, see Léon Lagrange, *Joseph Vernet, Sa vie, sa famille, son siècle* (Brussels: Imprimerie de A. Labroue et Compagnie, 1858), 29. Several artists bear Franck as a last name, see Antoine-Joseph Dezallier d'Argenville, *Abrégé de la vie des plus fameux peintres, avec leurs portraits gravés en taille-douce, les indications de leurs principaux ouvrages, quelques réflexions sur leurs caractères; et la manière de connoître les desseins et les tableaux des grands maîtres* (Paris: Chez de Burf l'Aîné, 1762), vol. 3, 90.

77 The image of this *kimpaba* is reproduced in Lehuard, *Art Bakongo: Insigne de pouvoir, le sceptre*, 916.

78 See Martin, "Family Strategies in Nineteenth-Century Cabinda," 71–73. Francisco Franque was born on January 2, 1777 and died on April 30

1875. See Martins, *Cabindas: história, crença, usos e costumes*, 45. His son Domingues José Franque was born in 1855 and died in 1941. See Pinto, *Nós, os Cabindas*, 11; 73.

79 On the rise of the illegal slave trade on the Loango coast, see Roquinaldo Ferreira, *Dos sertões ao Atlântico: Tráfico ilegal de escravos e comércio lícito em Angola, 1830–1860* (Luanda: Editorial Kilombelombe, 2012).

80 Roquinaldo Ferreira, "The Conquest of Ambriz: Colonial Expansion and Imperial Competition in Central Africa," *Mulemba* [online] 5, no. 9 (2015): http://journals.openedition.org/mulemba/439C1kX3QTaPoG28MhKT3Ue/Exmvoyhh22d.

81 See Martin, "Family Strategies in Nineteenth-Century Cabinda," 77–78.

82 See Martins, *Cabindas: história, crença, usos e costumes*, 31–34.

83 United Kingdom House of Commons Parliamentary Papers (hereafter UK HCPP), Inclosure 1 in no. 11 "Declaration of Mambuco Maniloembu," Africa. No. 2 (1883), *Correspondence Respecting the Territory on the West Coast of Africa Lying between 15° 12' of South Latitude: 1845–77* (London: Harrison and Sons, 1883), 17–18.

84 Jayme Pereira de Sampaio Forjaz de Serpa Pimentel, "O Congo Portuguez: Relatórios sobre as feitorias do Zaire, seu commercio, trabalhos de Stanley, missões inglesas e Cabinda," *Boletim da Sociedade de Geografia de Lisboa* 7, no. 4 (1887): 300.

85 Serrano, *Os senhores da terra e os homens do mar*, 116.

86 UK HCPP, Class A, Correspondence with the British Commissioners at Sierra Leone, Havana, the Cape of Good Hope, and Loanda, and Reports from British Vice-Admiralty Courts and from British Naval Officers Relating to the Slave Trade from April 1, 1854, to March 31, 1855, Loanda, No. 50 (London: Harrison and Sons, 1855), 68–69.

87 The paper trail of these conflicts and exchanges is extensive. See for example UK HCPP, "Count Lavradio to the Earl of Clarendon," September 17, 1853 and Inclosure 1 in no. 11 "Declaration of Mambuco Maniloembu," in Africa. No. 2 (1883), *Correspondence Respecting the Territory on the West Coast of Africa Lying between 15° 12' of South Latitude: 1845–77* (London: Harrison and Sons, 1883), 13–18.

88 UK HCPP, Class A, Class A, Correspondence with the British Commissioners at Sierra Leone, Havana, the Cape of Good Hope, and Loanda, and Reports from British Vice-Admiralty Courts and from British Naval Officers Relating to the Slave Trade from April 1, 1855, to March 31, 1856, Report from Naval Officers, West Coast of Africa Station, Inclosure 1 in no. 97, "Commander Need to Commodore Adams," January 30, 1855 (London: Harrison and Sons, 1856), 128.

89 See Martin, "Family Strategies in Nineteenth-Century Cabinda," 76.

90 Pechuël-Loesche, *Volkskunde von Loango*, 141.

91 Loesche, *Volkskunde*, 177.

92 See Julien Volper, "Trois cimpaaba d'argent: Échanges afro-européens sur les côtes kongo (XVIIe–XIXe siècles)," *Tribal Art magazine* XXV-4, no. 101 (2021): 83–95, at 86–89. Depending on the language, the company's name appears also as Valle e Azevedo, Valle y Azevedo, and Valle and Azevedo.

93 Luc de Heusch, "Essai sur la mythologie bantoue," *Journal des africanistes* 82, 1/2 (2012): 319–328.

94 See Blier, *Royal Arts of Africa*, 210 and Clara Saraiva, "Antepassados criadores: Representações entre a Europa e a África," in *As lições de Jill Dias: Antropologia, história, África, academia, The Jill Dias Lessons: Anthropology, History, Africa, Academy*, ed. Maria Cardeira da Silva and Clara Saraiva (Lisbon: Centro em Rede de Investigação em Antropologia, 2013), 193.

95 Beaujean, *L'art de la cour d'Abomey*, 237.

96 See Suzanne Preston Blier, "Le Musée Histoire d'Abomey: Colonial and Princely Prerogatives in the Establishment of an African Museum Milan," *Quaderini Poro: Arte in Africa* 2 (1991): 142, and Beaujean, *L'art de la cour d'Abomey*, 250–251.

97 Beaujean, *L'art de la cour d'Abomey*, 249–251.

98 Beaujean, *L'art de la cour d'Abomey*, 251.

CONCLUSION

1 Gaëlle Beaujean, *L'art de la cour d'Abomey: Le sens des objets* (Paris: Presses du Réel, 2019), 249.

2 Beaujean, *L'art de la cour d'Abomey*, 344–350.

3 ANF EM4 2014 4780/11 1819–1934, fl. 1. At that point Dodds had the rank of General.

4 I am grateful to Marie-Cécile Zinsou for sharing her notes with me and for calling my attention to the existence of Toffa's crown. As I finish writing this conclusion, we seem to have agreed that very probably there were two different crowns that both disappeared.

5 See "Emmanuel Macron's Speech at the University of Ouagadougou," *Elysée*, November 28, 2017, www.elysee.fr/emmanuel-macron/2017/11/28/discours-demmanuel-macron-a-luniversite-de-ouagadougou.

6 Felwine Sarr and Bénédicte Savoy, "*Rapport sur la restitution du patrimoine culturel africain. Vers une nouvelle éthique relationnelle*" (Paris: Ministère de la culture, November 2018).

7 Sarr and Savoy, "Rapport sur la restitution du patrimoine culturel africain," 55.

Bibliography

MUSEUM COLLECTIONS

Baltimore Museum of Art, Baltimore, United States
Metropolitan Museum of Art, New York City, United States
Musée d'Aquitaine, Bordeaux, France
Musée d'histoire de Nantes, Nantes, France
Musée du Nouveau Monde de La Rochelle, La Rochelle, France
Musée du Quai Branly, Paris, France
Museu da Ciência da Universidade de Coimbra, Coimbra, Portugal
Museu de Etnologia de Lisboa, Lisbon, Portugal
Muséum de La Rochelle, La Rochelle, France
Muséum d'histoire naturelle du Havre, Le Havre, France
Royal Museum for Central Africa, Tervuren, Belgium
Virginia Museum of Fine Arts, Richmond, United States

ARCHIVES AND LIBRARIES

Archives de la Chambre de Commerce, Marseille, France
Archives de la Marine, Rochefort, France
Archives départementales Bouches-du-Rhône, Marseille, France
Archives Départementales de la Charente Maritime, La Rochelle, France
Archives Départementales de la Loire Atlantique, Nantes, France
Archives du Musée d'Ethnographie du Trocadéro et du Musée de l'Homme, Paris, France
Archives nationales d'outre-mer, Aix-en Provence, France
Archives nationales de France, Paris et Pierrefitte-sur-Seine, France
Archives of the Royal Museum for Central Africa, Tervuren, Belgium
Arquivo Histórico Ultramarino, Lisbon, Portugal
Arquivo Nacional da Torre do Tombo, Lisbon, Portugal
Beinecke Rare Book & Manuscript Library, Yale University, New Haven, CT, United States

Biblioteca Nacional, Rio de Janeiro, Brazil
Bibliothèque Mazarine, Paris, France
Fundação Calouste Gulbenkian, Lisbon, Portugal
Getty Research Institute Library and Special Collections
Instituto Histórico Geográfico Brasileiro, Rio de Janeiro, Brazil
Library of Congress, Washington, DC, United States
Médiathèque Michel-Crépeau, La Rochelle, France
National Archives, Kew, United Kingdom
National Maritime Museum Manuscripts, Royal Museums Greenwich, United Kingdom
Princeton University Libraries, Princeton, United States
Sociedade de Geografia de Lisboa, Lisbon, Portugal

NEWSPAPERS AND MAGAZINES

Affiches américaines, Port-au-Prince and Cap Français, Saint-Domingue, France
Feuille maritime de Nantes, 1785
Mercure de France (1758), vol. 26

PUBLISHED PRIMARY SOURCES AND DATABASES

500 Ans: Arts décoratifs européens, Paris, Mercredi 7 novembre 2012. Paris: Christie's, 2012.

Adams, John. *Remarks on the Country Extending from Cape Palmas to the River Congo, Including Observations on the Manners and Customs of the Inhabitants*. London: G. and W. B. Whittaker, 1823.

"Angola: O Forte de Cabinda." Ministério das colônias, *Arquivos das colônias*, III July-December, no. 17 (1918).

Argenville, Antoine-Joseph Dezallier d'. *Abrégé de la vie des plus fameux peintres, avec leurs portraits gravés en taille-douce, les indications de leurs principaux ouvrages, quelques réflexions sur leurs caractères; et la manière de connoître les desseins et les tableaux des grands maîtres*. Paris: Chez de Burf l'Aîné, 1762. vol. 3.

Astley, Thomas, ed. *A New General Collection of Voyages and Travels Consisting of the Most Esteemed Relations, Which Have Been Hitherto Published in Any Language: Comprehending Every Thing Remarkable in Its Kind, in Europe, Asia, Africa, and America*. London: Thomas Astley, 1745. vol. 2.

Brásio, António, ed. *Monumenta Missionaria Africana: África Ocidental*. Lisbon: Agência Geral do Ultramar, 1952–1988. 15 vols.

Broecke, Pieter van den and James D. La Fleur. *Pieter van den Broecke's Journal of Voyages to Cape Verde, Guinea and Angola: (1605–1612)*. London: Hakluyt Society, 2000.

Burton, Richard F. *A Mission to Gelele, King of Dahome with Notes of the So Called "Amazons," the Grand Customs, the Yearly Customs, the Human Sacrifices, the Present Stat of the Slave Trade, and Negro's Place in Nature*. London: Tinsley Brothers, 1864. vol. 1.

Chavanne, Joseph. *Reisen und Forschungen im alten und neuen Kongstaate in den Jahren 1884 und 1885*. Jenna: Hermann Constenoble, 1887.

"Chronica das missões," *Portugal em Africa*. Lisbon: Typographia e Lithographia de A. E. Barata, 1896. vol. 3.

Cuvelier, Jean. *Documents sur une mission française au Kakongo, 1766–1776*. Brussels: Institut Royal Colonial Belge, 1953.

Dalzel, Archibald. *The History of Dahomy: An Inland Kingdom of Africa*. London: T. Spilbury and Son, 1793.

Dapper, Olfert. *Description de l'Afrique, contenant les noms, la situation et les confins de toutes les parties, leur rivières, leurs villes et leurs habitations, leurs plantes et leurs animaux; les mœurs, les coûtumes, la langue, les richesses, la religion et le gouvernement de ses peuples*. Amsterdam: Chez Wolfang, Waesberge, Bom & van Someren, 1686.

Dapper, Olfert. *Naukeurige beschrijvinge der Afrikaensche gewesten van Egypten, Barbaryen, Lybien, Biledulgerid, Negroslant, Guinea, Ethiopiën, Abyssinie*. Amsterdam: J. van Meurs, 1676. vol. 2.

Diderot, Denis and Jean le Rond d'Alembert, ed. *Encyclopédie ou Dictionnaire raisonné des sciences, des arts et des métiers par une société de gens de lettres*. Neuchâtel: Samuel Faulche, 1765. vol. 11.

"Emmanuel Macron's Speech at the University of Ouagadougou," *Elysée*, November 28, 2017, www.elysee.fr/emmanuel-macron/2017/11/28/discours-demmanuel-macron-a-luniversite-de-ouagadougou.

Forbes, Frederick E. *Dahomey and the Dahomans: Being the Journey of Two Missions to the King of Dahomey, and His Residence at the Capital, in the Years 1849 and 1850*. London: Longman, Brown, Green, and Longmans, 1851. vols. 1 and 2.

Grandpré, Louis-Marie-Joseph Ohier de. *Voyage à la côte occidentale d'Afrique: fait dans les années 1786 et 1787, contenant la description des mœurs, usages, lois, gouvernement et commerce des états du Congo; suivi d'un voyage au cap de Bonne-Espérance: contenant la description militaire de cette colonie*. Paris: Dentu, 1801. vol. 1 and vol. 2.

Journal d'un voyage sur les costes d'Afrique et aux Indes d'Espagne avec une description particulière de la Rivière de La Plata; de Buenosayres, & autres lieux; commencé en 1701 & fini en 1706. Amsterdam, 1723.

Journal encyclopédique par une société de gens de lettres, tome V, troisième partie. Liège: Everard Kints, 1757.

Lagrange, Léon. *Joseph Vernet, Sa vie, sa famille, son siècle*. Brussels: Imprimerie de A. Labroue et Compagnie, 1858.

Law, Robin, ed. *Dahomey and the Ending of the Trans-Atlantic Slave Trade: The Journals and Correspondence of Vice-Consul Louis Fraser, 1851–1852*. Oxford: Oxford University Press, 2012.

Ledward, K. H., ed. *Journals of the Board of Trade and Plantations*. Vol. 5, January 1723–December 1728. London: H. M. Stationery Office, 1928.

Le commerce de l'Amérique par Marseille ou Explications des Lettres-Patentes du Roi, portant règlement pour le Commerce qu'il se fait de Marseille aux Isles Françoises de l'Amérique, données au mois de Février 1719 et des Lettres-Patentes du Roi, pour la liberté du Commerce à la Côte de Guinée. Données à Paris au mois de Janvier 1716. Leiden and Aix: Pierre Chambon, 1782. vol. 2.

Mascarenhas, José Freire de Montarroyos. *Relaçam da Embayxada, que o poderoso Rey de Angome Kiayy Chiri Broncom, Senhor dos dila- tadissimos Sertõs de Guiné mandou ao Illustrissimo e Excellentissimo Senhor D. Luiz Peregrino de Ataide, Conde de Atouguia, Senhor das Villas de Atouguia, Peniche, Cernache, Monforte, Vilhaens, Lomba, e Pa,co da Ilha Dezerta, Cõmendador das Cõmendas de Santa Maria de Adaufe, e Villa velha de Rodam, na Ordem de Christo, do Conselho de Sua Magestade, Governador, e Capitão General, que foy do Reyno de Algarve & actualmente Vice-Rey do Estado do Brasil: pedindo a amizade, e aliança do muito alto; e poderoso Senhor Rey de Portugal Nosso Senhor*. Lisbon: Na Officina de Francisco da Silva, anno de 1751.

Mettas, Jean, Serge Daget, and Michèle Daget, ed. *Répertoire des expéditions négrières françaises au XVIIIe siècle*, tome I: Nantes. Paris: Société française d'histoire d'outre-mer, 1978.

Mettas, Jean, Serge Daget, and Michèle Daget, ed. *Répertoire des expéditions négrières françaises au XVIIIe siècle*, tome II: Ports autres que Nantes. Paris: Société française d'outre-mer, 1984.

Mission de Loango. Mémoire sur l'établissement d'une mission dans les royaumes de Loango, Kakongo en Afrique. Paris: Knapen, 1772.

Norris, Robert. "A Journey to the court of Bossa Ahadee, King of Dahomy, in the year 1772." In *The History of Dahomy: An Inland Kingdom of Africa*, ed. Archibald Dalzel. London: T. Spilbury and Son, 1793.

Oettinger, Johann Peter Craig Koslofsky, and Roberto Zaugg. *A German Barber-Surgeon in the Atlantic Slave Trade: The Seventeenth-Century Journal of Johann Peter Oettinger*. Charlottesville: University of Virginia Press, 2020.

Pechuel-Loesche, Eduard. *Volkskunde von Loango*. Stuttgart: Stecker and Schroder, 1907.

Pires, Vicente Ferreira. *Viagem de África em o Reino de Dahomé escrita pelo Padre Vicente Ferreira Pires no anno de 1800 e até presente inédita*. São Paulo: Companhia Editora Nacional, 1957.

Proyart, Abbé Liévin-Bonaventure. *Histoire de Loango, Kakongo et autres royaumes d'Afrique*. Paris: C. P. Berton, 1776.

Purchas, Samuel. *Hakluytus Posthumus or Purchas His Pilgrimes in Twenty Volumes, Contayning a History of the World in Sea Voyages and Lande Travells by Englishmen and Others*. Glasgow: James MacLehose and Sons, 1905. vol. 6.

Rinchon, Dieudonné. *Pierre-Ignace-Liévin Van Alstein: Capitaine négrier, Gand 1733–Nantes 1793*. Dakar: Institut de l'Afrique noire, 1964.

Rossini, Maison. *Dessins, tableaux anciens, art d'Asie, arts décoratifs du XXe, céramiques, montres, horlogerie, instruments scientifiques et de marine, objets d'art et d'ameublement*. Paris: Hôtel Drouot, salle Rossini le 5 juin 2015.

Sertchly, J. A. *Dahomey as It Is; Being a Narrative of Eight Months' Residence in That Country with a Full Account of the Notorious Annual Customs and the Social and Religious Institutions of the Fons; Also an Appendix on Ashantee and Glossary of Dahoman Lords and Titles*. London: Chapman and Hall, 1871.

Société des archives historiques de la Saintonge et de l'Aunis. *Bulletin de la So-ciété des archives historiques de la Saintonge et de l'Aunis.* Paris and Saintes: A. Picard and Mme Z. Mortreuil, 1896.

SlaveVoyages. Houston: Rice University, www.slavevoyages.org.

United Kingdom House of Commons Parliamentary Papers, Class A, Correspon-dence with the British Commissioners at Sierra Leone, Havana, the Cape of Good Hope, and Loanda, and Reports from British Vice-Admiralty Courts and from British Naval Officers Relating to the Slave Trade from April 1, 1854, to March 31, 1855. London: Harrison and Sons, 1855.

United Kingdom House of Commons Parliamentary Papers, Class A, Correspon-dence with the British Commissioners at Sierra Leone, Havana, the Cape of Good Hope, and Loanda, and Reports from British Vice-Admiralty Courts and from British Naval Officers Relating to the Slave Trade from April 1, 1855, to March 31, 1856. London: Harrison and Sons, 1856.

United Kingdom House of Commons Parliamentary Papers, Africa. No. 2, *Correspondence Respecting the Territory on the West Coast of Africa Lying between 15° 12' of South Latitude: 1845–77.* London: Harrison and Sons, 1883.

Wing, J. Van Wing and C. Penders. *Le plus ancien dictionnaire bantu: Vocabu-larium P. Georgii Gelensis.* Louvain: Imprimerie J. Kuyl-Otto, 1928.

Yacou, Alain. *Journaux de bord et de traite de Joseph Crassous de Médeuil: De La Rochelle à la côte de Guinée et aux Antilles (1772–1776).* Paris: Karthala, 2001.

SECONDARY SOURCES

Adandè, Alexandre. *Les récades des rois du Dahomey.* Dakar: Institut de l'Af-rique Noire, 1962.

Akinjogbin, Isaac Adeagbo. *Dahomey and Its Neighbours, 1708–1818.* Cam-bridge: Cambridge University Press, 1967.

Alfagali, Crislayne Gloss Marão. *Blacksmiths of Ilamba: A Social History of Labor at the Nova Oeiras Iron Foundry (Angola, Eighteenth Century).* Berlin: De Gruyter, 2023.

Alpern, Stanley B. "What Africans Got for Their Slaves: A Master List of Euro-pean Trade Goods." *History in Africa* 22 (1995): 5–43.

Anselin, Alain. "Résistances africaines sur la Côte d'Angole au XVIIIe siècle." *Présence africaine,* no. 173 (2006): 189–205.

Appadurai, Arjun. "Introduction: Commodities and the Politics of Value." In *The Social Life of Things: Commodities in Cultural Perspective,* edited by Ar-jun Appadurai, 3–63. New York: Cambridge University Press, 1986.

Araujo, Ana Lucia. *Brazil through French Eyes: A Nineteenth-Century Artist in the Tropics.* Albuquerque: New Mexico University Press, 2015.

Araujo, Ana Lucia. "Dahomey, Portugal, and Bahia: King Adandozan and the Atlantic Slave Trade." *Slavery and Abolition* 3, no. 1 (2012): 1–19.

Araujo, Ana Lucia. "Did Rodney Get It Wrong? Europe Underdeveloped Africa, But Enslaved People Were Not Always Purchased with Rubbish." *African Eco-nomic History Review* 50, no. 2 (2022): 22–32.

Araujo, Ana Lucia. "History, Memory and Imagination: Na Agontimé, a Dahomean Queen in Brazil." In *Beyond Tradition: African Women and Their Cultural Spaces*, edited by Toyin Falola and Sati U. Fwatshak, 45–68. Trenton, NJ: Africa World Press, 2011.

Araujo, Ana Lucia. *Public Memory of Slavery: Victims and Perpetrators in the South Atlantic*. Amherst, NY: Cambria Press, 2010.

Araujo, Ana Lucia. "The Death of Brazil's National Museum." *The American Historical Review* 124, no. 2 (2019): 569–580.

Bakewell, Peter John. *Silver Mining and Society in Colonial Mexico, Zacatecas 1546–1700*. Cambridge: Cambridge University Press, 1972.

Bastide, Tristan Arbousse. *Du couteau au sabre: Armes traditionnelles d'Afrique. From Knife to Sabre: Traditional Arms of Africa*. 2. Oxford: Archaeopress, 2008.

Bay, Edna G. *Asen, Ancestors, and Vodun: Tracing Change in African Art*. Urbana and Chicago: University of Illinois Press, 2008.

Beaujean, Gaëlle. "L'art de la cour d'Abomey: le sens des objets." PhD dissertation, École des Hautes Études en Sciences Sociales, 2015.

Beaujean, Gaëlle. *L'art de la cour d'Abomey: Le sens des objets*. Paris: Presses du Réel, 2019.

Beaujean, Gaëlle. "Le cadeau dans les relations diplomatiques du Royaume du Danhomè au XXe siècle." *Politique africaine* 1, no. 165 (2022): 73–94.

Bennett, Herman L. *African Kings and Black Slaves: Sovereignty and Dispossession in the Early Modern Atlantic*. Philadelphia: University of Pennsylvania Press, 2019.

Berbain, Simone. *Le comptoir français de Juda (Ouidah) au XVIIIe siècle*. Paris: Librarie Larose, 1942.

Binter, Julia T. S. "Becoming Imperial: The Politicisation of the Gift in Atlantic Africa." In *Exploring Materiality and Connectivity in Anthropology and Beyond*, ed. Phillip Schorch, Martin Saxer, and Marlen Elders, 53–71. London: University College London Press, 2020.

Blier, Suzanne Preston. *African Vodun: Art, Psychology, and Power*. Chicago: University of Chicago Press, 1995.

Blier, Suzanne Preston. *Asen: Mémoires de fer forgé. Art vodun du Danhomè*. Geneva: Musée Barbier-Mueller, 2018.

Blier, Suzanne Preston. "Europa Mania: Contextualizing the European Other in Eighteenth and Nineteenth-Century Dahomey Art." In *Europe Observed: Multiple Gazes in Early Modern Encounters*, edited by Kumkum Chaterjee and Clement Hawes, 237–270. Lewisburg, PA: Bucknell University Press, 2008.

Blier, Suzanne Preston. "Le Musée Histoire d'Abomey: Colonial and Princely Prerogatives in the Establishment of an African Museum Milan." *Quaderini Poro: Arte in Africa* 2 (1991): 140–158.

Blier, Suzanne Preston. *Royal Arts of Africa: The Majesty of Form*. London: Lawrence King Publishing, 2012.

Blier, Suzanne Preston. "The Art of Assemblage: Aesthetic Expression and Social Experience in Danhomè." *RES: Anthropology and Aesthetics*, no. 45 (2004): 186–210.

Blier, Suzanne Preston. "Words about Words about Icons: Iconologology and the Study of African Art." *Art Journal* 47, no. 2 (1988): 75–87.

Bohorquez, Jorge. "Linking the Atlantic and Indian Oceans: Asian Textiles, Spanish Silver, Global Capital, and the Financing of the Portuguese-Brazilian Slave Trade (c. 1760–1808)." *Journal of Global History* 15, no. 1 (2020): 19–38.

Borucki, Alex. "The US Slave Ship Ascension in the Río de La Plata: Slave Routes and Circuits of Silver in the Late Eighteenth-Century Atlantic and Beyond." *Colonial Latin American Review* 29, no. 4 (2020): 630–657.

Bostoen, Koen and Gilles-Maurice de Schryver. "Seventeenth-Century Kikongo Is Not the Ancestor of Present-Day Kikongo." In *The Kongo Kingdom: The Origins, Dynamics and Cosmopolitan Culture of an African Polity*, edited by Koen Bostoen and Inge Brinkman, 60–102. New York: Cambridge University Press, 2018.

Brault, Solange and Yves Bottineau. *L'orfèvrerie française du XVIIIe siècle*. Paris: Presses universitaires de France, 1959.

Brauner, Christina. "Connecting Things: Trading Companies and Diplomatic-Giving on the Gold and Slave Coasts in the Seventeeth and Eighteenth Centuries." *Journal of Early Modern History* 20 (2016): 408–428.

Brauner, Christina. *Kompanien, Könige und caboceers: Interkulturelle Diplomatie an Gold- und Slavenküste im 17. und 18. Jahrhundert*. Cologne, Weimar, Vienna: Böhlau Verlag, 2015.

Brauner, Christina. "To Be the Key for Two Coffers: A West African Embassy to France (1670/1)." *Institut français de recherche en Afrique Nigeria*, E-papers series, no. 30, October 10, (2013): 1–26.

Broadhead, Susan Herlin. "Trade and Politics on the Congo Coast: 1770–1870." PhD dissertation, Boston University, 1971.

Brummell, Paul. *Diplomatic Gifts: A History in Fifty Presents*. London: Hurst, 2022.

Caillé, Alain. *Anthropologie du don*. Paris: La Découverte, 2007.

Caldeira, Arlindo. "Learning the Ropes in the Tropics: Slavery and the Plantation System on the Island of São Tomé." *African Economic History* 39 (2011): 35–71.

Candido, Mariana P. *An African Slaving Port and the Atlantic World: Benguela and Its Hinterland*. New York: Cambridge University Press, 2013.

Candido, Mariana P. *Wealth, Land and Property in Angola: A History of Dispossession, Slavery, and Inequality*. New York: Cambridge University Press, 2022.

Candido, Mariana P. "Women's Material World in Nineteenth-Century Benguela." In *African Women in the Atlantic World: Property, Vulnerability and Mobility, 1660–1880*, edited by Mariana P. Candido and Adam Jones, 70–85. Woodbridge: Boydell and Brewer, 2019.

Chabaud-Arnault, Charles. "Études historiques sur la marine militaire de France. XIV: La marine française avant et pendant la guerre de sept ans (suites)." In *Revue maritime et coloniale*, 482–501. Paris: Librairie Militaire de L. Baudoin, 1892.

Chichi, Sandro Capo. "On the Origins of the Récades of the Kings of Dahomey." *African Arts* 56, no. 2 (2023): 10–19.

Clark, John C. *La Rochelle and the Atlantic Economy during the Eighteenth Century*. Baltimore, MD: Johns Hopkins University Press, 1981.

Cook, Jr., Edward S. *Global Objects: Toward a Connected Art History*. Princeton, NJ: Princeton University Press, 2022.

Cooksey, Susan, Robin Poynor, Hein Vanhee, and Carlee S. Forbes, ed. *Kongo across the Waters*. Gainesville: University Press of Florida, 2014.

Cornet, Joseph. *Pictographies Woyo*. Milan: PORO, Associazione degli Amici dell'Arte Extraeuropea, 1980.

Covo, Manuel. *Entrepôt of Revolutions: Saint-Domingue, Commercial Sovereignity, and the French American Alliance*. New York: Oxford University Press, 2022.

Curtin, Philip D. *Cross-Cultural Trade in World History*. Cambridge: Cambridge University Press, 1984.

Curtin, Philip D. *The Atlantic Slave Trade: A Census*. Madison: University of Wisconsin Press, 1969.

Curto, José. *Enslaving Spirits: The Portuguese-Brazilian Alcohol Trade at Luanda and Its Hinterland, c. 1550–1830*. Leiden: Brill, 2004.

Daniels, Jason. "Recovering the Fugitive History of Marronage in Saint-Domingue, 1770–1791." *The Journal of Caribbean History* 46, no. 2 (2012): 121–153.

Davis, Natalie Zemon. *The Gift in Sixteenth-Century France*. Madison: University of Wisconsin Press, 2000.

Delobette, Édouard. "Ces Messieurs du Havre. Négociants, commissionnaires et armateurs de 1680 à 1830." PhD dissertation, Université de Caen, 2008.

Denbow, James. "Heart and Soul: Glimpses of Ideology and Cosmology in the Iconography of Tombstones from the Loango Coast of Central Africa." *The Journal of American Folklore* 112, no. 445 (1999): 404–423.

Dermigny, Louis. "Circuits de l'argent et milieux d'affaires au XVIIIe siècle." *Revue Historique* 212, no. 2 (1952): 239–278.

Deveau, Jean-Michel. *La traite rochelaise*. Paris: Karthala, 2009.

Dobie, Madeleine. "Patrimoine mobilier: entre colonialisme et orientalisme." *In Situ: Revue des patrimoines* 20 (2013): 1–13.

Eddins, Crystal. *Rituals, Runaways, and the Haitian Revolution: Collective Action in the African Diaspora*. New York: Cambridge University Press, 2022.

Eltis, David and David Richardson. *Atlas of the Transatlantic Slave Trade*. New Haven, CT: Yale University Press, 2015.

Establet, Colette. *Répertoire des tissus indiens importés en France entre 1687 et 1769*. Aix-en-Provence: Institut de recherches et d'études sur les mondes arabes et musulmans, 2017.

Fauvelle, François-Xavier. *The Golden Rhinoceros: Histories of the African Middle Ages*. Princeton, NJ: Princeton University Press, 2018.

Fee, Sarah, ed. *Cloth That Changed the World: The Art and Fashion of Indian Chintz*. Toronto and New Haven, CT: Royal Ontario Museum and Yale University Press, 2019.

Fennell, Christopher C. "Kongo and the Archaeology of Early African America." In *Kongo across the Waters*, ed. Susan Cooksey, Robin Poynor, and Hein Vanhee, 229–244. Gainesville: University of Florida Press, 2013.

Ferreira, Roquinaldo. "Central Africa and the Atlantic World." *Oxford Research Encyclopedia of African History*, 30 October 2019, https://oxfordre.com/africanhistory/view/10.1093/acrefore/9780190277734.001.0001/acrefore-9780190277734-e-53.

Ferreira, Roquinaldo. *Cross-Cultural Exchange in the Atlantic World*. New York: Cambridge University Press, 2014.

Ferreira, Roquinaldo. *Dos sertões ao Atlântico: Tráfico ilegal de escravos e comércio lícito em Angola, 1830–1860*. Luanda: Editorial Kilombelombe, 2012.

Ferreira, Roquinaldo. "The Conquest of Ambriz: Colonial Expansion and Imperial Competition in Central Africa." *Mulemba* [online] 5, no. 9 (2015): http://journals.openedition.org/mulemba/439.

Franque, José Domingos and Manuel de Resende. *Nós, Os Cabindas, pelo príncipe negro*. Lisbon: Editora Argo, 1940.

Freeman, David. *A Silver River in a Silver World: Dutch Trade in the Río de la Plata, 1648–1678*. New York: Cambridge University Press, 2020.

Fromont, Cécile. "Common Threads: Cloth, Colour, and the Slave Trade in Early Modern Kongo and Angola." *Art History* 41, no. 5 (2018): 838–867.

Fromont, Cécile. "From Image to Grave and Back: Multidisciplinary Inquiries into Kongo Christian Visual Culture." In *The Kongo Kingdom: The Origins, Dynamics and Cosmopolitan Culture of an African Polity*, edited by Koen Bostoen and Inge Brinkman, 143–164. Cambridge: Cambridge University Press, 2018.

Fromont, Cécile. *The Art of Conversion: Christian Visual Culture in the Kingdom of Kongo*. Chapel Hill: University of North Carolina Press, 2014.

Fromont, Cécile. "The Taste of Others: Finery, The Slave Trade, and Africa's Place in the Traffick of Early Modern Things." In *Early Modern Things: Objects and their Histories, 1500–1800*, edited by Paula Findlen, 273–294. New York: Routledge: 2021.

Furtado, Júnia Ferreira. "The Eighteenth-Century Luso-Brazilian Journey to Dahomey: West Africa Through a Scientific Lens." *Atlantic Studies: Global Currents* 11, no. 2 (2014): 256–276.

Graeber, David. *Toward an Anthropological Theory of Value: The False Coin of Our Dreams*. New York: Palgrave, 2001.

Graeber, David and Marshal Sahlins. *On Kings*. Chicago: HAU Books, 2017.

Graincourt, Alfred. *Histoire des hommes illustres de la marine française, suivie de l'expédition française au Mexique en 1863*. Niort: Robin et L. Favre, 1863.

Green, Toby. *A Fistful of Shells: West Africa from the Rise of the Slave Trade to the Age of Revolution*. Chicago: Chicago University Press, 2019.

Green, Toby. *The Rise of the Transatlantic Slave Trade in Western Africa, 1300–1589*. New York: Cambridge University Press, 2011.

Gregg, Amanda and Ruderman, Anne. "No. 333: Cross-Cultural Trade and the Slave Ship the Bonne Société: Baskets of Goods, Diverse Sellers, and Time Pressure on the African Coast." In *Economic History Working Papers*, 1–60. London: Department of Economic History, London School of Economics and Political Science, 2021.

Gril-Mariotte, Aziza. "Indiennes, toiles peintes et toiles de Jouy, de nouvelles étoffes d'ameublement au XVIIIe siècle." *Histoire de l'art*, no. 65 (2009): 141–152.

Gril-Mariotte, Aziza. "La consommation des indiennes à Marseille (fin XVIIIe-début XIXe siècle)." *Rives méditerranéennes*, no. 29 (2008): 141–152.

Gualdé, Krystel. *L'abîme: Nantes dans la traite atlantique et l'esclavage colonial, 1707–1830*. Nantes: Musée d'histoire de Nantes et Fondation pour la mémoire de l'esclavage, 2021.

Guilet, Bertrand. *La Marie-Séraphique: Navire négrier.* Nantes: Musée d'histoire de Nantes, 2009.

Guthrie, Malcolm. *The Classification of the Bantu Languages.* Oxford: Oxford University Press, 1948.

Guyer, Jane I. *Marginal Gains: Monetary Transactions in Atlantic Africa.* Chicago: Chicago University Press, 2004.

Harms, Robert W. *The Diligent: A Voyage through the Words of the Slave Trade.* New York: Basic Books, 2002.

Hawthorne, Walter. *From Africa to Brazil: Culture, Identity, and an Atlantic Slave Trade, 1600–1830.* New York: Cambridge University Press, 2010.

Heintze, Beatrix. "Traite de 'pièces' en Angola: Ce qui n'est pas dit dans nos sources." In *De la traite à l'esclavage: Actes du colloque international sur la traite des Noirs, Nantes 1985,* tome 1: Ve-XVIIIe siècle, edited by Serge Daget. 147–172. Nantes and Paris: Centre de recherche sur l'histoire du monde atlantique and Société française d'histoire d'outre-mer, 1985.

Herbert, Eugenia W. *Iron, Gender, and Power: Rituals of Transformation in African Societies.* Bloomington: Indiana University Press, 1993.

Herbert, Eugenia W. *Red Gold of Africa: Copper in Precolonial History and Culture.* Madison: University of Wisconsin Press, 1984.

Heusch, Luc de. "Essai sur la mythologie bantoue." *Journal des africanistes* 82, no. 1/2 (2012): 319–328.

Heywood, Linda M. "Slavery and Its Transformation in the Kingdom of Kongo: 1491–1800." *Journal of African History* 50 (2009): 1–22.

Heywood, Linda M. and John K. Thornton. *Central Africans, Atlantic Creoles, and the Foundation of the Americas, 1585–1660.* New York: Cambridge University Press, 2007.

Holland, Dorothy Garesché. *The Garesché, De Baudy, and Des Chapelles Families: History and Genealogy.* St Louis, MO: Schneider Printing Company, 1963.

Homer. *The Odyssey,* trans. Emily Wilson. New York: W. W. Norton, 2018.

Hoopes, Thomas T. "French Silver of the Eighteenth Century." *Bulletin of the City Art Museum of St. Louis* 39, no. 1 (1954): 4–15.

Howe, Ellen. "Fon Silver Jewelry of the 20th Century." *Met Objectives: Treatment and Research Notes* 1, no. 2 (2000): 4–5, 8.

Inikori, Joseph E. *Africans and the Industrial Revolution in England: A Study in International Trade and Development.* Cambridge: Cambridge University Press, 2002.

Jambu, Jérôme. "La circulation de la monnaie métallique et des métaux monétisables en Europe au XVIIIe siècle." In *Les circulations internationales en Europe, années 1680–annees 1780,* edited by Pierre-Yves Beaurepaire and Pierrick Pourchasse, 151–165. Rennes: Presses universitaires de Rennes, 2010.

Kisluk-Grosheide, Daniëlle and Jeffrey Munger. *The Wrightsman Galleries for French Decorative Arts: The Metropolitan Museum of Art.* New York and New Haven, CT: The Metropolitan Museum and Yale University Press, 2010.

Krebs, Verena. *Medieval Ethiopian Kingship, Craft, and Diplomacy with Latin Europe.* Cham: Palgrave Macmillan, 2021.

Krieken, Gérard van. *Corsaires et marchands: Les relations entre Alger et les Pays-Bas, 1604–1830.* Saint-Denis: Éditions Bouchène, 2002.

Kriger, Colleen. *Making Money: Life, Death, and Early Modern Trade on Africa's Guinea Coast.* Athens: Ohio University Press, 2017.

Kriger, Colleen. *Pride in Man: Ironworking in Nineteenth-Century West Central Africa.* Westport, CT: Greenwood Press, 1999.

Laman, Karl Edward. *Dictionnaire Kikongo-Français avec une étude phonétique décrivant les dialectes les plus importants de la langue dite Kikongo.* Brussels: Georges van Campenhout, 1936.

Lane, Kris. *Potosí: The Silver City that Changed the World.* Oakland: University of California Press, 2019.

Law, Robin. "A Lagoonside Port on the Eighteenth-Century Slave Coast: The Early History of Badagri." *Canadian Journal of African Studies* 28, no. 1 (1994): 32–59.

Law, Robin. "The Slave-Trader as Historian: Robert Norris and the History of Dahomey." *History in Africa* 16 (1989): 219–235.

Law, Robin. *Ouidah: The Social History of a West African Slaving 'Port' 1727–1892.* Athens: Ohio University Press, 2004.

Le Glaunec, Jean-Pierre. *Esclaves mais résistants: Dans le monde des annonces pour esclaves en fuite, Louisiane, Jamaïque, Caroline du Sud (1801–1815).* Paris: Karthala, 2021.

Le Herissé, Auguste. *Royaume du Dahomey: Moeurs, Religion, Histoire.* Paris: Emile Larose, 1911.

Lehuard, Raoul. *Art Bakongo: Insigne de pouvoir, le sceptre,* vol. 4. Arnouville: Arts d'Afrique Noire, 1998.

Lovejoy, Paul E. *Transformations in Slavery: A History of Slavery in Africa.* New York: Cambridge University Press, 2011.

Luís, João Baptista. "O comércio do marfim e o poder nos territórios do Kongo, Ngoyo e Loango: 1796–1825." MA thesis, Universidade de Lisboa, 2016.

Luna, Kathryn M de. "Sounding the African Atlantic." *The William and Mary Quarterly* 78, no. 4 (2021): 581–616.

Macgaffey, Wyatt. "Os Kongo." In *Na Presença dos espíritos: Arte Africana do Museu Nacional de Etnologia, Lisboa,* edited by Frank Herreman, 35–60. New York: Museum for African Art and Gent: Snoek-Ducaju, 2000.

Mancal, Carlos. "The Spanish-American Silver Peso: Export Commodity and Global Money of the Ancien Regime, 1550–1800." In *From Silver to Cocaine: Latin American Commodity Chains and the Building of the World Economy, 1500–2000,* edited by Steven Topik, Carlos Marichal, and Zephyr Frank, 25–52. Durham, NC: Duke University Press, 2006.

Manker, E. "Niombo. Die Totenbestattung der Babwende," *Zeitschrift für Ethnologie* 64, no. 4–6 (1932): 159–172.

Mann, Kristin. *Slavery and the Birth of an African City: Lagos, 1760–1900.* Bloomington: Indiana University Press, 2007.

Manning, Patrick. *Slavery, Colonialism and Economic Growth in Dahomey, 1640–1960.* Cambridge: Cambridge University Press, 1982.

Marshall, Bill. *The French Atlantic: Travels in Culture and History.* Liverpool: Liverpool University Press, 2009.

Martin, Phyllis M. "Family Strategies in Nineteenth-Century Cabinda." *The Journal of African History* 28, no. 1 (1987): 65–86.

Martin, Phyllis M. "Power, Cloth and Currency on the Loango Coast." *African Economic History, no.* 15 (1986): 1–12.

Martin, Phyllis M. *The External Trade of the Loango Coast 1576–1870: The Effects of Changing Commercial Relations on the Vili Kingdom of Loango.* Oxford: Clarendon Press, 1972.

Martin, Phyllis M. "The Kingdom of Loango." In *Kongo: Power of Majesty,* ed. Alisa Lagamma, 47–85. New York: The Metropolitan Museum of Art, 2015.

Martinetti, Brice. "La traite rochelaise et la côte des esclaves: des coopérations locales aux prises d'otages, des décalages sociétaux aux intérêts divergents." *Dix-huitième siècle* 1, no. 44 (2012): 79–95.

Martinetti, Brice. *Les négociants de La Rochelle au XVIIIe siècle.* Paris: Presses universitaires de Rennes, 2013.

Martins, Joaquim. *Cabindas: história, crença, usos e costumes.* Cabinda: Comissão de Turismo da Câmara Municipal de Cabinda, 1972.

Martins, Padre Joaquim. *Sabedoria Cabinda: Símbolos e provérbios.* Lisbon: Junta de investigações ultramar, 1968.

Masgnaud, Francis. *Franc-maçonnerie et francs-maçons en Aunis et Saintonge sous l'Ancien Régime et la Révolution.* La Rochelle: Rumeur des Ages, 1989.

Mauss, Marcel. *Essai sur le don: Forme et raison de l'échange dans les sociétés archaïques.* Paris: Presses universitaires de France, 2002.

Mauss, Marcel. *The Gift: The Form and Reason for Exchange in Archaic Societies.* London and New York: Routledge, 2002.

McWatters, Cheryl Susan. "Investment Returns and la traite négrière: Evidence from Eighteenth-Century France, Accounting." *Business & Financial History* 18, no. 2 (2008): 161–185.

Merlet, Annie. *Autour du Loango (XIVe–XIXe siècle): Histoire des peuples du sud-ouest du Gabon au temps du royaume de Loango et du "Congo français."* Libreville: Centre Culturel Français de Libreville, 1991.

Meuwese, Mark. *Brothers in Arms, Partners in Trade: Dutch–Indigenous Alliances in the Atlantic World, 1595–1674.* Leiden: Brill, 2012.

Meyer, Jean. *L'armement nantais dans la deuxième moitié du XVIIIe siècle.* Paris: Éditions de l'École des Hautes Études en Sciences Sociales, 1999.

Miller, Joseph C. *Way of Death: Merchant Capitalism and the Angolan Slave Trade 1730–1830.* Madison: University of Wisconsin Madison, 1988.

Miyazaki, Hirozaku. "Gifts and Exchange." In *The Oxford Handbook of Material Culture Studies,* edited by Dan Hicks and Mary C. Beaudry, 246–264. Oxford: Oxford University Press, 2010.

Mobley, Christina Frances. "The Kongolese Atlantic: Central Africa Slavery and Culture from Mayombe to Haiti." PhD dissertation, Duke University, 2015.

Monroe, J. Cameron. *The Precolonial State in West Africa: Building Power in Dahomey.* New York: Cambridge University Press, 2014.

Mulinda, Habi Buganza. "Aux origines du royaume de Ngoyo." *Civilisations: Revue internationale d'anthropologie et des sciences humaines,* no. 41 (1993): 165–187.

Nganga, Arsène Francoeur. "La Compagnie royale d'Afrique et les commerçants négriers anglais sur la baie de Loango (entre 1650 et 1838)." *Études caribéennes* 42 (2019), https://journals.openedition.org/etudescaribeennes/15466.

Nganga, Arsène Francoeur. *La traite négrière sur la baie de Loango pour la colonie du Suriname*. Saint-Denis: Edilivre, 2018.

Notter, Annick. "Un témoignage de la traite rochelaise sur la 'côte d'Angole'." *La Revue des Musées de France, Revue du Louvre*, no. 4 (2016): 57–62.

Nwokeji, G. Ugo. *The Slave Trade and Culture in the Bight of Biafra: An African Society in the Atlantic World*. New York: Cambridge University Press, 2014.

Oliveira, Mário António Fernandes de. "Insígnias do poder entre os Cabindas." In *Angola: Os Símbolos do Poder na Sociedade Tradicional*, edited by Manuel Laranjeira Rodrigues de Areia, 13–26. Coimbra: Coimbra University Press, 1983.

Palmer, Jennifer L. *Intimate Bonds: Family and Slavery in the French Atlantic*. Philadelphia: University of Pennsylvania Press, 2016.

Parani, Maria G. "Intercultural Exchange in the Field of Material Culture in the Eastern Mediterranean: The Evidence of Byzantine Legal Documents (11th to 15th Centuries)." In *Diplomatics in the Eastern Mediterranean 1000–1500: Aspects of Cross-Cultural Communication*, edited by Alexander D. Beinammer, Maria G. Parani and Christopher D. Schabel, 349–372. Leiden: Brill, 2008.

Parés, Luis Nicolau. *O rei, o pai e a morte: A religião vodum na antiga Costa dos escravos na África Ocidental*. São Paulo: Companhia das Letras, 2016.

Phipps, Elena, Johanna Hecht, and Cristina Esteras Martín, ed. *The Colonial Andes: Tapestries and Silverwork, 1530–1830*. New York and London: The Metropolitan Museum of Art and Yale University Press, 2004.

Pimentel, Jayme Pereira de Sampaio Forjaz de Serpa. "O Congo Portuguez: Relatórios sobre as feitorias do Zaire, seu commercio, trabalhos de Stanley, missões inglesas e Cabinda." *Boletim da Sociedade de Geografia de Lisboa* 7, no. 4 (1887): 269–310.

Piqué, Francesca and Leslie Rainer. *Palace Sculptures of Abomey: History Told on Walls*. London: The J. Paul Getty Trust, Thames and Hudson, 1999.

Postrel, Virginia. *The Fabric of Civilization: How Textiles Made the World*. New York: Basic Books, 2020.

Queguiner, Jean-Pierre. "Jean-Amable Lessenne, Louisbourg 1739-La Rochelle 1818. Capitaine de navire négrier, président trésorier au bureau des finances de la généralité de La Rochelle, propriétaire du château de La Tourtillère (Puilboreau) et de l'hôtel particulier du Petit-Val (La Rochelle)." *Écrits d'Ouest* 12 (2004): 107–127.

Rademarkers, Frederik W., Nicolas Nikis, Thierry de Putter and Patrick Degryse. "Copper Production and Trade in the Niari Basin (Republic of Congo) During the 13th to 19th Centuries CE: Chemical and Lead Isotope Characterization." *Archaeometry* 60 (2018): 1251–1270.

Raveux, Olivier. "The Coral Trade in Smyrna at the End of the 17th Century as Seen through Several of François Garnier's Business Deals." *Rives méditerranéennes* no. 59 (2019): 135–151.

Revue de Saintonge et d'Aunis: Bulletin de la Société des archives historiques. Saintes: Mortreuil, 1896.

Richardson, David. "Consuming Goods, Consuming People: Reflections on the Transatlantic Slave Trade." In *The Rise and Demise of Slavery and the Slave*

Trade in the Atlantic World, edited by Kristin Mann and Philip Misevich, 31–63. Rochester, NY: Rochester University Press, 2016.

Richemond, M. Meschinet de. *Inventaire sommaire des Archives départementales antérieures à 1790: Charente-inférieure serie B (art 1829 à 2661), Jurisdictions secondaires relevant des présidiaux de La Rochelle et de Saintes*. La Rochelle: Eugène Martin, 1906.

Rinchon, Dieudonné. *Les armements négriers au XVIIIe siècle d'après la correspondance et la comptabilité des armateurs et des capitaines nantais*. Brussels: Académie royale des sciences coloniales, 1955.

Roberts, Allen F., Tom Joyce, Marla Berns, William Joseph Dewey, Henry John Drewal, and Candice Lee Goucher, ed. *Striking Iron: The Art of African Blacksmiths*. Los Angeles: Fowler Museum at UCLA, 2019.

Roman, Alain. *Mes ennemis savent que je suis Breton: La vie d'Ohier de Grandpré, marin de Saint-Malo (1761–1846)*. Saint-Malo: Éditions Cristel, 2004.

Roman, Alain. *Saint-Malo au temps des négriers*. Paris: Karthala, 2001.

Santos, Lyndon de Araújo dos. "Os Brácaros Chapeleiros Mundos e representações dos chapéus no Rio de Janeiro (1825–1898)." *Varia História* 31, no. 57 (2015): 787–818.

Saraiva, Clara. "Antepassados criadores: Representações entre a Europa e a África." In *As lições de Jill Dias: Antropologia, história, África, academia, The Jill Dias Lessons: Anthropology, History, Africa, Academy*, edited by Maria Cardeira da Silva and Clara Saraiva, 186–206. Lisbon: Centro em Rede de Investigação em Antropologia, 2013.

Sarr, Felwine and Bénédicte Savoy. *Rapport sur la restitution du patrimoine culturel africain. Vers une nouvelle éthique relationnelle*. Paris: Ministère de la culture, November 2018.

Saugera, Éric. *Bordeaux port négrier: XVIIe–XIXe siècles*. Paris: Karthala, 2002.

Schildkrout, Enid and Curtis A. Keim. "Objects and Agendas: Re-Collecting Congo." In *The Scramble for African Art*, edited by Enid Schildkrout and Curtis A. Keim, 1–136. New York: Cambridge University Press, 1998.

Schrag, Norm. "Mboma and the Lower Zaire: A Socioeconomic Study of a Kongo Trading Community, c. 1785–1885." PhD dissertation, University of Indiana, 1985.

Schryver, Gilles-Maurice de, Rebecca Grollemund, Simon Branford and Koen Bostoen. "Introducing A State-of-the-Art Phylogenetic Classification of the Kikongo Language Cluster." *Africana Linguistica* 21 (2015): 87–162.

Sénéchal, Louis Esnoul de. "Un manuel du parfait traitant au XVIIIe siècle." *Mémoires de la société d'Histoire et d'archéologie de Bretagne* 13 (1932): 197–209.

Serrano, Carlos. "Símbolos do poder nos provérbios e nas representações gráficas Mabaya Manzangu dos Bawoyo de Cabinda, Angola." *Revista do Museu de Arqueologia e Etnologia* (1993): 137–146.

Serrano, Carlos. "Tráfico e mudança no Reino Ngoyo (Cabinda no século XIX)." *Estudos Afro-Asiáticos*, 32 (1997): 97–108.

Shumway, Rebecca. *The Fante and the Transatlantic Slave Trade*. Rochester, NY: Rochester University Press, 2011.

Silva Jr., Carlos da. "Enslaving Commodities: Tobacco, Gold, Cowry Trade and Trans-Imperial Networks in the Bight of Benin (c. 1690s–c.1790s)." *African Economic History* 49, no 2 (2021): 1–30.

Silva, Daniel Domingues da. *The Atlantic Slave Trade from West Central Africa, 1780–1867*. New York: Cambridge University Press, 2017.

Silva, Daniel Domingues da. "The Supply from Luanda, 1768–1806: Records of Anselmo da Fonseca Coutinho." *African Economic History* 38 (2010): 53–76.

Silva, Daniel Domingues da. "The Transatlantic Slave Trade from Angola: A Port-by-Port Estimate of Slaves Embarked, 1701–1867." *International Journal of African Historical Studies* 46, no. 1 (2013): 105–122.

Silva, Filipa Ribeiro da. *Dutch and Portuguese in Western Africa: Empires, Merchants and the Atlantic System, 1580–1674*. Leiden: Brill, 2011.

Snodgrass, Mary Ellen. *An Encyclopedia of History, Culture, and Social Influence*, vol. 1. Abingdon: Routledge, 2014.

Soares, Mariza de Carvalho. *A coleção Adandozan do Museu Nacional: Brasil-Daomé, 1818–2018*. Rio de Janeiro: Mauad, 2022.

Soares, Mariza de Carvalho. "Trocando galanterias: a diplomacia do comércio de escravos, Brasil-Daomé, 1810–1812." *Afro-Ásia*, no. 49 (2014): 229–271.

Sommerdyk, Stacey Jean Muriel. "Trade and Merchant Community of the Loango Coast in the Eighteenth Century." PhD dissertation, University of Hull, 2012.

Soumonni, Élisee A. "Dahomean Economic Policy Under Ghezo 1818–1858: A Reconsideration." *Journal of the Historical Society of Nigeria* X, no. 2 (1980): 1–11.

Soumonni, Élisée Akpo. "Trade and Politics in Dahomey, 1841–1892, With Particular Reference to the House of Regis." PhD dissertation, University of Ife, 1983.

Soumonni, Elisée. "The Compatibility of the Slave and Palm Oil Trades in Dahomey, 1818–1858." In *From Slave Trade to 'Legitimate' Commerce: The Commercial Transition in Nineteenth Century West Africa*, edited by Robin Law, 78–92. Cambridge: Cambridge University Press, 1995.

Sparks, Randy J. *Where the Negroes Are Masters: An African Port in the Era of the Slave Trade*. Cambridge, MA: Harvard University Press, 2014.

Spring, Christopher. *African Arms and Armor*. Washington, DC: Smithsonian Institution, 1993.

Staller, Jared. *Converging on Cannibals: Terrors of Slaving in Atlantic Africa, 1509–1670*. Athens: Ohio University Press, 2019.

Stein, Robert Louis. *The French Slave Trade in the Eighteenth Century: An Old Regime Business*. Madison: University of Wisconsin Press, 1979.

Thomas, Nicholas. *Entangled Objects: Exchange, Material Culture, and Colonialism in the Pacific*. Cambridge, MA: Harvard University Press, 1991.

Thornton, John K. *A Cultural History of the Atlantic World, 1250–1820*. New York: Cambridge University Press, 2012.

Thornton, John K. *A History of West Central Africa to 1850*. New York: Cambridge University Press, 2020.

Thornton, John K. "The Origins of Kongo: A Revised Vision." In *The Kongo Kingdom: The Origins, Dynamics and Cosmopolitan Culture of an African*

Polity, edited by Koen Bostoen and Inge Brinkman, 103–122. Cambridge: Cambridge University Press, 2018.

Thornton, John K. "The Regalia of the Kingdom of Kongo, 1491–1895." In *Kings of Africa: Art and Authority in Central Africa*, edited by Erna Beumers and Hans-Joachim Koloss, 57–63. Maastricht: Foundation Kings of Africa, 1992.

Thornton, John K. and Linda M. Heywood. *Central Africans, Atlantic Creoles, and the Foundation of the Americas, 1585–1660*. New York: Cambridge University Press, 2007.

Thuile, Jean. *L'orfèvrerie en Languedoc du XIIe au XVIIIe siècle. Géneralité de Montpellier*. Montpellier: Causse & Castlenau, 1966.

Tiberini, Elvira Stefania. "La Recade Del Dahomey: Messagio-Simbolo D Potere." *Africa: Rivista trimestrale di studi e documentazione dell'Instituto italiano per l'Africa e l'Oriente* 37, no. 1–2 (1982): 54–74.

Trimble, Jennifer. "The Zoninus Collar and the Archaelogy of Romany Slavery." *American Journal of Archaeology* 120, no. 3 (2016): 444–472.

Trivellato, Francesca. *The Familiarity of Strangers: The Sephardic Diaspora, Livorno, and Cross-Cultural Trade in the Early Modern Period*. New Haven, CT: Yale University Press, 2009.

Um, Nancy. *Shipped But Not Sold: Material Culture and The Social Protocols of Trade during Yemen's Age of Coffee*. Honolulu: University of Hawai'i Press, 2017.

Vansina, Jan. "On Ravestein's Edition of Battell's Adventures in Angola and Loango." *History in Africa* 34 (2007): 321–47.

Vansina, Jan. *Paths in the Rainforests: Toward a History of Political Tradition in Equatorial Africa*. Madison: The University of Wisconsin Press, 1990.

Vansina, Jean. "Notes sur l'origine du Royaume du Kongo." *The Journal of African History* 4, no. 1 (1963): 33–38.

Verger, Pierre. *Fluxo e refluxo do tráfico de escravos entre o Golfo do Benin e a Bahia de Todos os Santos dos séculos XVII a XIX*. São Paulo: Editora Corrupio, 1987.

Vignols, Léon. "El asiento francés (1701–1713) e inglés (1713–1750) y el Comercio franco-español desde 1700 hasta 1730." *Anuario de historia del derecho español*, no. 5 (1928): 266–300.

Volavka, Zdenka and Wendy Anne Thomas. *Crown and Ritual: The Royal Insignia of Ngoyo*. Toronto: Toronto University Press, 1998.

Volper, Julien. "Trois cimpaaba d'argent: Échanges afro-européens sur les côtes kongo (XVIIe-XIXe siècles)." *Tribal Art Magazine* XXV-4, no. 101 (2021): 83–95.

Zaugg, Roberto. "Le crachoir chinois du roi: Marchandises globales, culture de cour et vodun dans les royaumes de Hueda et du Dahomey (XVIIIe– XIXe siècle)," *Annales: Histoire, Sciences Sociales* 73, no. 1 (2018): 119–159.

Index